...pencer is one of the best-known faces on British television, ...presenting the hit Channel 4 series *Location, Location, Location* ... *Relocation, Relocation* and presenting *Relocation: Phil Down Under*. ... trained as a general practice surveyor and, in 1996, was one of the first people to set up a property-buying agency. He has written ...umns for, among others, *The Sunday Times*, *GQ* and *Country Life* ... appears regularly on radio to discuss property issues.

www.philspencer.tv

HOW TO BUY YOUR FIRST HOME

(and how to sell it too)

Phil Spencer

Vermilion
LONDON

7 9 10 8

Published in 2011 by Vermilion, an imprint of Ebury Publishing

Ebury Publishing is a Random House Group company

Copyright © Phil Spencer with Cheryl Markosky 2011

The Random House Group Limited Reg. No. 954009

Addresses for companies within the Random House Group can be found at
www.randomhouse.co.uk

A CIP catalogue record for this book is available from the British Library

The Random House Group Limited supports The Forest Stewardship
Council® (FSC®), the leading international forest-certification organisation.
Our books carrying the FSC label are printed on FSC®-certified paper.
FSC is the only forest-certification scheme supported by the leading
environmental organisations, including Greenpeace. Our
paper procurement policy can be found at
www.randomhouse.co.uk/environment

MIX
Paper from
responsible sources
FSC® C016897

Printed and bound in Great Britain by Clays Ltd, St Ives plc

ISBN 9780091935375

Copies are available at special rates for bulk orders.
Contact the sales development team on 020 7840 8487 for more information.

To buy books by your favourite authors and register for offers,
visit www.randomhouse.co.uk

*To all my family for being so inspiring,
amazing and supportive*

Contents

Acknowledgements

First and foremost, I'd like to thank my good friend and writing colleague Cheryl Markosky, without whom this book would never have happened. She's been absolutely fantastic and I'm hugely grateful for her help and dedication in translating years of my thoughts into a fantastic and coherent book.

I'd also like to acknowledge and thank all the first-time buyers I've worked with over the years. It's only through them that I have the experience necessary to write this book. The whole team at Vermilion have been outstanding, so thanks to them for publishing my words once again. Also to Channel 4, to Jonathan Conway at Mulcahy Conway Associates and especially to Hilary Murray at Arlington. She's the best TV agent in the world.

A big thank you also to my gorgeous boys, Jake and Ben, who never fail to make me proud to be their dad, and to Fiona, my truly amazing wife. I love you so much.

Introduction

Buying your first home is probably one of the biggest things you'll ever do in your life. It's up there with other momentous life events, such as starting your first job, getting married and having your first child. No one should underestimate the importance of such a move.

In most cases, buying a first property is also one of the most expensive purchases you will make. Later purchases as you climb the property ladder are likely to cost more, but that feeling of parting with a significant amount of cash for the first time will leave its mark on you. When I bought my first place, I felt like a grown-up doing a very grown-up thing. Just as I was chuffed to bits to have a car, I was also chuffed to bits to have my first flat.

Naturally, many first-time buyers are terrified at the prospect of taking on the responsibility of a first home. It's never been an easy task – ask your parents and grandparents and they'll tell you the sacrifices they had to make to get onto the property ladder – but it's not as daunting as you think. When times get tough, remember that we're really all rooting for you, even though it might not seem that way at the time. Believe me, it's so worthwhile owning your own home that, a bit like childbirth or exams, you forget all the pain when you see the great result afterwards.

Every homeowner was a first-time purchaser once and I see this as almost a rite of passage you have to go through. It's worth knowing that first-time buyers are the darlings of the property business. Without them, moving up and down the property ladder would be impossible for everyone else, so they're regarded with fondness by estate agents, house finders, developers, property research-experts and, frankly, everybody in the property world. Politically, it is viewed a clever and popular move to back and help first-time buyers, and such support has helped many a Member of Parliament or local councillor to a powerful place governing a county, or even the country.

As a presenter on *Location, Location, Location*; *Relocation, Relocation*; and other property specials for Channel 4 television, and as a property finder helping people find their dream homes, I have worked with a number of first-time buyers over the years and done much to alleviate their fears and worries. I have seen every phobia and panic attack known to first-time buying man and can reassure first-timers that everything generally works out all right in the end. I hope this book will calm frayed nerves with its information, advice and encouragement. When times get tough, pick it up and find the section or sections most relevant to you and read on.

Buying for the first time can appear complex, with some of the terminology appearing like gobble-de-gook from a Martian that has just landed in his spaceship. The seemingly complicated buying process is explained in full in this book, along with the terms people use that are most puzzling to first-time purchasers. I've broken everything down into easy-to-understand steps, making that mammoth task more bite-sized and achievable.

The book is divided into logical and chronological sections, taking you through the buying process. Topics covered include:

- Getting a mortgage in place
- How to view a property
- Making an offer
- Getting the best from your solicitor (who carries out searches and surveys to see if there are any legal problems with your home or its surrounding area)
- A survey (an inspection of the property by a surveyor) and how it can help you decide whether to buy
- Exchange of contracts (the swapping of contracts between the buyer's and seller's solicitors)

- Completion (the final stage of the sale when ownership changes hands from the seller to the buyer)

I want to help first-time buyers using this book to focus clearly on one stage at a time, without fretting about the tasks that lie ahead. There's no point in having sleepless nights about the font for the change of address cards when you haven't yet had an offer accepted on a property, for instance. It's all about priorities and identifying them, and this sort of lucid thinking is one of my strong points.

Also, I hope this book will help first-timers think creatively about how to get onto that first rung of the property ladder. My own example of buying a first home wasn't typical, but it was nothing if not imaginative.

I did a deal with a friend, who had bought a building in London that could be divided into two flats. I rented the place from him at a reasonable rate so I had somewhere to stay, while overseeing the building work to split it into two flats. We then sold one flat, which he got the proceeds for, and I ended up with the other flat for my efforts.

This might not be regarded as the most straightforward way to get onto the ladder, but it certainly worked for me. It involved a certain amount of time and hard graft to get the building work sorted, and I had to make sure I didn't fall out with my mate, but it all worked out and I ended up with a newly converted first home.

There are a number of ways you can get your hands on that elusive first property, even when the task appears impossible in leaner economic times. Once you remove the confusion and get your head round the baffling bits, hey presto, you find you can do it.

An added bonus is a final chapter on how to sell your first home, too, to give you some idea about what you should do the first time you sell a property. The book also contains a glossary defining all those baffling terms property types bandy about, and an appendix explaining permitted development rights: what you can do without having to seek planning permission when you want to carry out that first bout of building work.

Don't forget: I'm here to help you with every step along the way. So, happy house hunting and happy days in your first home. It's a once-in-a-lifetime opportunity – and I hope you will enjoy it as much as I enjoyed buying and living in my first home.

CHAPTER ONE

Deciding to Buy

Deciding if now is the right time for you to
buy a home is the first step – are you ready?

Before you get excited about looking at tempting homes for sale in estate agents' windows and on the Internet, you need to ask yourself whether you are truly ready to buy. If you haven't first asked yourself some fundamental questions about your circumstances and lifestyle, it's too early to start admiring old sash windows and cornices of a period property or to get excited by an up-to-the-minute flat in a smart development.

If you've been thinking about buying, though, perhaps you are ready to become a hunter of a first home. What you must do is identify whether this is the right move for you and whether it's the right time to buy a home. Only you will know, and much depends on your own personal circumstances. A good way to work out if this is the right move for you right now is to ask the following questions. If you can't say yes to the majority of them, then maybe you need to hang on for a bit longer.

Are you ready?

- Do you have enough money to buy a home?
- How likely is it you will be able to borrow money to buy your home?
- Is it tax efficient for you to buy now?

- Does it make sense for you to make this move now?
- Will you be in one spot long enough to make it worthwhile?
- Are you eager to put down roots?
- Can you cope with the responsibilities involved?
- Are you happy to make the commitment to be a homeowner?

You do need to be careful that you are buying a home for the right reasons. I believe some people feel it's what they should be doing by a certain age or when they get married. Also, you might feel pressure from friends and family. If a number of your friends are buying their first home, or your mother thinks it's time you 'settled down' – these might not be the best reasons for you to be thinking of scrambling onto the property ladder.

Is it a good time to buy?

You could probably rightly argue that this is a bad time for first-time buyers to be trying to get any form of permanent accommodation. Some experts even believe the UK is in danger of creating an entire generation of people who will never be able to buy their own homes. Unless you have wealthy parents or are in a highly paid job, you'll probably have to save for decades, suggests a recent study from the University of York.

One problem is saving enough for a deposit. Until the last few years, a number of people could borrow 90–100% of their home's worth without a great deal of trouble. But now a bank or building society is unlikely to consider lending money to a buyer unless they've saved at least a minimum of 25% of the price of the home. Many are even demanding more – 25–50% in some cases.

It can be difficult for many first-timers to come up with this sort of cash, despite saving for long periods of time. Inevitably, parents and grandparents often end up helping out. Four out of five first-time buyers under the age of 30 currently get help with deposits (the cash you put down on a mortgage) from their parents – the Bank of Mum and Dad, as the newspapers call it.

But these days, even the Bank of Mum and Dad is restrained by how much it can hand over. The 'sandwich generation' – those that find themselves caring for both their children and their parents – has to decide whether to spend its savings on long-term care for their elderly parents, funding their own retirements or helping their sons and daughters acquire educations and property of their own. A recent report by Oxford Economics said that if younger people had to save up for a 20% deposit it would take them on average 40 years to do so.

Also, the average age of a first-time buyer not given a helping hand by affluent parents has risen sharply. Back in October 2007, when the credit crunch started, the average age of a first-time buyer was 33. By April 2009, the average age rose to 36. Many property experts estimate it is more likely to be closer to 37 or 38 by now. And while the number of first-timers has remained at about the same rate over the last three years (80,200 in 2006, contrasting with 80,700 in 2009), those not given any financial assistance by their parents has dropped from 120,900 to only 20,200 over the same period of time.

This might make depressing reading for some, but it's important to know where first-time buyers stand. And it's not all bad news. The property market needs first-time buyers to keep the whole buying and selling process going. If there's no one at the bottom of the property ladder, it can severely restrict movement up and down the rungs, affecting everyone from young families and downsizers (those wanting to move down to smaller homes), to retirees leaving family homes for the last time.

First-timers by numbers

- **£166,769** – average price of a home in England and Wales
- **£18,600** – average deposit required for a first home
- **80,200** – number of first-time buyers in the UK

- **36** – average age of a first-time buyer
- **4 out of 5** – number of first-time buyers under 30 who get parental help towards a deposit
- **22–25%** – average deposit needed by first-time buyers to get a mortgage
- **40 years** – the time it would take the average first-timer to save a 20% deposit

If it's so difficult, why bother?

Surely, it can often be a struggle to come up with the cash for a deposit on a property, let alone cough up mortgage payments every month. But first-time buyers have always lamented how hard it is to get that first property. Even in tougher times, many have somehow accomplished this feat.

Your parents' generation made quite large sacrifices to buy their first home. I believe the difference now is that most people are not used to waiting for things. If you want the latest plasma screen, you hand over your credit card and take one home. Equally, if you feel like going out for dinner, you do so. Earlier generations tended to save up to get married and buy a first home.

In difficult economic times, it might not be so easy to splash the cash so readily, and one must feel sympathy for young first-time buyers with other debts that their parents and grandparents might not have accrued. For example, many first-time buyers today are trying to pay off student loans, and day-to-day costs and standards of living were generally lower in the past. Now, you're hard-pushed to get by without the presumed 'basics' of a laptop, mobile and other technology required for work and play.

Equally, people are settling down later, moving around more and not sticking in the same jobs for lengthy periods of time. In the past, it was assumed most people would work in the same job in the same company for life, or most of their life, anyway. In today's society, many workers will reinvent themselves and change jobs frequently over the course of their career, which means a very mobile workforce travelling internationally and upping sticks a great deal more than previous generations.

Not having a job for life and travelling to different jobs and places has an effect on our house-buying patterns. But despite living in these volatile, changing times, I would still encourage everyone who can to get on the property ladder as soon as possible. All the time you're paying rent, you're paying someone else's mortgage, which does not benefit you in the slightest. If the costs are relatively similar, why not pay off your own mortgage?

I would approach buying a first home as a reasonably medium-term decision. You can always rent your home out for a year if you do go to work in another city or country. It gives you an asset, and I think there's a lot to be gained from the personal comfort and security of knowing that's home and that's mine. And when it comes to building up a credit rating (how you are rated when it comes to borrowing money), there's no better way than owning a home and making regular payments on it. It will make it easier to get a loan for a car or another property one day.

And don't get bogged down with thinking your first home has to be perfect. It doesn't have to be what I call your 'forever house' – the place where you will ultimately spend the greatest proportion of your life. Some first-time buyers have told me that if they can't buy what they want, then they won't bother at all. This seems to be a bit blinkered to me, as this is your first home and a start in life, after all. It might not be ideal and should be equated to your first car. Most of us probably won't be in a position to pick up the latest BMW or Mercedes as a first motoring purchase, so why would you expect to walk into a snazzy penthouse or large country rectory?

Besides, life can pass you by if you're always waiting for the perfect job, the perfect relationship and the perfect home. You will have to compromise on something – even the very wealthy don't always get everything they want – and I seriously think it's better to get something, rather than miss the boat and end up with nothing at all. In this book, I'll explain how you can get the best you can, even if you have limited funds. Through tips, advice, case studies and contacts from my little black book, I want to help you acquire a good first home that you will enjoy and benefit from when it comes time to move on.

And even if you feel it's a bit premature for you to be looking for a first home quite yet, do remember everything takes time. I find many first-timers underestimate the time it takes to get a home and actually move in. If you say you want to be in a flat by Christmas and start looking in September, I doubt you'll pull it off. If you want to be in by Christmas, you most likely need to start looking at least six months earlier.

Why to buy

Pros of owning your own home

You might ask, 'Why shouldn't I just keep on renting? It's easier, there's less responsibility and I won't need to worry about endless maintenance.'

It might sound less taxing to let a property, but I think there are many pluses to owing your own home:

- **You get to choose the wallpaper**
  As basic as this might sound, it can be very exciting having something that is yours, and not someone else's. This is your place and you can fill it with whatever you want and decorate it any way you want. Not having to put up with the landlord's somewhat suspect taste in brown, post-war furniture and swirling-patterned carpets can be a huge bonus. You can also convert the loft, dig out the basement and carry out other projects that add value and make living in your home more pleasurable.
- **You aren't throwing away 'dead money'**
  When you rent, you have nothing to show for your money once the rental lease ends. If the value of the place increases, or you put your hand in your pocket to redecorate or install some shelves, you won't see any of the value added.
- **Also, you don't have to move every six months**
  There comes a time in your life that it's no longer quite so fun upping sticks with all your belongings and settling in somewhere

new. And, you don't need to worry about your flatmate doing a runner and leaving you to somehow find all of the rent. Equally, if you have a difficult or unreliable landlord, you no longer have concerns over how the property is being looked after.

- **Once you've finished making all the payments on your home, you will be rewarded with a property that is all yours**
  This means if you pay everything off before you retire, you can live rent- and mortgage-free – a huge boon when you're on a limited income later in life.
- **It can be very fulfilling living in an environment you've chosen, paid for and invested a large part of yourself in**
  You'll feel satisfied coming home from a hard day's work through your own front door and making yourself at home, literally. Remember, your home is your sanctuary, a private place where you spend time with your loved ones.
- **You can take on the maintenance**
  Instead of waiting for a landlord to come and sort out the dry rot or the leaky guttering, you can get on with the work yourself. Equally, you can control how much you pay, instead of having to put up with eye-wateringly high bills that are difficult to question from a landlord.

I feel whenever I've rented property, no matter how pleasant it might appear, I've never had the same feeling that it's mine. Small things can really matter – like, can I have pets? Most landlords aren't all that keen on furry friends. I remember when I got my first home, I would say to myself, 'I've been to work and I deserve this.' Hopefully, you will too when you've put the keys in the door and entered your new home for the first time.

PHIL'S TOP TIP

Property is a good investment. Over a period of time, prices inevitably rise. Buying your first home today should ensure you a decent profit when it's time to sell.

Why not to buy

Cons of owning your own home

You have to be confident enough with your income and ability to pay the mortgage before you take a major step like owning your own home. There's no denying that a home of your own is a commitment and responsibility you can't ignore. Here are some of the biggest disadvantages to being a home owner:

- **You can't move out and on as easily**
  If you rent a property, you can move out and move on quite quickly, which you can't do if you own the title deeds. You might have to give a few weeks' or months' notice as a tenant, dependent on your contract with the landlord, but renting is not the same major tie as being in possession of a property. As long as you don't mind the impermanence of the situation, you can sleep on friends' floors or sofas without the worry or bother of the future.

- **You could fall into negative equity**
  This is when your home is worth less than it was when you bought it, or for the sum you borrowed. In a downturn, property prices can drop and you can find it hard to move on. You might not be able to sell your home for a large enough sum to clear your debts so you will be stuck and going up the ladder will be difficult.

- **Another trap can be coming up with the initial deposit**
  Finding 25% of a £225,000 home is £56,250, which is a lot of cash for most first-timers to find. Some get discouraged and give up at this point.

- **You're committed to working and earning to keep up with your mortgage payments**
  As they say in all the advertisements for lenders' deals, if you don't keep up your payments you are in danger of having your home repossessed. There will be obligations you need to accept and it's all about being encouraged, or forced, to grow up, which I don't think is necessarily a bad thing.

- **You have to pay for any maintenance yourself**
  This includes having to regularly book in plumbers, heating engineers, electricians and builders to carry out set tasks, such as annual checks on the boiler, clearing out guttering and making sure the electrics are up to scratch.

And yet, if the free spirit inside you cries out to remain free and not be tied to home-owning responsibilities, then maybe buying a home is not for you. Or, not right away, anyhow.

Do keep in mind, however, that owning a home can be liberating and a rite of passage, similar to learning to drive. It's a very specific moment in your life, where you get your first piece of Britain. But, the duty and complications involved in the buying process might not suit everyone. And only you will know if buying your first place is the right step to take.

CASE STUDY

LONG-TERM RENTER

Marion Stuart is a full-time renter with no desire to become a homeowner. 'I rent a lovely one-bedroom flat at £325 a week in south-west London, and can't see myself buying anything, to be honest. It's convenient and I don't need to get stressed about looking after the place, because the landlord does everything from fix the boiler to repaint every couple of years.'

Marion, a 38-year-old marketing executive for the sports industry, declares herself a 'dedicated townie' that needs to be close to great shops, restaurants and bars. 'What's the point of buying something miles from the city centre, which is what I would have to do to afford a decent-sized place? I'd rather pay a bit more and live only a few minutes' walk from the action.'

When asked whether Marion thinks she's missed the boat by renting for more than 15 years rather than buying her own home, she says it doesn't bother her. She sees her friends scrimping and saving to come up with enough for a deposit, and then struggling to pay the mortgage when they take the leap and purchase a place. This is enough to put her off ever having to worry about such a responsibility.

'However, my father's worried I'm forking out a great deal of money for something I'll never own. I guess he has a point, although I still don't feel I'm ready to buy something,' she points out.

Her brother, who's an accountant, suggests she could have paid off nearly a third of her mortgage by now if she'd chosen to go down the home-owning road. 'And yet, I wouldn't have had the same experiences travelling abroad and enjoying a full and fun life in the capital. I guess I've made my choice and have to live with it.'

Marion does admit it might be a good idea to one day invest in a small studio flat nearby, so she does have an asset of sorts. 'And if the landlord of my rentals flat ever wanted to sell, I'm sure I'd consider buying – that is, if I can afford it, as prices have nearly doubled in the area.'

PHIL'S TRADE SECRET

My philosophy for a good first-time buy is to get something you will enjoy living in for several years. You might sell sooner, or even rent out your place depending on your situation, but look at this as a pleasurable experience rather than a money-spinner. Keep in mind that you are likely to make a profit when you move to the next rung of the ladder.

In this early phase of debating whether you should take the leap or not, I would advise doing as much research as possible on the Internet, reading newspapers and magazines and talking to friends and family. A good local estate agent should be able to guide you with regards to property types and prices.

One thing you need to be aware of is that the press often talks about how expensive starter homes can be and how hard it is to get on the ladder. Often, national statistics are quoted. Don't be put off, however, and check what prices are doing in the specific area or areas where you hope to buy a home. For instance, the press might say prices are rising, but when you check this out it could refer to London and the south-east (as typically is the case), and not elsewhere in Britain. Getting access to a starter home in Newcastle can vary hugely with access to a first home in London, so do your homework.

Buying with a partner, friend or family member

When you have decided that you're ready to buy, you need to consider whether to go it alone or buy jointly with someone else, such as a friend, partner or relative.

As the song goes, 'You've gotta have friends on whom you can rely.' Buying with a friend, especially a reliable one, might be a clever way to get onto the ladder. Whether you view this as a short-term step until you can afford to get your own place, or a longer-term idea, buying a place with a good chum can be a sensible financial proposition, as well as a fun way to start off life as a homeowner.

I find the main problem with buying with a mate is if something goes wrong and you start to fall out with one another. It is bad enough having problems with a professional colleague, but it's truly heart-breaking 'splitting up' with a very good friend. As well as being emotionally upsetting, it can turn into a financial and practical disaster, too. And don't think that it's only friends who can have a major falling out – a large number of people buy with a family member, thinking that – especially as they've already experienced living together – it won't be as troubled. But believe me: you can suffer many of the same issues with a brother, sister or cousin as you can with a friend. Make sure both of you know what you are getting into.

I've come across a number of first-time buying couples over the years, too. Buying with your boyfriend or girlfriend can be fraught with disaster if the couple splits up. It is a huge commitment buying a home with someone you're in a relationship with. So, do not go ahead with the purchase unless you are certain you can be rational and grown-up about what happens if the love affair flounders and even collapses. Getting an agreement in writing is just as important, if not more so, for a couple as it is for friends buying together. See the below advice on how to put together an agreement to save a lot of rowing and bad blood between you later on.

PHIL'S TOP TIPS

BUYING WITH A PARTNER, FRIEND OR FAMILY MEMBER

- Sit down together and really work out what you both want. If you can't agree on the basics before you start looking for a property, maybe this is a sign this wasn't meant to be and I recommend you pull out now.
- If you are buying together (and won't be sharing a room), make sure you get two double bedrooms in your flat or house, so there are no spats about room sizes and who gets the bigger space. And if you do buy somewhere with a smaller bedroom, then it might be a good idea for the person in the less generous-sized bedroom to pay slightly less towards the mortgage or the bills.
- Get a contract in place so one person can buy the other one out if one of you moves on.
- You should also agree on how the mortgage will be paid and who is responsible for making sure bills are paid on time.
- Also, put in writing what happens if one of you moves out temporarily or if a relationship breaks down. Will the room be rented, and if so, does your co-owner get any say as to who the tenant will be?

- Make a list of simple rules you will both adhere to, so there won't be petty arguments over house cleaning or noise issues.
- A household 'kitty' (a small amount of money put into a pot to cover basic items) is a good idea, as are ways to share some costs, such as food, Internet set-ups and the television licence.

Pros of buying with a partner, friend or family member

- You can share saving up for the deposit. Joining with another person means you don't have to wait quite so long to save up the money.
- You share costs. Buying a home incurs solicitor's fees, survey costs and removal costs. But purchasing with a friend means you'll only pay half.
- You can get a bigger mortgage (some lenders even offer special mortgages). With a co-buyer on board, you can borrow more money, which could mean living in a better neighbourhood, or even in a bigger property.
- You get help with maintaining the property. All of your bills – including any building work, decorating and maintenance costs – are shared by the two of you.
- You can draw up an agreement. A formal contract can make it easier to resolve disputes, compared with buying with a partner or spouse.

Cons of buying with a partner, friend or family member

- You pay higher legal fees. Arranging a formal agreement and deed for co-purchasers costs more, so you'll be paying the solicitor more.
- You could end up disagreeing on certain matters. Despite your written formal agreement, disputes can arise when sharing a home. If someone wants to sell their portion of the property before the other person also wants to move, there could be some friction.

- Your finances are more complex. Although you are sharing costs, working everything out will be more complicated than if you were just doing this on your own.

BUYING WITH A FRIEND

Alexander Wall and Sadat Haryana have known each other since they were 10-year-olds living in the same city. Their parents worked together in Hong Kong, where they were brought up as young boys. They went to the same school and played together every day after the final school bell rang.

They both ended up back in Britain to do their A levels and kept in touch while they studied at Leeds and Birmingham Universities, respectively. Now, Alexander, a junior doctor, and Sadat, a corporate lawyer, have together bought a £350,000, two-bedroom top-floor flat, with a good-sized study and roof terrace, in the heart of Manchester. It costs them £450 a month each to cover the mortgage.

'It wasn't realistic for me to buy a place on my own, so I asked Sadat to come in with me,' explains Alexander. 'He was looking for something quite similar to me, so it made good sense for us to chip in and share a home.'

Although they are getting on well – the duo has even got a train set, not a million miles different from one they played with years ago when they were both still in short trousers – Alexander and Sadat regard this as a short-term step to each getting their own place one day. 'It could take a while, however, as we will need to be in a position to fund a property by ourselves, which can be difficult with prices of property rising or staying steady, and prices for food, utilities and other expenses going up, too,' points out Sadat.

There haven't been any major squabbles to date, although Alexander said they had to put a stop on 'sticky note syndrome'.

'If something was annoying one of us, we had this tendency to complain on bright yellow sticky Post-it notes, which ended up plastering the walls and kitchen counter. It was a bit silly and we sat down and talked about how it would be much better to voice issues and resolve problems as they came up, without resorting to the sticky notes.'

Sadat says he's learned to accept Alexander's 'squeaky violin practice sessions', while Alexander 'has had to put up with my early morning grunts from sit-ups and press-ups.'

'It's a bit like an odd-couple marriage, but without any rings or anniversaries to worry about celebrating,' jokes Alexander. 'On a serious note, we did get a contract drawn up to resolve any potential future disagreements, and if one of us leaves he has to give the other six months' notice. Also, there's an option so one of us can buy the other one out.'

It helps that Sadat's a legal graduate too, as he understands the importance of such an agreement in case there are any disputes at a later date.

Buying with strangers

I've noticed some websites and other social-networking sites trying to match people up to buy a property together. I must admit I'm not convinced that buying your first home with a total stranger is a very good idea, and I'd need some coaxing into believing otherwise.

Buying your first home is a big step, and to undertake this with someone you barely know could be a big mistake. If you are thinking of going down this route at all, do be careful and really check the other person out. You will need to be reassured this is the right thing to do and it might not be a bad notion to ask for some references – personal and financial.

Under these circumstances, it is imperative you get a very formal and tightly written agreement drawn up by a solicitor you trust. Who knows, you might prove me wrong and find buying with a 'pseudo-friend' works out okay for you, but I would not recommend it personally. This is certainly not anything like a rental flat-share, so please keep this in mind before you take the plunge.

YOUR DECIDING-TO-BUY CHECKLIST

☐ Decide if you're ready to buy
☐ Have you got a deposit in place?
☐ If not, is there a friend, family member or partner who would also like to buy a property with you?
☐ List the pros of buying
☐ List the cons of buying

PHIL'S CONTACTS BOOK

- Sharedspaces.co.uk – a terrific website helping first-time buyers invest in property together
- Sharingaccommodation.co.uk – useful information, such as how to buy together, how to sell a shared property and 'ask the experts'
- Loot.com – classified ads for buying and selling
- www.gumtree.com – free classified ads in the UK for buying and selling

CHAPTER TWO

Money, Money, Money

There is no need to be over-awed by financial terminology. Arm yourself with knowledge and the process of getting accepted for a mortgage will seem much less intimidating

Perhaps the most daunting aspect of buying your first home is sorting out your finances. Not only are you making that first exciting step on the property ladder, you're also making a financial commitment that will stay with you well into the future. It's important to understand exactly what you are getting yourself into, from the different sorts of mortgages that are on offer to what other costs you will have to pay, including Stamp Duty.

As you don't want to get yourself tied into an agreement that means you are paying a higher rate of interest than you should, having a clear understanding about the various types of interest that are available to you is essential.

As I mentioned in the last chapter, increasingly first-timer buyers are finding it tough going it alone. They are clubbing together with someone else to buy a home, or borrowing money from a friend or relative to top up the difference if the bank won't lend them enough cash.

There are a number of methods helping first-timers climb onto the property ladder as well, such as the current government-funded shared ownership and HomeBuy schemes, where you can get help from the state towards purchasing a private home (see pages 39 and 82 for more on this).

The process of applying for a mortgage may not be the most enjoyable part of buying a house, but it is essential, and I hope that the tools you find in this chapter will make it as pain-free as possible.

Mortgages explained

I meet a number of first-time buyers who are somewhat blinkered when it comes to understanding exactly what a mortgage entails. Don't be scared by mortgages and other related financial concepts.

Basically, a mortgage is money lent to you by a bank or building society towards the overall cost of your home. These days, it's unlikely you can borrow 100% of the purchase price, so you will have to save towards a deposit on the mortgage.

There are two main kinds of mortgages – **repayment mortgages** and **interest-only mortgages** – and it's pretty straightforward getting to grips with both.

Repayment mortgage

This is a fairly steady-as-you-go mortgage, and is perceived as the safest way to pay off your debts. With a repayment mortgage, you pay some of the loan and the interest on the loan every month. At the end of the allotted mortgage period (which is typically 25 years, but it can be longer), the entire loan will be repaid.

Interest-only mortgage

An interest-only mortgage means that you only pay the interest to the lender each month, so at the end of the mortgage term you will need to repay the entire amount you've borrowed from the lender. In order to do this, you will also put money into an investment scheme each month in order to pay this remaining amount back. The overall monthly amount is therefore less than a repayment mortgage, but there's a risk that the money placed in the investment plan (an endowment, personal pension plan or an ISA, or individual savings account) might not be enough to pay off the entire mortgage at the end of the mortgage term.

Interest-only mortgages suit people like first-time buyers who might not have a great deal of money at the outset. They prefer paying less with an interest-only deal, but I would suggest this is a good idea for only a certain amount of time – usually a few years. Otherwise, you could be stuck trying to pay off the mortgage at a later date. On the plus side, however, you might find that your investment scheme does well and you could end up paying off your mortgage sooner than you thought.

Interest rates

When you choose a mortgage type, you'll be faced with an array of further options for interest rates. Interest is the money you have to pay on top of the loan. So, as well as borrowing the sum required to help pay for your new home, you also have to take into account the rate you are paying to borrow the money.

For instance, you might want to take out a mortgage for £50,000. If you are getting the money with a 6% interest rate, you will be paying back more than a mortgage at a lower interest rate of say, 3% or 4%. Usually, if you put down a lower deposit, you will end up with a mortgage with a higher interest rate, so make sure you understand what you will be paying in total.

Interest rates go up as well as down, so be careful that when you work out what you can afford to repay you take into account the fact that interest rates could rise. Then, you will be required to pay more. You could be in big trouble if your salary isn't enough to cover the mortgage. Before you sign on the dotted line, get advice from a trustworthy financial expert so you don't overstretch yourself.

Interest rates can be worked out in different ways. Here are the main rates and what they mean:

Variable rate

All this means is that the interest rate on your mortgage can vary and go up and down. So, the lender could ask you to pay more or less, depending on what is happening with the economy and financial markets. You need to be prepared to pay more if the rates go up without crippling yourself and losing your home.

Fixed rate

The rate is fixed for a certain period of time, normally for one to five years. This is a sensible approach because you can work out your budget in advance and you won't be worrying what could happen if the rate goes up, as could happen with the variable rate.

If you can afford to go down this route, this is a safe approach. You will know how much you have to pay and it won't alter for a set time.

Interest rates and payments

Take advantage of guides on lenders' websites (if you can't easily access the Internet, you can ask them to post you the guides). These list what you should expect to pay on an interest-only mortgage and repayment mortgage, along with interest rates.

Interest rates are important, of course, but don't forget to check out other things, too. How secure your lender is, particularly in less buoyant economic times, is crucial. You might pay a bit more, but knowing the lender has a good reputation and isn't about to fold will give you peace of mind. Upfront costs and how much you have to pay to get out of an arrangement – it could happen, so bear it in mind – are worth considering as well.

There are a number of variations on the two basic repayment and interest-only mortgages. Lenders are dreaming up new mortgage types – often the main models with a few tweaks around the edges – all the time. You need to ask questions to find out what really is on offer and whether it will work for you.

Here are some examples:

Tracker

A variation on the variable is a tracker mortgage, which moves up and down in tandem with the Bank of England mortgage base rate. Cheaper tracker mortgages might be a bit of a risk at times when it looks like the base rate is about to rise. But when the base rate is steady, your mortgage rate stays where it is.

Capped rate

A capped rate is a mix of variable and fixed rates, if that doesn't sound like a contradiction. What this means is the interest rate is variable (it can go up and down), but it cannot go over a certain amount for an agreed period of time.

Discount rate

A discount rate based on the lender's variable rate (again, one that goes up and down) is given to a buyer for a set amount of time. For instance, you might be offered a discount rate deal where you get 1% off the variable rate for one or two years.

Remember, a building society or bank is more likely to offer you an attractive discount rate if you put down a decent-sized deposit.

Cashback mortgages

You get an extra lump sum of money at the start of your mortgage to spend on anything you want, but usually it has to be linked to the house. This can help first-timers that need money upfront to buy furniture, pay solicitor's fees or cover removal costs. Cashback mortgages are typically linked with a variable-rate mortgage.

Offset mortgages

An offset mortgage literally lets you 'offset' savings from you, or maybe from friends or family, to cut down the interest you pay on your mortgage debt. Say, you have a mortgage of £120,000 and you can hand your lender savings of £20,000, then you only pay interest on £100,000, rather than on the total amount. This saves on the interest and might cut down on the length of time it takes you to pay off the entire mortgage.

I think a good idea, if it works for you, is to perhaps start out with an interest-only mortgage for a few years, and then change to a repayment scheme where you are paying off the amount you have borrowed and the interest. But you need to get proper advice from an expert, as everyone's situation is different.

PHIL'S TOP TIP

Do talk to a good financial adviser, and also sound out your parents and friends who have already bought a home. And remember, what worked for someone else might not always be right for you. A lot depends on how much you earn, how steady your job is and how often you will be moving.

Where to get a mortgage

There are a number of people who can help, from mortgage brokers, special advisers and even Independent Financial Advisers (known as IFAs). But, be careful, as some advisers are less independent than others.

Some might want to push their employers' mortgages, which might not be the best deal for you.

What to ask a mortgage adviser

It's easy to tell first-time buyers to ask plenty of questions to ensure they are getting the right mortgage for them, but what are the right questions to ask? Here are some of my suggestions:

- What are your rates?
- Are there any other costs involved, such as a reservation fee, broker fee or product fee?
- Can I pay any costs upfront or are they tied into the mortgage?
- What will I be charged for a valuation or survey on the property?
- What happens after the initial agreed term is finished? Will I have to pay higher rates?
- If I pay off my mortgage early, do I have to make any payments to the lender?
- If I want to move at some point, can I transfer the mortgage to another property?
- Do I have to buy insurance from the lender?
- Do you offer advice on mortgages from the entire market, or just from a select group of lenders?

PHIL'S TOP TIP

Make sure that anyone you speak to is regulated by the FSA (the Financial Services Authority). It's worth checking out your adviser if you have any concerns. The FSA, the government body that regulates the financial services industry in the UK, keeps a register of everyone regulated, and it is available to the public. Contact details are provided in my Contacts Book at the end of this chapter.

What price can I afford?

It's all very well deciding you want to buy a home. But first, you have to sort out how you will pay for it. As I mentioned in the last chapter, buying a first home isn't always easy in a poor economic climate, with banks frightened to lend money in case they don't get it back, and the difficulties of saving when interest rates remain low.

I don't think there's much point going out shopping for accommodation, though, if you can't pay for it. If you estimate that a typical couple will need in the region of £30,000 for a deposit, you also need to remember to factor in other costs, such as Stamp Duty (a government tax based on the purchase price), solicitor's fees and removal costs. If you choose to get help from a house finder, that's another added cost. And don't forget that you will need a certain amount of money to kit your home out. Even if you beg, borrow and steal from friends and family, there are still some costs that are likely to crop up.

So, if the couple's raised only £20,000, they could be wasting their time looking at property until they stump up more cash; a £10,000 difference in savings can mean ending up with a lender willing to give you £280,000 for a home, instead of one at a lesser £200,000.

It can be dispiriting being able to scrape together only a small amount over a two- to three-year period if your salary isn't rising exponentially and prices are soaring. Relative to earnings, first-time buyers 25 years ago could borrow 90% of the value of a home, compared to about 75% today. Equally, the house price to earnings ratio was 2:9, while now it is 4:6. The average deposit, according to figures from the Nationwide Building Society, was only £1,321 a quarter of a century ago, while today you have to save £35,614.

Mortgage calculations

A good way to discover if you can afford a home right now is to go on the Internet and put your earnings and outgoings into a bank's or building society's online mortgage calculator. This gives you an indication of how much you can borrow.

For instance, let's say a couple earns £44,400 a year between them, and has saved a deposit of £25,000. Outstanding loans total £1,500 paid out annually for a car and student loan repayments. Taking all of this into account (the lender also might want other details, such as your planned retirement age and information on pension schemes), a leading building society will lend the first-time buying couple up to £310,000.

Even though things can look grim for today's first-timers, you can usually find a way through. Good research to find out what deals are on offer is key, along with understanding how the whole financial process works. The New Homes Marketing Board advises saving regularly, which not only accumulates cash towards a deposit, but provides you with some emergency funds for repairs and maintenance on a new property.

PHIL'S TOP TIP

It's easy working out how much you can afford to spend on a home. Find out how much the lender will give you (usually three or four times the average salary). Add this figure to the amount you've saved. Then, subtract the total from the price of the property. If it doesn't add up, you need to find a way to cover the deficit.

Hidden costs

Here's my list of costs first-time buyers must remember. You will need to put aside money to cover them. They can add up, so be sensible and make sure you're not caught short.

- **Estate agent's fee**
  Normally (and mercifully), this is paid by the vendor, but you might engage a property finder to help you find a home.
- **Solicitor's fee**
  This can vary, but you should allow from about £400. Make sure you get a quote upfront. Some solicitors will do the job for a set fee, while others charge by the hour.
- **Valuation**
  The lender will send someone to check out the property to ensure it's worth the sum they are lending you.
- **Survey**
  You might want a simple ('walk through') survey, or a full-blown survey to see what kind of shape the property is in. A lender usually wants a survey to be carried out.
- **Searches**
  Searches looking for anything unusual or untoward (rights of way or clauses linked to the property's usage) are carried out by the solicitor. The costs are usually included in the solicitor's fee.
- **Land Registry**
  The property will have to be registered with the government's Land Registry. A small fee is charged, depending on the property's value.
- **Mortgage arrangement**
  You will have to pay the bank or building society a small fee for arranging your mortgage. This varies according to the lender, but can be a couple of hundred pounds.
- **Removal costs**
  It can cost anything from about £50 to hire a small van, right through to several thousand pounds, depending on how many services you request (are you happy to pay extra for someone to wrap up all of your belongings, for instance). This is a cost most first-time buyers forget to factor in, so you have been warned.

- **Stamp Duty**
  A purchase tax from the government charged on all purchases of houses, flats and other land and buildings (see page 36 for more information).
- **House-finder fee** – An optional extra, if you employ a house finder to help you find a property. This could cost anything from a few hundred pounds to several thousand, depending on how much assistance you require and how much a particular house finder charges. Expect to pay about 1–2% of the purchase price.

How much will I have to pay?

The amount you will need to cough up depends on a variety of factors that determine value, including the location, size and state of the property. Other issues can push up the price too, such as whether the property is brand new (new homes cost more, typically) or it's a period home with character.

If you end up fighting over a home because other buyers want it as well, you could well pay more for it. You need to be careful under these circumstances and stick to a price threshold you won't go beyond. It's easy to get carried away and pay an over-the-top price if you fall head over heels with a particular place. But, you could end up struggling to make the mortgage payments, and even go into debt if you're not careful.

What can I afford to pay on my mortgage per month?

As boring as it might sound, learning to budget is massively important. It's not that difficult working out what your outgoings are and how much money is coming into your personal piggybank. Some lenders, such as the Nationwide, have fantastically good charts (check on the Internet and you can download them) where you can determine what you have to pay for various items and how much money you need to cover these costs. Other good websites with household budget calculators are: www.thisismoney.co.uk and the Cooperative Bank's goodwithmoney.co.uk.

A typical chart lists your income – your salary, any gifts and interest from your savings – and personal costs going out. The latter includes items such as:

- Food and drink
- Transport
- Clothing
- Telephones
- Entertainment
- Credit card payments

You need to think of what your mortgage will cost, and other set costs, including:

- Council tax
- Insurance
- Electricity
- Gas or oil
- Water rates

You can add up all of your costs, take the total away from your income and then you'll know if you can manage. I would suggest allowing for the odd treat and also some money for emergencies and repairs. You will need to maintain your new home and should allocate some money towards the upkeep. This amount would vary depending on the size of your property and the state it is in, but I'd estimate from about £750 a year for a small flat in a reasonable condition, and £1,000 plus for something larger needing more work.

Are you credit worthy?

Banks and building societies do not want to take big risks when lending money. They're often more cautious when it comes to first-time buyers without much of a credit history.

When you fill in your mortgage application, you will receive a score – a bit like in an exam – based on how successfully and promptly you have paid off any debts. This could include credit cards, store cards and any other payments you have regularly made when you have 'borrowed' money for items.

Being credit worthy means getting a good 'credit score'. A good way to build up credit worthiness is to pay off debts quickly and efficiently. This means when a check is carried out on you, you will come up trumps and be more attractive to a lender.

PHIL'S TRADE SECRET

You can improve your credit status in several ways, including getting store cards and making sure you make payments every month. This way, you do not have to pay any interest, while at the same time you build up a credit rating. Another simple way is to register to vote.

And if you are concerned about your status, you can hire credit-rating agencies that will check out your record for a small sum (typically, £20–£100). Sometimes mistakes are made that can blight your credit rating and agencies can wipe this from your record. Details of agencies are in my Contacts Book at the end of the chapter.

Applying for a mortgage

The first step is getting an agreement in principle from the lender for the amount you want to borrow. For this initial stage, you will need to supply a certain amount of information, including where you are employed, your income and outgoings, and if you've already got this far, the property you hope to buy and your solicitor's details.

You will be expected to produce several pay slips if you have a staff job, or tax returns for the last couple of years if you are self-employed. There tends to be a lot of form filling, but don't be put off. The lender can explain anything that is a bit baffling, so just be patient and do your best to provide the information required.

Once you've made an offer on a property you fancy, you will need to go back to the lender to provide more detailed information, so they can make up their minds about really lending you the money. This process can take some time, so stay calm and get back to the lender (or broker, if you're using an in-between source to help you get the best mortgage) as quickly as you can with any additional facts they need. If you linger too long and don't get on with it, you might well lose the place you like. So, be efficient and do your best to supply everything fast.

What will the lender want?

- Passport details and National Insurance number
- Proof of address, such as utility or council tax bills
- Your employer's name and contact details (including your own, if you're self-employed)
- Proof of income (pay slips, P45 slip, etc)
- Last few bank statements and outgoings, debts and loans
- List of assets, including other bank accounts and investments
- Details of the property you want to buy
- Your solicitor's details
- Mortgage requirements
- Valuation and/or survey requirements
- Mortgage protection requirements
- Insurance requirements

PHIL'S TRADE SECRET

To help this whole process go smoothly, prepare everything beforehand. It can be terribly time-consuming and annoying having to hunt down old pay slips and tax returns, and your lender is likely to ask for other details, too. You could miss out on a good home if you can't supply what is needed and you end up delaying the entire process.

Fill out everything you're asked to fill out, and don't be shy if you need to ask questions. Your broker and/or lender will help you, so you're not alone.

FINANCIAL PHOBIC

Don Riley, a 29-year-old radio producer in Norwich, says he's always been a bit blinkered when it comes to financial matters. 'I don't know why, but I always tense up at the thought of talking to my bank manager, or anyone else who might expect me to do some maths. I know it's a bit childish, but I'm pretty scared of getting to grips with pretty much anything to do with money.'

While he believes the time has come for him to get his own flat, helped by a small legacy of £25,000 from his aunt, Don's reluctance to face up to financial matters means that he hasn't done his research to discover how to raise the money to buy his first home.

'I don't even know if that would cover the deposit, but now I must swallow my fears and do my homework. The hardest part is knowing who to ask for help and how best to get started in my search for a mortgage.'

Don thinks the best approach is for him to check out what two of his friends, both mates from university, have done to get on the ladder. One has bought a two-bedroom flat in London with his sister, and the other has just made an offer on a new studio flat in Ipswich, where he's recently accepted a job as a teacher.

'My mother's recommended a broker she used to remortgage the family house in Cambridge. He's also found her good insurance for her car, so it seems a great place to start,' says Don.

Don has also checked out some first-time buyers' guides on several bank and building society websites. 'I'm becoming less frightened about everything and have even found myself playing with the mortgage calculator on these sites. At this rate, I will get over my financial phobia, I hope, and get on with it. My mum thinks it's all to do with growing up and accepting more responsibility. She's probably right.'

Don's elder sister, who bought a small one-bedroom cottage in Lincolnshire with her fiancé, says what worked for her was actually going into her bank and a local building society and having a good chat with financial advisers.

'Inspired by my far braver sister, I've booked an appointment with my mum's broker and my building society manager. And, I've printed off a chart of outgoings and incomings from the building society's website that I can start filling out. Who knows? By this time next year, I might actually be living somewhere as an owner, rather than a tenant.'

Stamp Duty – what it is and why we have to pay it

One of the costs that, depending on the price of the property, you may have to stump up is Stamp Duty. It can be a fairly hefty amount of money, so it's important to factor this into your calculations.

Stamp Duty is an ancient tax first introduced in the UK in 1694 during the reign of William and Mary to raise money for the war against France. At first, it was a tax, or duty, on documents (like the transfer of ownership of land) that required the royal seal (or stamp) to be legally valid.

When you buy a property, the change in land ownership has to be legally registered at the Land Registry. This process requires a certificate from the HMRC (HM Revenue & Customs), which they only issue on receipt of the Stamp Duty Land Tax due on the purchase of the property. If you don't pay the Stamp Duty, you can't buy your new home.

How much will I pay?

Stamp Duty is a tax charged on all land and property transactions in the UK. It can also apply to buying shares. When you buy a property, you almost always pay Stamp Duty (known as Stamp Duty Land Tax). The version for shares is known as Stamp Duty Reserve Tax.

The amount of Stamp Duty Land Tax buyers pay varies depending on the price of the property, which falls into a band grouping, and you have to pay the tax related to that band, as per the table below.

Purchase price:	Stamp Duty rate:
Up to £125,000	0%
Over £125,000, to £250,000	1% (0% for first-time buyers)
Over £250,000, to £500,000	3%
Over £500,000	4%
Over £1 million	5% (from 6 April 2011)

As you can see from the table, purchasers buying a freehold or leasehold property (see page 46 for the differences between the two) for a purchase price more than £125,000 pay Stamp Duty Land Tax (SDLT) of between 1% and 4% of the entire purchase price.

However, if the purchase price of the property is £125,000 or less, the property is exempt from Stamp Duty.

The rates above apply to all buyers, except first-time buyers. The good news is that the threshold for when you start to pay Stamp Duty is now £250,000. This only applies if you've never owned a house or flat in the UK or anywhere else in the world. If you're buying with someone else, they also must never have owned property before to be exempt. This higher threshold relates to purchases made on or after 25 March 2010 and before 25 March 2012.

It's worth keeping an eye on the threshold for first-time buyers. The government tends to tweak this every so often, as it's a bit of a vote-winner if you're the political party being seen to help out beleaguered first-time purchasers.

This information was correct at the time of going to print, but could change in the near future. You can check out the current rates of

Stamp Duty Land Tax on the HM Revenue & Customs (HMRC) website (www.hmrc.gov.uk).

There are a couple of other ways where first-time buyers are either exempt or pay less Stamp Duty:

Disadvantaged Areas Relief

If you buy a home in an area designated by the government as 'disadvantaged', you might qualify for Disadvantaged Areas Relief. In this case the threshold for Stamp Duty Land Tax is £150,000. If you're a first-time buyer, it's unlikely you need to apply, as currently the threshold for first-time buyers is higher at £250,000. You can get more details on Disadvantaged Areas Relief from the HM Revenue & Customs website (www.hmrc.gov.uk), as above.

Zero-carbon homes

Another way you can escape paying Stamp Duty and help save the planet at the same time is to buy a 'zero-carbon' home. All qualifying homes under £500,000 are exempt, and houses at or above £500,000 will have their Stamp Duty bill reduced by £15,000.

The government definition of a zero-carbon home is one that can be connected to the mains electricity and gas, but needs to have sufficient additional renewable power to cover the average consumption of a house over a year. To achieve this, the fabric of the building has to be insulated and built to very high standards and the house needs to incorporate renewable energy technologies. Additionally, the house must be zero-carbon over the course of the year.

Don't be discouraged, but I come across very few zero-carbon homes when house finding or filming for my television series. But as more builders start to erect zero-carbon homes, this might become a possible Stamp Duty saver in the future for first-time purchasers. For more information, again go to the HM Revenue & Customs (HMRC) website (www.hmrc.gov.uk).

I get by with a little help from the government

For anyone feeling discouraged about ever gathering together enough money to buy a home, there are other options to consider that offer help to first-timers. At various times, the government injects cash to subsidise projects and make it easier for first-time purchasers struggling to buy a property.

At the time of going to press, the central government was still offering some government-backed schemes to help first-time buyers get onto the ladder, such as **HomeBuy Direct**. This is where first-timers can buy new homes from house builders that are partly funded by the government. There is more information about how different house builders set out these government-sponsored projects below. However, depending on budgets set in the future these initiatives could change, so do check out government (www.direct.gov.uk) and house-builder websites to see what's still on offer and gauge how long the funding is likely to run.

In essence, different house builders across the UK have given different first-time buyer schemes different names. This might sound confusing, but it's more marketing and advertising bravado to help these units sell, rather than anything else. The principles behind the incentives are fairly similar, but they're mapped out in a variety of ways. I've outlined some to give you an idea of what developers are suggesting.

Essentially, you can borrow up to 20% of the price, which you pay back interest-free over a 10-year period. Also, you might get half of the 10% deposit paid, too. The schemes differ slightly, so it's worth talking to developers to see what help they're giving on their sites.

And remember that, to a degree, these schemes are negotiable. Basically, the house builder just wants to shift the property as soon as possible. If it means throwing in a few extras, they might certainly consider this – especially in a downturn or quieter market.

The following government-funded schemes were in place when this book went to print. It's worth double-checking whether these schemes, or variations on them, are still operating.

Easy Start

This plan from house builder Taylor Wimpey lets first-time purchasers buy a new home for 85% of the full market value, 5% of which is put down as a deposit. The remaining 80% is found through a mortgage the buyer has arranged in advance, while the rest of the 15% equity is covered by an interest-free loan from the developer. The buyer has to pay this back over a 10-year period.

Deposit Match

This is another Taylor Wimpey idea that was designed to help those first-timers who are finding it hard to save enough money for a deposit. They need to come up with a 5% deposit and then the house builder will match a further 5% towards the overall deposit through a 10-year, interest-free loan. The higher the deposit, typically the more you can borrow, so this could help by doubling the deposit.

Friends and Family Advantage

If you can get friends or family to help with a maximum of 20% towards the full purchase price of a new property, they will get 5% interest a year on this investment over the next five years. This is another Taylor Wimpey offer, and it's worth talking to other developers to see if they'll do something similar. You have to weigh up whether this is a good return for the family and friends who have come to the rescue, of course, by comparing interest rates directly with banks and building societies.

Parent Power

A variation of Friends and Family Advantage, Barratt Homes says it will match any contribution from a parent or parents up to a maximum of 5% of the value of the home. The extra money can be used as cash towards the deposit, or to help with buying furniture and furnishings.

Head Start

A hard-pressed first-time purchaser can buy a new property for 85% of the asking price, and the remaining 15% can be paid back to Barratt Homes over 10 years in the form of an interest-free loan. If you sell the property, you have to pay the remainder before you move on. This could help cut down on upfront costs and give you a chance to get a better mortgage deal from a lender, as you only need an 80% mortgage then (with only a 5% deposit required).

David Wilson Homes also offers a Head Start programme, very similar to Barratt's. This one is a deferred payment scheme, where buyers pay 85% of the asking price and the developer again covers the remaining 15% with an interest-free loan that has to be paid back in 10 years. The house builder might also pay 5% of the deposit through its 5% deposit paid incentive.

Helping Hand

The developer, this time Hillreed Homes, defers 10% of the value of the home, and like the other schemes, you pay back the money at any time over the next decade. Also, the house builder offers to put up 5% towards your deposit.

EasyBuy

Again, you own 100% of your property right off the bat by only coming up with 85% of the purchase price upfront, while the house builder, Crest Nicholson, lends you the other 15% that you have to pay back within a 10-year period. The developer will pay 5% of the deposit, like many of the others, while it combines this with a 90% mortgage deal with a lender.

MyWay

First-timers pay 80% of the price, while Miller Homes offers the remaining 20% that the buyer has to pay back within a decade. Miller also will double any deposit saved, up to a maximum of £5,000.

Bank of Mum and Dad

You might be keen to buy your first home, so you can escape the clutches of Mum and Dad, and all that living under the roof of the family home entails. This is completely understandable, but increasingly getting parental help is a way of getting onto the property ladder.

As Winston Churchill once wryly observed, 'Saving is a fine thing. Especially when your parents have done it for you.'

CASE STUDY

FAMILY FORTUNES

Siblings Philip and Amelia Cronin are unlikely to disagree with Winston, as they have been given a leg up from their parents Judy and Gareth Cronin. Mr and Mrs Cronin are giving their two offspring the sum of £47,000 for the deposit and money to carry out building work on their first joint home – a £250,000, two-bedroom flat in west London.

Philip, 28, has been renting with friends nearby, and Amelia recently moved back home in order to save some money after travelling in the Far East. 'We were both desperate to get our own place, so we asked our parents for help,' explains 26-year-old Amelia, who works as an administrator for a children's charity.

As well as stumping up a quarter of a million pounds to buy the flat, the younger Cronins also need the wherewithal to knock out a wall between the kitchen and living area, update the bathrooms, sort out a damp problem and replace the windows. 'It just wouldn't be possible without our parents' assistance,' Amelia adds.

Research from the Alliance & Leicester Building Society reveals that the Cronins are not alone in helping their progeny. Nearly half of all parents are forking out close to £18,000 to help their children buy their first homes, with some surpassing their offspring's expectations, offering on average £4,000 more than they were expecting.

It's not surprising that first-time buyers generally on lower salaries are looking for extra funding from their parents to get on the housing ladder. That crucial first rung of the ladder does seem to be slipping out of reach for a number of first-time buyers, and if parents are willing to either loan or give their children some of their inheritance in advance in the form of a deposit on a house, it does make sense.

Taking the parents' income and/or savings into account can certainly help a first-time buyer trying to get a mortgage. There are even special mortgages you can take out, called guarantor mortgages, where the parents essentially guarantee the payments if the lender is concerned about the ability of the first-time buyer to keep up payments. As these change on a regular basis, I can't really include them here, but it's worth checking what is available at the time you are interested in exploring this way of funding a mortgage.

PHIL'S TOP TIP

Just like buying with a friend, you really don't want to fall out with your mum and dad. I think it's worth drawing up an agreement clearly outlining what you are borrowing from your parents, how you will pay it back (if it's a loan) and how any profit will be distributed, if this is part of the deal. I've seen too many family wrangles over money and it would be a shame to end up fighting over one of the finer points of this contribution to a first-time buyer's home.

YOUR FINANCES CHECKLIST

☐ Work out how much you can afford to spend
☐ Find the best mortgage offer for you
☐ Get an offer lined up from a lender
☐ Work out other costs you will have to cover

- ☐ Get all the paperwork (lender's forms and bank statements) in place
- ☐ Gather up identification (driving licence, passport and references, if required) for the lender
- ☐ If buying jointly, get an agreement drawn up to settle any disputes, or if one of you wants to sell his share
- ☐ Get a certificate from the lender stating how much you can borrow
- ☐ Check to see what government schemes are in place and whether you can get assistance

PHIL'S CONTACTS BOOK

- www.godirect.co.uk – particularly helpful for working out mortgage quotes for joint owners
- Council of Mortgage Lenders (CML) – 020 7437 0075, www.cml.org.uk – trade association for UK mortgage lenders
- www.moneysavingexpert.com – the extremely useful website by money expert Martin Lewis that helps save you money and offers tips, advice and other consumer information
- www.moneysupermarket.com – a site where you can compare the cost of financial products, including mortgages
- Association of Independent Financial Advisers – aifa.net – to help you find a financial adviser
- Financial Services Authority (FSA) – 0845 606 1234, www.fsa.gov.uk
- British Bankers' Association (BBA) – for information leaflets, go to www.bba.org.uk
- Building Societies Association (BSA) – for general information from building societies, go to www.bsa.org.uk
- Experian.co.uk and equifax.co.uk – two sites where you can get easy access to your credit rating

Different Types of Homes

There's a plethora of different types of homes you can buy in Britain – which one is right for you?

It's all very well talking about buying a first home, but what sort of place should you buy? A great deal depends, of course, on who you are, where you want to buy, how much money you have and your likes and dislikes.

There is a huge variety of property you can invest in, from a small flat or maisonette (a flat on two levels with internal stairs, and often, its own entrance at street level), to a house in a row of terraces, to a semi-detached (pairs of houses built side-by-side) or detached house.

As well as a house type, you need to think about the age of the property. You can buy a period home that is many hundreds of years old, or opt for a brand-new home. Most of the UK's first-time purchases lie somewhere in the middle in Victorian terraces, twentieth-century purpose-built blocks or post-war housing estates that are comprised of starter homes (small one-, two- or three-bedroom homes) that are ideal for a first-time buy.

Of course, there are pros and cons for old and new, or detached or semi-detached property. Here are some of the questions you should ask with regards to house type and age:

- How noisy is the terrace? Are there soundproofed floors, or at least carpets to absorb some of the sound?
- How roomy is the new flat? Keeping in mind that the measurements of most new homes have diminished over the years, will you have enough space?
- Is the purpose-built block above a shop or restaurant? If so, will you be bothered by noise or cooking smells from the business premises below?
- As detached property costs more than semi-detached or terraced homes, is it worth paying the extra money to live separately and own an asset others will want in the future?
- A semi-detached property can be the next best thing to a detached home, as long as you get on with your neighbour. Have you checked out who lives there?
- The success of living in a new development block or converted older building often relies on good property management. Who owns and looks after the building, and does it look well tended?

Freehold vs leasehold

Getting to grips with what you are buying and understanding key terms is essential. Two you will need to know about are **freehold** and **leasehold**, which are terms that refer to different ways property in England and Wales can be owned. Scotland has its own version ('feuhold'). Leasehold does exist in Scotland, but it isn't as common as in England and Wales.

A **freehold** property is one that includes both the property and the land where it is built. You do not have to pay ground rent or any service charges, because you are the owner and what is known as the freeholder. You will own the property and the land forever as the freeholder, and if you die, it is part of your estate and can be left to your heirs. Your entitlement to do what you want with your freehold property is only limited by planning and other laws. You are totally responsible for the property and its upkeep.

A **leasehold** property, which applies mainly to flats (houses are almost always freehold), means that you own the property for a certain period of time as specified on the lease or contract with the freeholder, but not the land on which the property is built. Someone else, the freeholder, owns the land. You will have to pay an annual ground rent (usually a nominal sum of no more than a few hundred pounds, but it can be more) to the freeholder.

Equally, you will be charged service (or maintenance) charges (this is typical for flats in a building) to cover the cost of insurance, cleaning and upkeep on the communal parts of the building and the land. Usually, the freeholder will take out insurance for the whole building, so you could argue you are saving some money on insurance.

You only have the right to occupy the property for the amount of time that is written on the lease agreement with the freeholder. This could be anything from a few years in the case of a short leasehold or up to 999 years on a long leasehold. In Scotland, few homes are leasehold, with the vast majority freehold.

Some foreign buyers, particularly Americans, can be wary of leasehold properties, as they're used to property in their own countries being freehold. This could affect a sale, so it is best to have all agreements with the freeholder transparent and easy to understand. A good property solicitor should check into the leasehold agreement for you when you're buying the property.

It can sometimes be more difficult getting a mortgage from the bank or building society on a leasehold property compared to a freehold. A lot can depend on how much time is left to run on the lease after the end of the mortgage term

– the shorter the lease, the trickier it might be. Also, don't forget that it can take longer to get information about leasehold properties, which could slow down the process of getting a mortgage and gathering information for a search and survey.

New rules introduced under the 1993 Leasehold Reform Housing and Urban Development Act and its amendments have given flat owners the chance to extend their leases. Typically, lease extensions are granted in 90-year blocks and a tenant must have owned the property for two years before the date of the claim to extend the lease. You do not have to occupy the property, however, and the original lease must have been for a term of over 21 years.

The rules apply to all the Estates, bar the National Trust, English Heritage and the Crown Estate. Different Estates seem to apply different rules as to how long they'll grant leases. For instance, the Grosvenor Estate won't grant a long lease for a 20-year short lease, but usually tops it up by another 20 years; while the Crown Estate will negotiate, but is not forced by law to comply.

Choosing the right type of property usually comes down to matching something to how you live your life. A new inner-city flat might appeal to someone who works long hours in a nearby office, for example; while a keen gardener might be willing to commute from further away, simply to have a small patch of garden where she can grow sweet peas and cabbages, and maybe even have a few chickens scratching around.

Second-hand homes (or resales)

Many people favour new homes, which can be a good option, but there are a number of good reasons why a second-hand property can be a good buy, too.

Just like going to a charity shop to buy a perfectly good used suit, you can buy a slightly worn second-hand home. One of the main advantages is price: second-hand homes (or resales, as agents call them) are generally cheaper than new homes. Also, although you might have to carry out a bit of work to freshen them up, you can stagger the work dependent on when you have the funds to pay for it, and you can turn a bit of a profit when it comes time to sell.

One shouldn't be daunted by a home that needs a bit of work. As long as the structure is sound, the work is likely to be more decorative, which can be quite fun to carry out. You ensure you get the look you want and feel you have a real stake in the property as you add your personal touches to it. Besides, it's amazing and quite inspiring what a lick of paint and some small repairs can add to a dated property.

Taking on something requiring more in terms of refurbishment needn't be alarming either. You do need to be realistic about how much you can do, of course, but a bit of time and energy invested in tackling a resale could be a sound investment.

Also, you don't need to do everything in one go. Just like developers build large schemes in phases, you can come up with a similar staggered plan for your own mini-refurbishment. If you don't have all the money at the beginning, divide up what needs to be done and do it in sections.

For instance, you might want to fix the leaking gutter and get the boiler sorted when you first move in, so there's no damp and you're warm. Then, you can tackle the cosmetics, such as repainting and putting down some new carpet. It makes sense, obviously, to carry out any structural work first, so you don't have to undo what you've just done. Repainting first to only have the job ruined when you dig into the walls to sort out the wiring would be not only a waste of time, but a waste of money, too.

It might even be worth paying for a session with an architect (it won't cost more than a few hundred pounds to get advice) and he could explain how you could best do the work in stages. It would be money well spent, which you'd probably get back in the long run. Once you've found your property and have moved in, check out chapter 11 for tips on how to fix up your new home.

PHIL'S TRADE SECRET

Keep an eye out for ex-council property. It might be dated — from the 1950s onwards — or even in an older converted period building. Check out the building, the estate (if it's on one) and the area. Some ex-local authority property can be quite good and the estate where it sits friendly and well established — recently I passed a well-tended council estate in Bristol, for instance, that was all neatly planted with lovely flowers and shrubs. Neighbours were chatting and children were out playing with one another.

Equally, I've come across some local authority property that's perched up on the sixteenth floor of a graffiti-sprayed 1960s concrete block where the lift rarely works. It is likely you would feel less secure and more alienated here, so be cautious where you buy. And even if you feel relatively safe, a future tenant or the next buyer might not agree.

You can find some good deals, however, and as an area — and the council building — is upgraded, you could do well in the long run.

What to look for when buying a golden girl

- **Guttering and roof**

  If there are leaks and rust on metal gutters, water might have seeped into the house, rotting the wooden timbers.

- **Slates**

  Are any missing or have they slipped out of place? This might be a sign that you have to replace the roof, which could be pricey.

- **Chimney**

  Is the stack sealed at the joint, with the roof, and is the brickwork intact? Look for cracked mortar and any leaks.

- **Dry rot**

  It's easy to spot dry rot simply by sniffing. If there's a musty scent and you can see cracked woodwork, this could mean there's dry rot. Dry rot is caused by a fungus (*Serpula lacrynens*), which can be very expensive to sort out, as you have to replace all the wood that has been infested. Mind, you could get a big discount on the property if you're prepared to take the risk that the problem can be fixed.

- **Leasehold vs freehold**

    I've talked about the difference between leasehold and freehold property earlier in this chapter (see page 46). To recap, freehold refers to the property and the land on which it is built, while leasehold means you own a property for an agreed number of years as set out in a lease. With older properties, however, there could be complications with **restrictive covenants**, a legal reference where you aren't allowed to do something, or go somewhere. One common example is a restrictive covenant inserted into a lease regarding rights of way. This could mean the public is allowed to access your property to get to a road or footpath. Generally, any anomalies are more likely to be found in older properties, so get a good solicitor to check everything out before you buy.

PHIL'S TOP TIP

A good way to find a property is to walk or drive around an area you like the look of, keeping your eyes open for 'For Sale' signs displayed outside.

New homes

A good way to get onto the property ladder is to buy a new home from a house builder. In chapter 2, I outlined a number of deals available aimed at first-time buyers in particular, which can be advantageous in a number of ways. See page 39.

I find that some first-time buyers can be frightened of buying a new home, but developers love you. You aren't in a chain, which means you don't have a home to sell first, and therefore, you aren't waiting for someone else to sell his home so you can move. This is good news for a developer that doesn't like complications, long chains or deals falling through.

In public relations terms, it can also look good for a house builder to be seen to be helping first-time buyers. Nothing can be more heart-warming than a story about a developer, generally regarded by the public as a money-grabbing chancer just out to make a quick buck, selling a first home to a young purchaser.

We've all seen the photographs in the press of a nice young person or couple, sitting on the sofa in their lovely new home (usually staged in the show flat so the pictures look better). To be fair, some house builders really do care about first-timers, and you can identify them pretty quickly by going onto developers' websites to see what initiatives and guides they have for first-time buyers.

A new starter home in Britain ordinarily means a one- or two-bedroom flat. Some developers call them apartments, making them sound terribly posh, but apartment means the same thing as flat. The marketing departments of new-build homes prefer to use the word apartment, as it makes the property sound more luxurious.

As many first-time buyers are buying later in life now, they're starting to miss out a rung, or even two, on the leap up the ladder into a larger flat, or a small starter house. This gives more options, and often, you get better value from a larger flat or small house than a one-bedroom flat. As one-bedroom flats are popular with first-timers and investors wanting to rent them out, the prices can appear higher for the space you're actually getting. The catch, of course, is you need that extra bit of cash in the first place to buy a bigger place.

Whatever you choose, you need to understand the pros and cons of buying something brand-new.

New beginnings: the pros of buying a new home
- No one has ever lived in your home before and you'll be the first person to enjoy its unsullied freshness.

- There's no work for you to do, saving time, effort and money.
- New homes are more eco-friendly and up to four times more energy efficient than older properties, leading to a smaller carbon footprint and lower bills.
- New homes often come with the latest design and technology: fitted kitchens and bathrooms, high-pressure showers and wiring for sound and home entertainment systems.
- Security is generally better, from secure double-glazed windows, fire-resistant materials and circuit breakers, to smoke alarms and modern locks, knocking down insurance premiums and giving you more peace of mind. There might even be a concierge or porter in a reception area (or foyer).
- Modern materials mean you don't have to worry about leaks and woodworm.
- Forget about surveys and upward chains, delaying when you move in.
- Often, you can personalise your home by choosing carpets, curtains, tiling and paint colours.
- Sometimes, plumbed-in new appliances are included in the price, which means not having to choose, buy and install them yourself.
- You're unlikely to be confronted with many nasty surprises, such as problems with the electrics or bad plumbing, as most new homes are covered by 10-year building warranties. However, beware of developers cutting corners and giving you a polished look that hides a tired infrastructure.

You're covered: building warranties

Most new homes or newly converted homes are covered by a 10-year building warranty, so if there are any problems the company that's provided the warranty can make an inspection and see to any repair work that's required. This raises standards in the new-build industry and gives consumers protection from shoddy workmanship or rogue builders.

Keep in mind that most lenders will not give you a mortgage on a new or newly converted home unless you have some form of cover. A leading developer will have a contract with an established building warranty firm, building in the price of the insurance into the selling price of the property. Typically, this is based on a scale of charges relating to the sales value of each home.

One example of a building warranty company is NHBC (0844 633 1000, nhbc.co.uk) that insures over 80% of all the new homes in Britain. Currently, around 1.7 million new homes in the UK are covered by NHBC's Buildmark warranty.

A building warranty doesn't cover everything (you will need separate general home insurance to cover the contents of your place), but it ensures backup if you are having concerns about a builder not delivering a product that's up to scratch, or they're not readily fixing something that has gone wrong.

If a builder goes bust, you'll be insured, too. If you believe your builder is no longer trading prior to completion, you can contact the NHBC, or another company providing the warranty, direct.

After completion and during the builder's liability period (usually a 10-year period), you will contact the builder first to get him to resolve the problem. If the work isn't carried out to your satisfaction, you can then go to the likes of NHBC for them to remedy it. And, after the liability period, you can go direct to the building warranty company and they might still be able to help, depending on how your contract is worded.

If you sell your home before the 10-year liability period is up, the insurance cover transfers automatically to the new owner – a good selling point to reassure your new buyer.

Before you buy a home, you are advised to check with the house builder if you will be given a building warranty. You or your solicitor can check if a builder is covered, if you are concerned. Larger firms, such as NHBC, have a register of developers and house builders who are covered. You can search by company name, county and NHBC registration number on the website (nhbc.co.uk/Builders), or through Customer Services, on 01908 747255 (email: cssupport@nhbc.co.uk).

Providing warranties is big business, so if you want to take out cover yourself (if it's not automatically provided by a developer), there are a variety of firms from which to choose. A good solicitor can probably recommend a company, and remember, if you go down the self-build route (building your own home), you can take out insurance as well.

The cons of buying a new home

- A new home usually costs more than an older property. You are paying extra, because it has been untouched and there won't be anything for you to do.
- Depending on when you move in, it is likely you will have to put up with noise, dust and other disruptions while the rest of the scheme is completed. Typically, this can take two to three years.
- Even in the best of new homes, you have to expect some 'snagging'. This means tradesmen will have to come back to sort out glitches and problems with the building work. It can be frustrating and time-consuming if they have to return several times to right a wrong.
- You might not yet be part of an established community and there might not be all the promised facilities – shops, cafés and leisure amenities – on site or nearby. And if the developer starts to run

out of money, some might not be how they looked on the brochure, or they might not appear at all.

- As you could be buying your home 'off-plan' – which means buying a home before it's actually built – you are taking a risk that it might not turn out exactly as you expected. Also, you have to wait until it's ready before you get to move in.

So, should I buy a new home?

The quality and care of new property has improved a great deal over the last decade, but do keep in mind that the size of homes has shrunk. If you are into buying every square foot you can for your money, a new home might then not be for you.

I think you need to consider longevity, too. Ask yourself how long the property will work for you. If there's not a lot of storage and you're about to get married and start a family, perhaps you should think about other options, like buying a second-hand property you can do up and extend.

Off-plan buying

Buying off-plan is where a buyer purchases a property before it's built. Because you can't see your home, you have to rely on the architect's plans, brochures and other information from the developer, as well as computer-generated images (mocked-up pictures on a computer to give you an idea of the real thing).

In some instances, a show flat or show home will be constructed to give you a better indication of what your home will look like. You can get a good idea of space and how different areas will look, so a show home can be useful if you're buying off-plan.

PHIL'S TRADE SECRET
Don't be fooled by a show home, however. A show home is there essentially to sell the development, and will be kitted

out in the best way possible to shift units. Tricks of the trade include:

- Putting smaller beds in bedrooms to make them appear bigger
- Removing doors from hinges so the home looks larger
- Using the interior decoration to distract a viewer from any problems, such as bad layout or shoddy workmanship
- Installing more up-market items – wooden flooring, smart appliances or built-in cabinetry – that aren't 'standard', which means you'd have to pay extra to have them in your own place

Buying off-plan can be a canny thing to do when prices are going up. You buy at an agreed price before the property is built, and by the time it's finished the property is worth more. Naturally, in a falling market the opposite could be true. Your home might be worth less than when you did the deal with the developer a year or two earlier.

Off-plan homes are marketed pretty much the same as homes that have already been constructed, directly through developers or via estate agents. But, you have to read the fine print of any agent's instructions or developer's literature.

Questions to ask when buying off-plan

- What guarantee or compensation is offered if the dimensions of your home change during the building process?
- How do you know the builder will build what is promised?
- What materials will be used? Ask if you can see samples.
- Is the building all privately owned, or is there a housing association share where people rent as well?
- Who will maintain the building and what is the managing company's track record like?

- If the residents want to swap the managing company for a different one at some point, is this possible?
- When will the development be totally finished?
- Is there any parking?
- Will there be any amenities and services on site, such as a swimming pool, gym, communal garden, concierge, shop or café?
- How often will the communal areas and windows be cleaned, and the gardens weeded?
- What kind of service charges – the annual amount paid to cover costs of communal facilities, insurance and maintenance – will you have to pay? And, what will they cover exactly?
- Will there be a residents' association and how much say will it have in the running of the building and overall site?
- Which local authority covers the area and how much will the council tax cost?

How to buy off-plan

Buying a home off-plan requires research. The developer and/or agent should be able to give you the property's layout and room sizes.

Before you take the plunge and sign on any dotted lines, however, go and check out other schemes the house builder has created. This is extremely important, because you can actually see what the design is like, and how good the quality of materials and construction will be on your own site. Talk to residents that live there if you can, to get their take on the developer. If anyone has moved into your own scheme already, do have a chat with fellow-residents there, too.

PHIL'S TOP TIP

Beware of the catch when seemingly free goodies or money-off enticements are on offer. Most, if not all, of these initiatives apply only to selected properties. So, find out which ones apply before you set your heart on a particular place. It's worth trying to get a deal no matter what, though, as the house builder might be keen to sell and will try to come up with an arrangement to help you – and his sales figures.

Also, I would only buy from someone with a well-established reputation. So, check out a small house builder or larger developer by doing some, or all, of the following:

- Go on the Internet to see what you can find out about the builder: a Google search, or similar, can be quite revealing. Check out his website, go to chat rooms and read the local and national press to see if there's anything you need to be wary of.
- Talk to local estate agents, who usually know who is good and who is not. They might even be able to recommend house builders in your area that they rate.
- You can glean a lot by talking to people in local pubs or cafés.
- Walk around an area you like to see what is being built. Talk to other house builders on the patch about their rivals.
- Check out what's on the planning section of your local authority's website. Anyone applying for permission will be listed, along with what they hope to do. You could get the inside track on something that's coming up, and find out if there are any disputes or problems by monitoring the site.
- Talk to local architects, who might know what your developer or house builder is like. They should be in tune with new schemes in the locale, too.

Keep in mind that some lenders are now reluctant to lend on off-plan properties, so you will need a decent-sized deposit of about 20%. Buying off-plan is proving trickier than it was before the recent financial crisis. With some inflated valuations in the past, the worth of new-build properties fell fast and by larger sums than second-hand properties. This means the maximum loan-to-values (LTVs) – the amount a lender's willing to give you based on value – has been lowered, so you can't borrow more than 80% LTV.

PHIL'S TOP TIP

Find an independent mortgage broker to give you advice. A broker who knows about the entire market, and not just one part with which he's being paid to be associated, will know about the lenders willing to lend money for an off-plan property. Some might even consider higher loan-to-values, even if you only have a small amount saved for a deposit.

The next step will be choosing a plot: a piece of land where the house will be built, or in the case of a flat, which unit you will occupy. The trick here is to really walk around the site and this is when you want your compass to hand. Which way the flat or house is facing is crucial, and depending on when you want the sun facing a balcony, terrace or even a main living room window is all-important. Some people want sun in the mornings and some the evenings. Only you know how you live and which you prefer.

Be careful where the traffic flows (do you really want to be on the side of the building where rush hour occurs?), and be aware of what is near your home. Avoid being close to the dustbins, maintenance area or too close to a parking lot. It is believed a first-floor flat or higher can be safer than a basement place. However, if there's no lift it might be hard to coax future buyers to scale six flights of steps if you're on the top floor.

Which new flat do you choose?

Personally, I'd go for a flat on the top floor on the corner. You'll get extra light flooding in here, and as you're above everyone else, there's unlikely to be a noise issue. A lot depends on how mobile you are and whether there will be a lift in the building, but it would be a good spot to be up on the top of your new world.

Again, the earlier you buy into a scheme, the better position your flat is likely to be in, as you'll have first call on what you want. You might pick up good deals at the end of the sales cycle, too, but you won't get the same good positions for property.

Check for any future development plans round the site. I remember visiting a new scheme in south-east London not far from the Thames and a keen young salesman reassuring me the view of the river was there forever. Of course, I knew it wasn't as I'd heard another scheme was about to be built right in front of the building. A quick search by you, or a solicitor, of the local authority's planning website is likely to unearth future plans and proposals.

PHIL'S TRADE SECRET

You can play the developers and estate agents by taking advantage of the fact that they have to account for their sales every month, and at certain points in the year. If you get in early, you not only get first pick, but you get a good deal as a first buyer in an early phase of the development. It makes the bank balance look good to have some initial sales, and it's a psychological boost to sales staff and investors, too.

Another clever ploy is to find out when the developer's year-end figures need to be posted. Many are eager to do a deal to make the annual sales figures look impressive. You might even get away with simply making the offer and delaying payment until the next operating year.

This trick works with estate agents too, who also have to account for sales at certain times. And, making an offer during dead periods, such as leading up to Christmas and in the summer when everyone's on holiday, could net you a bargain and a sympathetic negotiating stance from sales staff.

PHIL'S TOP TIP

I know that as a property search agent I haggle for a living, but you too can haggle over the price of your new home. Also, you can haggle over the specifications. You can always be cheeky and try to get your kitchen, bathrooms and some appliances upgraded. It's always worth asking to see what you can get.

When you reserve the plot, you'll be asked to put down a reservation fee, normally in the region of £1,000. Contracts are exchanged typically in about three or four weeks, when you'll need to pay a 10% deposit. If you fail to complete the sale, you lose your deposit.

And be warned: some buyers who put down deposits for off-plan property before the downturn and then withdrew from the purchase are being chased through the courts by some developers thinking they should carry on with the sale. When times are tough, you might find some developers are less understanding, as they're keen to make sales at the best prices they can.

Then, you play a waiting game until the property is finished. This can take anything from a few months to two to three years. Don't forget that the mortgage deal you have in place when you make the initial offer might not still stand a few years later. In a falling market, the lender might even decide the initial valuation is no longer accurate and might lend you less money.

You should be contacted several weeks before the final completion date to give you time to check the snagging (checking and getting any problems sorted after the building work is finished) of the property and that everything is in order. There are professional snagging companies now that will carry out an inspection and make sure the snagging's done properly, if you feel it's necessary to hire one. Prices are in the region of about £250 for a one-bedroom flat, and up to £450 for a five-bedroom house. Contact details are at the end of this chapter.

What is snagging?

As a building settles down on its foundations after building work has been carried out, the building can shift slightly, which could lead to a sticking cupboard or small hairline cracks in the paintwork. Sometimes, everything isn't tested properly by the builders, so a drain isn't working the way it should, or an electrical circuit keeps fusing.

Snagging means checking out the entire property to make sure all of these problems are rectified. It is a normal and expected phase at the end of building work, so don't be alarmed.

On completion, your solicitor will transfer the funds from the lender – the bank or building society – and remember, you will have to pay Stamp Duty at this point, too. After that, the new home is yours.

After-sales care

Another good indicator of a well-run business and good client support is what kind of after-sales care is provided. Check this out on the website and ask the developer what's provided, and what would be done to help you if something goes wrong.

PHIL'S TOP TIP

You might want to consider renting your new home back to the developer. By entering into a deal such as this, the developer, typically, uses your home for the show flat or show house while selling the whole development off. Then, the property reverts back to you when everything's sold. Sometimes, developers use homes as offices while they're on site, too.

This is a clever plan, as long as you have somewhere else to live while the developer's using your flat. By camping out at your mum and dad's, or at a friend's place, you escape the dust and disruption of the early stages of development and earn money at the same time, too.

Other new incentives

Some house builders will also throw in freebies to attract first-time buyers. For example, you might be given free carpeting throughout your new home, or all of the appliances (washing machine, drier, refrigerator and dishwasher) could be included in the price.

Another classic is having the landscaping all carried out for free. This might consist of the house builder laying the lawn, and planting shrubs, trees, flowers and even hedging. Some house builders could incorporate some 'hard' landscaping as well, which means you could have a small brick or stone terrace built where you could have a barbecue, and put out a table and a few chairs to enjoy the sun in the summer.

I think some of these offers sound okay, but ideally, I would want more money knocked off the price rather than these extras. The reason the developer comes up with these wheezes is to get you to buy, and usually, these incentives don't cost the developer much money at all. Carpeting is bought in bulk, for instance, so the price per unit is very low. But, you won't get much choice, if any, in colour or pattern. But, if the developer won't budge on lowering the price any further, at least you get some items *gratis*, which could be a help for struggling first-timers.

More attractive, I believe, are deals where the developer offers to pay all, or some, of your deposit, Stamp Duty and solicitor's fees, or gives you cash back when you buy. This helps you lessen the burden financially, and the more you can put forward in cash, the better the arrangement with your mortgage lender.

Converted homes – old with a touch of new

Don't always think completely brand-new when you think of new developments. Some that are brand-new are criticised for being soulless and uninspiring, yet a number of them are very interesting conversions. This means the developer's bought an old building – say, a Victorian school – and has converted it into a number of flats and maybe townhouses. Sometimes, new housing might be built alongside the old property in the grounds, too.

Many old buildings have great proportions – high ceilings and big rooms – that you can benefit from. And if you're lucky, there might be a number of original features (or at least features that have been partially restored), such as tall skirting boards, dado rails (where pictures originally hung) or floor-to-ceiling windows, that will be fantastic to have and will add value when you later sell the property.

The joy of a converted property is that you really can have the best of both worlds: the old combined with the new. You get a lovely, old, period building with a wealth of character, while you also get modern conveniences that our forebears weren't fortunate enough to enjoy.

Keep in mind, however, that well-converted properties don't come cheap, and typically, cost more than a straightforward new-build. You will be expected to pay extra for the conversion work and for the honour of owning some older features that add character. But at the end of the day, I believe these dual-purpose old-new combo homes will hold their value better than a simple new-build.

What are service charges?

I mentioned service charges earlier in this chapter. Although some might be fair, at other times you need to be wary of what you're being asked to pay. It's difficult for a developer to be accurate about service or maintenance charges, as they're sometimes called.

This might not be a problem if you feel the building's being looked after properly and the charges are reasonable for the number of and quality of the services provided. However, do you really need 24-hour concierge cover, lifts and a car park? If you don't, then maybe a smaller scheme with fewer amenities might make sense.

Sometimes, service charges can be quite outrageous, so you need to ask the developer, or managing company that's going to look after the building, how they arrived at the eye-wateringly high figures. Also, check when charges can be increased and if there's some sort of cap on them. Having the power to stand up for themselves is invaluable if residents feel they're being ripped off, and the power to vote out a bad managing company to lower service charges is a good option to have.

Often, first-time buyers think service charges apply only to new buildings, but converted older or post-Second World

War purpose-built buildings have service charges attached to them, too. When major work needs to be carried out (reroofing the building, for instance), the charges can climb steeply. A 'sinking fund' (a reserve of money collected over the years from the residents to cover large jobs) can make this less painful, but you will still be paying out, just in smaller chunks.

PHIL'S TOP TIP

Even if you can't afford the expensive conversion inside the former hospital, you could still do reasonably well with the new-build in the grounds next to it. You can use the extensive communal gardens and other amenities on site even if you don't live in the old period pile. With older property, there might be a library or billiards room, or something similar, that's open for all residents to experience. And, it's great having a view of a former stately home, rather than a newer, often dull-looking, new building.

Whether you opt for a straight new-build or a conversion of something old into something newer, remember that a property is only old once or refurbished to this degree once. Effectively, you are paying the builder's premium, but you do get on the ladder at least.

Tenants vs owners

I would also advise keeping an eye out for the proportion of owner-occupiers (buyers who will live there) to investors (buyers who plan to rent out the property). You won't necessarily get a straight answer from the house builder, but it is better if you can try to buy in a scheme where there are more owner-occupiers. Otherwise, the turnover of tenants will make the place feel itinerant, with nomads wandering in and out.

For all the negative press you might read, living in a new scheme can be great fun. You will meet people, a number of which will be first-timers, too. You're all in the same place, and it's new and exciting for everyone. A decent developer will host a few social evenings so you can meet one another. Failing that, you can set something up yourselves. Some schemes have their own websites or Facebook pages, where you can exchange information and suggestions, contributing greatly to the beginnings of new communities.

Storage: where do I put my skis?

Storage is always under-valued and isn't something first-timers often look for. It can be scarce in new schemes where homes generally are not as well proportioned as older properties (although there are exceptions to this rule, of course).

If you're offered the chance to buy, or rent, a storage space on site, I'd go for it if you can afford it. Not only will you then have somewhere to put skis, luggage and other bulky items, this will be a great extra to offer when it comes time to sell. And, if for some reason you end up renting your property for a period of time, you can put some personal items in your storage area, clearing out your home for the new tenants.

Is there a car park? Again, if you have the money, I'd pay extra for a car parking space, if it doesn't automatically come within the purchase price. If you don't need to use it, you can always rent it out.

There's good money to be made in renting out car parking spaces, particularly in towns and cities where car parking is a precious commodity. You can earn hundreds of pounds a month letting out the space and there are a number of websites that list rentable private parking spaces for free. I really don't think purchasing a car parking space will ever be something you'll regret.

Buying a wreck: will it ruin me?

Buying a wreck and doing it up can be a good way of getting that first foot onto the property ladder. But it's not an easy thing to do, so you have to be quite brave to take an utter ruin on. I do think this is quite ambitious for a first-time buyer, but at the same time, I applaud anyone undertaking such a project.

Firstly, lenders (in a less buoyant economy, in particular) do not like any impediments that could lessen a home's worth. If you borrow money to do up a crumbling property and don't finish the work, they're worried they won't get their cash back. So, some lenders might not be all that keen to hand out a mortgage, especially to a first-timer with little, or no, experience of renovating a property.

However, it's not impossible to borrow the money, if you have a good broker rooting for you. You also need to be able to lay out your case, demonstrating you really know what you're doing (initial plans or ideas for the work from a reputable builder or architect should show you're serious) and that you have done your sums.

PHIL'S TRADE SECRET

Keep in mind that if a property has no kitchen, it's defined as not being habitable. If a place isn't deemed habitable, it's much more difficult to get a mortgage. So, you could use the neat builder's trick of making sure the very basics are in place (for instance, fix the roof above the kitchen and connect the water tap) to make this room habitable to get a lender on side.

The other good reason for buying and doing up a ruin or a run-down property is because, ultimately, it will be worth more. This means you can end up having a bit more as well when you move on, increasing your chances of getting a better place when you move up the next rung of the ladder. This is how developers fund large projects. It's not about what they sell for necessarily, but how good the deal is in the first place when they buy.

To get an estate agent to help you find a wreck that you can add value to, you need to show you're more organised than any other buyers. Being prepared and ready to move quickly with the sale will enhance your chances. If you show any signs of flakiness, it's unlikely the agent will think you're up to such a project, and therefore, he won't suggest to his client that he should sell to you.

You'll need to show evidence of your earnings, as mentioned in the getting a mortgage chapter earlier. So, have all your pay slips and tax returns to hand. If you're freelance or self-employed, it could be more difficult proving you're the best person for this home-improvement job, but it's not impossible.

Take advice from an accountant or broker early on. If you are thinking about this well in advance, you might even want to do a few years accounting in a different way so you appear more attractive to a lender.

Remember that reconstructing a ruin will obviously take longer than something needing no, or only a small amount of, work. There will be a great deal more planning, and the more organised you can be, the better the result. But, I believe this could be very satisfying, and very profitable.

Such projects don't always go smoothly (as witnessed on television programmes, such as *Grand Designs*), and if you have a family member or friend you trust who can help out physically and/or financially, I think it's worth approaching him or her. Having a dad who's a chippy (carpenter), or a brother who's a sparky (electrician) could be immensely helpful, and it might also save you some cash in the long term.

A good pal of mine's an architect and when I had building work done he helped with the planning and even came up with the idea of incentivising the builder on the end result. There was a trusting relationship between the two of us and the builder.

Another way to get on the ladder with a wreck is to get someone to help with a particular project and you can pay him or her back (maybe with a certain amount of agreed interest) when you sell. For instance, you might want to extend the kitchen and your mum helps pay for it, reaping her share of the loan with some profit on top when you move on. Relatives could feel happy doing this at a time when they're bound to make more money this way than keeping their money in the bank when interest rates are low.

WRECK AND RUIN –
GETTING ON THE LADDER BY DOING UP A DISASTER

After searching for two years in Surrey, music teacher Marcus Carlisle and his fiancée Jennifer Martyn, 37, realised the only way to get on the ladder was to buy a wreck.

'We put down £15,000 to buy a £243,500, 1930s two-bedroom semi in need of work and spent weekends and evenings doing it up,' says Marcus, 24. 'We thought it would be easy, but it was really hard graft. But as most first-timers get pushed out of this expensive area in the south-east of England, at least we have managed to bag a home here.'

Marcus suggests anyone contemplating ruin renovation has to keep on top of the builders – 'Don't let them slack' – and a twentieth-century property is more affordable than a period one. 'Also, when it comes to borrowing money, building societies are a bit more amenable about giving you funding for a property that isn't too old.'

To cut down on some of the costs, Marcus and Jennifer rolled up their sleeves and pitched in along with the builders. They'd recommend first-timers at least do some of the work if they can, as it does help balance the books, and 'There's something primeval about working on your own home. I really felt I was in touch with the place and know a lot more about it now,' Marcus adds.

Jennifer concurs that she knew very little about building work, and how to deal with builders. 'You need to set the ground rules. At first, I was grovelling with gratefulness that they'd turned up and were deigning to work on our humble home, but it became ridiculous when I was pandering to them too much. They wrote off my new hoover the first few days on site – do not let them touch yours, they should bring their own.'

She learned about bigger issues, too, like how to keep track of all of the money spent on a spreadsheet. 'It was my responsibility to work out how much we were spending on the work, which was quite scary for me, as maths isn't my strong point. But, it made sense – if you don't keep an eye on things, money can disappear quite quickly.'

Jennifer advises always communicating with the builders in advance before any money is spent – she once ordered some bathroom sanitary ware with fittings that were too narrow. She said a regular weekly meeting was held with the builders to discuss what was going to happen that week and what that meant in cost terms. 'Because I was ordering most of the materials and fittings I could clearly see what items cost. If we wanted to spend a bit more on one thing, it would mean cutting back on something else. A good life lesson, really, as I think this is how we should all live, rather than permanently being in debt.'

Other tips from Marcus and Jennifer are:

- Do your homework – know exactly where you want to be.
- Rely on your own judgement and don't listen to your parents, who bought 30 years ago. Jennifer's mother was appalled by the price of their home, but she was comparing it to one she had bought several decades ago.
- You will need about a third to a half of the asking price to carry out all the work. Marcus says they spent £36,000 to renovate their first home.
- Make sure you have a contingency fund for unforeseen events (the builders discovered rotting floorboards hidden under the carpeting in two rooms, which involved replacing the wooden flooring that wasn't in the original budget).

Planning permission

You might need planning permission to carry out work on your home. Guidelines are set out by central government and planning officials in local authorities manage individual areas.

I find that a number of first-time buyers are intimidated by planning departments, but there's no need to be concerned about your dealings with them. Essentially, they are there to protect communities, with each local authority drawing up a framework outlining how they will oversee what is built in the region.

A really good source for anyone considering or undertaking building work is the government website www.planningportal.gov.uk. This is a great starting point to find out whether you require planning permission for a project, and what you are allowed, or not allowed, to do. I would recommend that for a large project you talk to an experienced builder, architect or surveyor about the planning guidelines and what they mean in relation to your own plans.

You must remember that if you own a listed building or live in a conservation area, different rules might apply. It's a criminal offence, for instance, to carry out work on a Grade-II listed building that affects its 'special characteristics', and you could be fined or even end up in prison if you disobey these rules.

An appendix on planning permission is on page 263 at the end of the book. It's a handy guide to various popular projects, including converting the loft, adding on an extension and building a conservatory, that you can dip into when you need to know more about how best to improve your home.

Auctions: Going, going, gone

First-time buyers have discovered auctions, where they can pick up down-at-heel or difficult-to-shift properties for reasonable prices. Auctioneers say they're seeing more first-timers come through auction house doors, but they do admit that the downside is getting mortgage lenders to cooperate. It's not unknown for them to hesitate when it comes to coughing up money to anyone buying their first home at an auction.

The reason lenders show some reluctance is that they want to know the first-time buyer has the determination and wherewithal to go ahead with improving the property. This isn't wildly different from the situation when you want to buy a wreck (which is dealt with earlier in this chapter).

Three golden rules

There are three golden rules when you buy a property at an auction:

1. **Check out the property**
   You must first see what the condition of the building is like with a good builder or surveyor, so you know what you're taking on. There's no point turning up to bid if you haven't properly checked out the property and haven't a clue what any work would involve.

2. **Legal package**
   Get hold of the legal package from the auctioneer with all of the conveyancing information for your solicitor to go through.

3. **Pay in full**
   Finally, you must remember that once the hammer falls (when the auctioneer bangs down his gavel to say the property is now yours), you have 28 days to pay all of the money in full.

I think buying at an auction can be a great idea for a first-time purchaser, as long as you realise that you must be highly organised and convey a certain amount of spirit to make the deal happen. If you are keen on DIY (doing it yourself), chummy with your builder or do not mind going for the kind of property not normally found on most estate agents' books, then bidding for your first home at an auction could be for you.

Around 30,000 properties are sold at auction in the UK every year, many at up to 40% below high street prices. A number of investors snap up homes this way. Typically, they buy something in need of some TLC (tender loving care), spruce it up, and then rent it out, or even sell it on at a bit of a profit.

A big plus for buying a property at an auction is that the whole process can be considerably quicker and less complicated than conventional purchasing methods, as contracts are exchanged with the successful bidder at the auction.

Also, if you take your cue from investors and small-scale developers and buy a slightly run-down home at auction and make improvements to it, you're likely to accrue more profits than if you bought a house in better shape in the traditional fashion direct from an estate agent.

PHIL'S TRADE SECRET

Personally, I'd plump for a flat in a small purpose-built block with only two or three properties in the building in total. This way, you escape paying high overheads and service charges that you would have to part with in newer and larger schemes.

I would also caution first-time buyers not to do anything too adventurous, unless you are a serious DIY addict who's extremely dexterous with a drill. Try to buy something reasonably clean and not too horrendous. Auctioneers tell me they've come across so many cases of people buying something beyond the pale and then giving up halfway through the renovations. Sadly, they then end up putting the property back up for auction again.

A sure-fire winner can be scooping up a property with an AST (assured short-hold tenant). This means that you buy a home with a short-term tenant in situ, usually for six months to a year. While you are sorting out builders, any planning applications (if applicable) and anything else to get going on the renovations that are probably required, at least some money is rolling in to help you out. You might even want to hold onto the tenant a bit longer to save towards funding the building work.

Do keep in mind that buying at an auction is not for the fainthearted. Most of the property has been either repossessed, is too odd or run-down to merit being sold through an agent in the normal way or has some other peculiarity you need to find out about. The flip side can be true, too. Sometimes, unusual and even rare property (such as a chocolate-box thatched cottage) is sold by auction, to see if keen competing buyers can push the price up. I've even known an auctioneer to hold an auction on a houseboat (interested parties had to be ferried there by boat), to generate the right atmosphere and get as much money as he could for this rare aqueous property.

Another neat trick by auctioneers is generally to fix the reserve price at a low enough value to get buyers' juices flowing. Some property is bid up considerably from this starting price, so make sure you have a predetermined cut-off point, so you don't go crazy and bid far more than you can afford. You must stick to this level and stop bidding then, no matter how exciting the whole event becomes.

PHIL'S TOP TIPS

It can be daunting if you haven't bought at auction before, so buy the catalogues of property for sale and go along and watch. Do your research and carry out a rehearsal. Pretend to go through the whole exercise in your head.

Whatever you do, however, do not be tempted to stick up your hand enthusiastically and wave it about if you do not have the cash. And remember, the job of an auctioneer (not unlike an estate agent representing the seller) is to ensure you pay more than you should have.

It's also important to check out an area first. Property is sold at auction because it's difficult to determine its value due to its situation or condition, so you must do your homework. Yes, you might save £50,000 by buying a flat on a busy road, but the *value of the property will be lower, too. And, do you really want to live on a noisy, dusty and unpleasant road? You might have to rent your property out for some reason as well, and you need to think of what a possible tenant will put up with – and not put up with.*

Another good tip is to decide whether you want to buy at 'a' price, or at 'any' price. It's best to make the hard business decision to buy at 'a' price – and no more. Every pound you pay over the asking or guide price, you are throwing out some of your profit.

Don't be scared, be prepared

You shouldn't be frightened by auctions, but as every good boy scout will tell you, being prepared is crucial. Be brave and don't be snobby about repossessions (properties that the banks have reclaimed, because the owners couldn't keep up the mortgage payments). It might feel a bit ghoulish, but you can get some good deals.

Auctions are quite high-pressure environments due to the energy and speed at which things happen. But if you understand what's going on and don't mind taking some calculated risks, this is a good way to make money. Get to know the behaviour and rhythm of an auction. As I mentioned before, watch and learn are the bywords here.

PHIL'S TRADE SECRET

A tip from an auctioneer is to ignore everyone else around you, other than the two people bidding (after all, only two people can bid at the same time). Don't put your hand up until one of them drops out. Don't get carried away and stick to the threshold you refuse to go beyond. Bidding is all about timing, so don't be tempted to bid too early.

If you are nervous about bidding, which is totally understandable, you can always get someone else to do the bidding for you. If he or she is not emotionally involved, it might be easier that way.

I would advise having an odd figure in mind (just like with sealed bids – see page 152). If you have the odd amount of £200,300 in your head, say, rather than £200,000, you might just win the property by only a few hundred pounds. Most people drop out at even increments, keeping you in the running.

Remember, you have to exchange contracts there and then if you win your bid, and you only have 28 days to complete. Can you, your mortgage company and your solicitor all be in position to tie the deal up on time? It's important you feel confident that this can happen. Otherwise, maybe buying at an auction is not for you.

What to think about before buying at auction:
- **Condition**
  Does the property require refurbishment? How much will this cost? Do you have the funding available?
- **Location**
  Will the property be safe for you, or future tenants (if you decide to rent it for some reason), or for future buyers (when it comes time for you to sell)?
- **Funding**
  How much can you borrow? Is the money in place?
- **Conveyancing**
  Have you put the legal aspect of buying a property into action?
- **Interest rates**
  What are they doing, and what effect will they have on your monthly repayments? Does it look like they're likely to rise in the near future, and have you factored this into your financial plans?

> ### PHIL'S TOP TIP
>
> *One way to finance the property is to get a 50–60% mortgage beforehand and top it up with family subsidies if you have relatives willing to invest. Then, you can remortgage once you have bought the property.*

Rent-to-buy

One of the biggest hindrances to buying that first home is getting together enough money for a deposit in the first place. An innovative, and not very well-known, way to get onto the property ladder is to rent-to-buy.

A rent-to-buy scheme means you rent a home, usually at a new development, with half the rent going towards the deposit to buy the property outright in a few years' time. Two years is the normal period, although this can vary.

This is a fairly new idea and one of the pioneers in rent-to-buy in the UK is the Acorn Property Group (www.acornpropertygroup.org). Why it can be a good idea is that you are getting a percentage of your rent back for a deposit, and you aren't just throwing money away as you would be in a private rentals home.

Generally, you need to let the company running the rent-to-buy scheme know that you want to buy within six months of first arriving as a tenant. You can't purchase the home before two years of letting is up, and you pay the market rate the home was first valued at when you first started renting.

Is there a catch? As companies that usually operate rent-to-buy are both developers and landlords with huge property portfolios round Britain, it is a good way for them to get a better class of tenant. They also avoid having to pay estate agent fees when selling.

This can be a good way for the landlord-developer to guarantee a tenant goes on to buy a property outright (although you don't have to, necessarily). You need to feel secure with the company you're dealing with, however, as there have been some reports of rent-to-buy tenants losing their deposits – and sometimes, their homes – in America, because they didn't keep up their payments. So, it's wise to get sound legal advice before you sign a contract.

Other advantages of rent-to-buy include no expensive removal costs – you live there already – and not having to send out change of address cards, or contact utility companies. At the end of the day, you're not really going anywhere.

CASE STUDY

FROM TENANT TO OWNER

Sales advisor Christopher Fox, who has been renting a flat in north London for £900 a month, found the biggest problem to getting onto the property ladder was trying to save up the deposit for a home.

Renting a home through a rent-to-buy scheme means he can now rent a one-bedroom flat worth £265,000 in a new development in Borough, south-east London, with half of the rent going towards the deposit to buy the property outright in two years' time.

'The difficulty I've had up to now is that I've needed £10,000–20,000 for a 5–10% deposit,' Fox, 45, says. 'And those amounts have started to rise even higher now, with lenders asking for higher and higher deposits to cover themselves. By the time I had saved the deposit amounts I discovered the deposit prices had gone up.'

For first-time purchasers like Fox who feel they're a bit old to be cadging money off their mum and dad, this scheme can give them the boost they require to scramble onto that distant first rung of the property ladder.

Fox believes he hasn't lost anything – 'I was renting before with little prospect of ever saving enough to put down a deposit' – and certainly has moved on in his fight to get a first home. 'At least I'm renting with a purpose now. It doesn't feel like I'm chucking a great chunk of my money down the drain and one day, I will actually own a property.'

Waiting for two years can sound like a long time, but Fox reckons there are advantages. 'For instance, I'm getting to know my neighbourhood before I buy, if you know what I mean. Most people go from rented accommodation to buying a place without knowing anything really about the area or the people in it. I feel ahead of the game in many ways, as I'm already settled into my home.'

As rent-to-buy schemes are relatively new, Fox recommends getting a good solicitor, preferably one who's dealt with rent-to-buy before, or at least has some knowledge of it. He also thinks it crucial to make sure the contract has some kind of safety net so you don't lose your deposit – or your new home – if you find yourself in a position where you miss a payment.

PHIL'S TOP TIP

You might consider getting an independent broker to help you find a mortgage. As rent-to-buy isn't a traditional way to buy a home, some lenders might be reluctant, particularly in a downturn. An enlightened broker should be able to help, however, and suggest a bank or building society that will evaluate your situation.

Shared ownership

At the time of going to press, we were at the fag end of the outgoing Labour Government's HomeBuy scheme, set up to help first-timer buyers onto the ladder (see page 39 in chapter 2 for more information). There is talk of new initiatives to replace HomeBuy, although no one could confirm what these might be quite yet. So, this book outlines schemes that have been helping first-time buyers, in anticipation of new plans that could extend some of these schemes, or come up with something similar, or more innovative.

The term 'sharing' in shared ownership refers to housing associations sharing in a new development scheme. This means that a certain number of units on site will be sold outright privately, while some other units come under shared ownership. Basically, you buy a portion of the property and rent the rest through a designated housing association or associations linked to the project. You can step up your share in the property, buying more bits of it when you can afford to do this.

For example, shared-ownership schemes under the current HomeBuy initiative allow first-timers to put down a percentage (typically, at least 25%) to buy a portion of their first place, with a housing association renting them the remainder. When they have more money, they can 'staircase' – buy larger shares until they own their home outright. When it comes time to sell, the housing association has first option to buy the home back at open market rates.

Key workers

You need to plan ahead when applying for shared ownership, which can favour you in some cases if you're what is known as a 'key worker'. A key worker is someone working in a job that's regarded as vital to public services. For instance, some key workers are: police officers, emergency workers (such as ambulance drivers), nurses and teachers.

You can register with your local authority to get onto a waiting list for shared-ownership opportunities. Some councils say you need to have been registered for a period of time (typically six months and up to two years), while others aren't so particular about a timeframe. Another way to be considered for shared ownership is to register with a local housing association or associations.

Most schemes stipulate that you must either live or work in the borough. Some exceptions can be made, depending on the property available and how many people are taking up the chance to be part of the shared-ownership scheme.

PHIL'S TOP TIP

Even if you think you'll have little chance of being accepted on a shared ownership scheme, do talk to the council and housing associations. You might discover that they haven't had a great take-up in certain places and they are happy to give you a chance to register and then buy a property.

I have found that some builders of schemes are even happy to consider you if you're not a key worker. A lot depends on individual circumstances, and what's happening in your area and with each scheme. Often, officials would rather there is someone who can keep up the payments and enjoy living in the property, compared to it standing empty for some time. So, by all means, do ask.

Make sure you also look in the area where you live and in the area where you work (if they're not in the same locale). This gives you two bites at the cherry, increasing your chances of qualifying for a shared-ownership home.

CASE STUDY

SHARED OWNERSHIP GOT ME A LUXURY FLAT

Mina Roche, a 29-year-old personal assistant, found renting a home a waste of money, but she couldn't afford to buy a place on her own.

'Luckily, although I'm not a key worker, I found I was still able to register with a shared-ownership scheme with a local housing charity here in Yorkshire,' she says. 'After only four months, I found a new two-bedroom flat with a balcony overlooking a stream.'

Because Mina had some savings, she was able to buy 60% of the £235,000 flat not far from the centre of York. She pays rent on the other 40% to the housing association, as part of the government's HomeBuy scheme, and she hopes to increase her share in the near future.

'I'm not that far from work – it's about 20 minutes on the bus, or a five- to ten-minute drive, depending on the traffic,' Mina adds. 'My friends – most of whom haven't even heard of shared ownership – are amazed. The ones that have an inkling of what it might mean think shared ownership is just for firemen and teachers, but it's for those who can't afford to buy a home outright.'

Mina's family and friends are equally amazed that she's in a brand-new flat in a development that has a small gym, pool and car park, which all residents – private and those in shared ownership – can use. Many people perceive housing association property to be dingy and rather run-down – terms that can't be applied to Mina's new flat.

Mina says she might well rent out the second bedroom to help pay for the running costs and extras for her flat. 'Or, I could save the rentals income and put it towards buying some more of the property. It certainly gives me options for the future.'

Property on a short lease

If you are eager to nail down that first home, you might want to snap up a property on a short lease. It can be a smart way for young purchasers to get a foot on the ladder, and is most common in London (but it might be possible in some other towns and cities too), where property is on a lease to an estate or freeholder (see page 46 for an explanation on the differences between freehold and leasehold properties).

You can lift the worth of your home by extending the lease on it, or by buying the freehold. The cost to extend the lease will be recouped when you go to sell your property, as a longer lease adds more value.

But isn't a short-lease property a risky buy?

Some buyers are wary of homes with brief leases – regarded by some as the equivalent of putting groceries with alarmingly short sell-by dates into the shopping cart – which can lessen the competition for these properties. Most people walk away from a short-lease property, other than builders or small developers who can do these places up and rent them out for the remainder of the lease, or sell them on at a profit.

Another big advantage of purchasing a short-lease home is you can pay for it in two tranches. If you buy a short lease now, then in a few years' time you can pay more to extend it. And if you buy a short lease in a rising market, you can essentially have it for free.

PHIL'S TOP TIP

It is important to have at least two years to play with on the lease. If it is too short, it is difficult to bargain with the Estate or freeholder.

Make sure you check early on that the person selling the property can assign the lease to you. A word of caution: if the lease is for only five years, they cannot. You would then have to go back to the landlord and get his consent to extend it.

I think picking up a short lease can be a good way to buy a first home, paying less than the market rate for it at the age of 25, for example, and then when you are earning more money at say, 35, you can pay for the extension.

The downside is you are relying on earning more money in the imme-diate future, but you might become side-tracked by marriage, children and other life experiences that can eat up your savings, which could make it tricky to find money in a hurry.

Also, as the clock ticks down for leases below 80 years, the 'marriage value' – the latent value released when the lease is extended – becomes more expensive. A general formula is applied where you pay for the existing unexpired lease term: half the marriage value and compensation for any loss in value of other property owned by the freeholder that would occur as a result of granting the extended lease.

As you can see, extending short leases can be a complicated business, so you must get specialist advice. Some of the larger estate agencies employ short-lease specialists, and a good property solicitor should be able to help, too. Also, small house builders that buy one-off short-lease homes to do them up and sell them on would be able to advise you, too.

This is a great way to get that first home, but sometimes, costs can be high. You could well end up paying the landlord's and your legal fees – and remember, the Estate's lawyers are not there to point out your mistakes.

Another negative, I'm afraid, is that you'd have to find a lender to give you a mortgage on a short-lease property, something that a number of them are reluctant to do. But, maybe you could borrow some money from a relative or friend in the first instance, or hunt down a good independent broker who might be able to come up with a sympathetic lender.

Live—work units

Some councils positively encourage what they call 'live-work units', which are typically built by small house-builders, or larger developers that include some of these units within a bigger scheme. These are a combina-tion of residential space and work space for those who work most or all of the time from home. Local authorities like them, because they ultimately cut down on traffic, because you work from home and don't have to commute. Also, they encourage small businesses into the area.

You might be subject to business tax rates, though, which can be higher than residential rates, so check this out before you consider purchasing a live-work unit. Equally, you must make sure you qualify, as a number of people have claimed they were going to run a business from home simply to get their hands on these units. If you tell a white lie and it's discovered you aren't working from home, you could be in trouble with the local authority.

A well-designed live-work unit can be a fantastic space. Most have a separate 'work' entrance, which is ideal if you are a practitioner of some kind (maybe an acupuncturist or counsellor) because your clients don't have to traipse through the residential part of the live-work unit to get to your work premises. Some live-work units are brand-new, while others are pleasingly converted spaces from old warehouses or factories.

It's worth checking with your local authority to see if any live-work units have been erected by developers in your area, or are planned for the future. Prices are generally not too over the top, as the local authorities want to attract good business people to live locally.

THE RIGHT-HOME-FOR-YOU CHECKLIST

- [ ] Match a property to how you live
- [ ] Consider old vs new homes
- [ ] Walk or drive round the area looking for 'For Sale' signs
- [ ] Check out new developments and converted homes
- [ ] Find an independent mortgage broker to give you advice
- [ ] Weigh up 'free' offers or other incentives from developers or private sellers
- [ ] Ask about service charges
- [ ] Check out storage and parking (even if you don't need them, you can rent them and get an income)

☐ Determine what's best for you: a wreck, buying at auction, rent-to-buy, a home on a short lease, live-work unit

☐ Research government schemes (shared ownership)

PHIL'S CONTACTS BOOK

• Check out the Association of Independent Financial Advisers – aifa.net – to find an adviser

• To find out more about government shared-ownership schemes, go to www.direct.gov.uk/en/homeandcommunity or www.shared-ownership.org.uk

• A good rent-to-buy company is the Acorn Property Group – www.acornpropertygroup.org

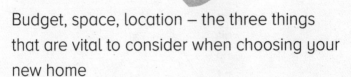

CHAPTER FOUR

What and Where to Buy

Budget, space, location – the three things that are vital to consider when choosing your new home

Once you get some notion of what you can afford and how much cash a mortgage lender is likely to give you, it's time to start checking out properties. A number of first-timers have asked me over the years: how is it best to get started on finding properties?

First, it's a good idea to make a list of sources that can help you find a property. These include:

- Local estate agents in the places where you want to buy, or think you might want to buy
- Estate agents' sites and other good property websites on the Internet
- Local newspapers and magazines
- New developments
- Auction houses, or auction divisions of estate agencies
- 'For Sale' signs that can be spotted outside homes
- Word of mouth from others who have bought recently
- Government schemes and websites

Phil's home triangle

You then need to determine what kind of property you should be looking for. I favour working out your priorities using the triangle approach, which is simple and clear. Basically, you draw a triangle and at the three points you insert the following:

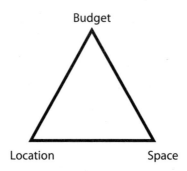

Budget

Location   Space

Budget

The first point of the triangle, the budget, is usually fixed. So, once you work out the amount you have to spend, put this sum down. Keep in mind your budget could vary a bit, if you are lucky enough to inherit some money from Aunt Agatha at the last minute, or you have discovered forgotten savings stuffed under the mattress. But generally for most first-time purchasers, once the lender says you can have this much money, that's it.

If the budget point of the triangle isn't as high as you would like, there are ways to up it. You could, for example, get a 'loan' from a relative or friend, and then repay it when you sell or acquire more cash. I wouldn't recommend this if you're worried about how it could affect the personal relationship you have with the person lending you the extra funds. There's nothing worse than falling out with someone over money. And, if you go down this route, do make sure you draw up a simple contract outlining a repayment structure and dealing with any pitfalls that might arise.

Space

When assessing space, it's best to concentrate on the amount needed opposed to the amount of space you'd ideally like to have. I always think it's best to be realistic to avoid later disappointment.

Space questions you should be asking include:

- **Do I really need a two-bedroom flat, or could I cope with a one-bedroom place?**
  If the answer is that you really do need two bedrooms (perhaps you plan to rent one out to make the equation add up), then maybe you need to look further afield in order to afford what you want. Or, possibly a one-bedroom flat makes more sense financially for the time being, and then you can work your way up the ladder, literally, to a two-bedroom home.
- **What sort of space is important to you?**
  I find a good debate or two, and discussions with friends and family, can be very useful. It also helps to write down what you think you want. For instance, perhaps a bright, airy reception room combined with a good kitchen space in an open-plan fashion is important to you. But if you do very little cooking and don't think counter space is a priority, then the kitchen size isn't as crucial.
- **Will you be working from home?**
  If so, it could be important to have a quiet and pleasant working space. This could be a corner of a decent-sized living room, or a separate office or small bedroom adapted for the purpose.

A good idea is to try to focus on your requirements. Think about the different angles – what do you really need and what sort of space layout best suits you – and blend them together. It is unlikely you will get everything on your tick list, but once you start researching what property is out there you'll get a good sense of what you will put up with – and what you won't.

I find most first-time buyers don't stop to think that this first home is not what I call a 'forever home'. A 'forever home' is your dream home, the one you want to buy one day where you will spend the biggest portion of your life. It is pretty rare, however, to be able to buy a 'forever home' at the outset, and if this is your aim, I'm afraid you'll be sorely disappointed.

However, because first-time buyers are getting older, as many young first-time purchasers are finding it difficult raising cash for deposits or getting lenders to lend them money, some might find themselves missing a step on the ladder. This could mean buying what would normally be perceived as a 'second-time home': one that is a bit bigger, perhaps, or has a garden or parking space. It depends on how much money has been raised and what you are earning.

PHIL'S TOP TIP

As a first-time buyer is usually on a tight budget, spotting possibilities is a fine art. Don't ignore that large hallway or mezzanine – you might be able to fit a home office there. I can't tell you how many times I've spotted an overly large wardrobe or corner of a bedroom that could easily be converted into a compact, but highly valuable, en suite bathroom. It's all about balance, though. Don't forget that as soon as you add a particular space (like an en suite), you've taken away another space (in this case, storage).

Location

As they say, location, location, location are the three main things to think about when buying a home. The upshot is that you can change many things about a place, but location isn't one of them.

This third point of your triangle is a key one, because if the house is in the wrong place to start with it could cause problems in the future – particularly when it comes time to sell. You might get a great reduction on the price if the property is on a busy main road, but you could well be limiting buyers when you want to move on. Weighing up the pros and cons of location is crucial. Sometimes it's a bit of a gamble, but you could come out ahead if you buy somewhere that looks like it's on the way up.

For instance, a friend of mine bought a small terraced house in a street in Lincoln that became a 'rat run' – a cut-through route for commuters going into the centre of the city. Luckily, the council cut the road off at one end while carrying out road repairs, and for some unknown reason, decided to leave the road as a cul-de-sac after the work was finished. The value of my mate's home increased considerably, as did his life in a much quieter spot. Yet, you cannot always foresee that such a positive change will occur.

Reasonably priced first homes are not always in the best locations, but you need to determine what is acceptable, and what isn't. I would advise against buying on an extremely busy road, or anywhere that suffers from undue train or Tube noise. In some instances you might be able to double-glaze a house to cut out some of the racket, but you are severely limiting the number of prospective buyers when you sell.

However, other major positives – wonderful period features, great accessibility to key places or a far larger property than you could realistically afford elsewhere – could make the flawed location appear less problematic. Do really think through whether you are making the right decision, however, as I believe location really is the most crucial point of the triangle.

CASE STUDY

A PERIOD GEM?

Two years ago, IT consultant Simon Terry bought a beautiful Arts & Crafts house in Cheltenham, Gloucestershire for £415,000 with his primary school teacher wife Louisa. The beautiful Victorian former artist's studio had many of its original features, including stained-glass windows, panelled walls and double-height leaded windows.

Despite the attractive pluses of being the proud owner of the 'Victorian jewel', as Simon calls it, the house sits on a very busy thoroughfare running through the spa city. Sitting in a concrete hinterland with traffic booming past, Simon says that in this case, he felt location wasn't as important as the house itself.

'I had to compromise somewhere – no one gets everything they want when they buy a property – and I was willing to give up living on a quieter road in order to get hold of this marvellous, interesting building,' explains Simon.

But does he ever worry though that he might find it hard to sell when he moves on? 'Well, maybe it will cut down on the number of willing viewers, especially these days with Google Maps on the Internet where people can see exactly where property sits, but I'm sure there are like-minded people out there that will appreciate the beauty and history of the place as much as I do.'

The noise is ever-present, as Simon and Louisa were not allowed to double-glaze the large windows, because the house is Grade-II listed with English Heritage. This means they can't change the 'special characteristics' of the building and have to get planning permission for any work that can affect them. Simon says they play music softly to deaden the sound of cars, buses and taxis racing by, which does help, and there is some dust from the road, but it doesn't really bother the couple.

A local agent says location is terribly important. 'But, at the end of the day, you just need one person who loves the place to walk in and make an offer. However, it is true as well that the house is blighted somewhat by its location, which cuts down the value to a degree.'

So, beware. Location, location, location isn't just an empty phrase, but in many cases, a warning. But one man's compromise could be his and another man's delight – as Simon and Louisa say they hope will one day be the case.

Viewing, viewing, viewing

Once you have determined your priorities, it really helps to kick off proceedings by just going to see a few properties. There's nothing better for getting an idea of what's out there in your price range and how you might have to tailor some of your original space expectations to make them fit the budget point of your triangle.

This is one of the fun parts of buying a first-home, I think. It can be terribly exciting going to look at the first few properties and these days, you can create a good sense of how best to use internal space by looking at floor plans on the Internet before you set out. Be warned, though. The danger is you can get too excited early on and make a decision about what you want before you've sorted out all three points of your triangle.

'Would like' and 'need' lists

Lenders, such as the Nationwide, often suggest you come up with 'would like' and 'need' lists. I think this is a great idea, as it helps you narrow down the property you want and where it ideally should be.

Simply draw up a list (you can print some of these off the Internet from lenders' websites, or ask them for the list), including different aspects, such as number of bedrooms, separate kitchen, central heating and separate dining area. Then, put a tick next to the ones you feel you 'need' and those you 'would like'. You might need to amend your list as you start viewing and parameters change.

This list essentially helps you ask the right questions, so you can tighten your search. Here are some questions to get you started:

- Where do you want to live – in the middle of a town, near your workplace and/or near schools?
- Why are you moving in the first place – to get on the ladder, because you're getting married or you have a new job?
- Do you want a garden?
- Is outside space essential (maybe you want to keep a pet)?
- Do you want off-road parking?

- Is the property near amenities and good transport?
- How many bedrooms do you need?
- Is a patio space important?
- Do you like living near shops?
- Do you need to be close to public transport?

I would advise then drawing up a list of the three main things you feel you **must** have. No more than three, however, or you'll become frustrated by not finding all the items on your wish list. It could be a second bedroom large enough to accommodate a paying lodger, as in order to pay the mortgage you need to rent it out. Or, maybe you need to live somewhere on the east side of a town or city, which is the right side of town to travel to your workplace.

Be prepared to amend and update your wish list as your house hunting proceeds. In some cases, you might have to become more flexible with regards to some features. The more open-minded you can be, the easier will be your search. Being as realistic as you can and accepting there are limits is important.

However, you need to get the balance right. There's no point buying a 'bargain' property that's on a main road and blighted by noise and dust if it will be impossible to sell when you need to move on. But, if you insist on being in a particular location and that's all you can afford, you might have little choice. I would advise trying to get the best place you can for your money. It might be better in some instances to move just that bit further out where prices are often cheaper to get more for your cash.

Price will dictate a great deal, as will what's actually on the market when you're searching for your first abode. Remember, no one will ever get absolutely everything on their wish list, even if they're spending millions of pounds on a property. And, if you're a first-time purchaser, it is likely that you'll have to compromise on some features.

Compromise

The art of compromise is a skill a first-time buyer needs to acquire quickly. It's unlikely you'll get all three points of the triangle in your first home:

budget, space and location. You will probably have to relent along the line and let something go. Some first-timers are lucky and do find a spacious property in a great location that still manages to fall within their budget, but I suspect they're playing with more cash than the majority is likely to have.

However, I think you should be able to get at least two out of three of the points in the triangle, while compromising on the third. For instance, you might find an airy flat with three spacious bedrooms for the amount of money you can borrow. The catch is it is in a dodgy neighbourhood that hasn't quite heard the word 'regeneration' yet. The gamble is whether the area will improve in the near future, but you can generally spot certain signs that indicate that a place is up and coming. Some of these signs are:

- New developments being built
- A new transport link, or improvements to current links
- The main shopping parade getting a facelift
- The council repaving streets and pavements and installing new street furniture
- Local residents planting and tidying verges and roundabouts
- Graffiti being cleaned up and the removal of old furniture and mattresses in the streets by the council and residents
- Gastropubs and other smart eateries opening up
- Plenty of skips in the streets, indicating locals are doing up their homes

Meeting compromises is a game most first-time buyers will have to play, but don't be disheartened. Even buyers with plenty of money don't always get absolutely everything they want. Another common compromise for first-timers is venturing out a bit further. Many choose an area where they want to live and find they can't afford to live there. By stepping over the boundary into the next neighbourhood, prices usually drop and you will get more space for your money, too. You will have a longer commute into work perhaps, but look at the bright side: you'll be more likely to get a seat on the train, as you're getting on board before many of the other commuters.

I would advise trying to get the best you can for your money. Certain things you can't change, such as location, and I think location is key. You can always refurbish a run-down house in a good location, but it is less tempting ending up with a smart house in a bad location, which you can do nothing to alter.

Compromise with a partner, relative or friend

One of the biggest problems I come across is when dealing with couples, friends or relatives buying a house together that are unwilling to compromise. You need to really listen to what your co-buyer wants, and equally, your co-buyer needs to listen to you. Often, the more vocal of the two wins out, which means the other person ends up frustrated and unhappy.

It's a good idea to get both parties to write down what they really want – a trick we use on *Location, Location, Location* – to make sure that some of the features are included from each wish list. For example, you might need a light and airy study space, because you work from home, while your partner, who is a dedicated gardener, is keen to have a decent-sized green patch where he can grow vegetables. Satisfying both of those desires as well as you can makes for harmonious living in your new home.

Education, education, education

I can't emphasise enough how much research you should do before going out viewing property. You will be more informed and able to see through any sales blarney or hyperbole about the property and neighbourhood.

Also, use my 'three to one' method. I think you should think about at least three different areas before you start property hunting. Then, you should eventually try to narrow this down to one area. This will make the entire process quicker, easier and more fun. Don't forget, this is probably the biggest shopping trip of your life.

Be aware that you might have to shift your search or widen it slightly (perhaps into the neighbouring, less-expensive area). Being open-minded to a degree is as important as narrowing down your search, if that doesn't sound contradictory. There might not be anything suitable or for sale in your chosen area on your budget, so you will have to think again. If you're finding you're disappointed frequently, then you have to change to a new area.

Some buyers, for whatever reason, insist on living in a three-bedroom flat or having a garden. If you fall into this category (and maybe it is for legitimate reasons to house a family or to grow vegetables to feed them, for instance), then you will have to go somewhere else to get this particular sort of property.

Really thinking about small details helps categorise property, too. As a motorcyclist, I am keen on side access to a property and somewhere to store my motorbike. If you do reduce the number of properties to a tiny proportion because of certain demands, remember that you will have to accept this and you can't be too fussy about the few you see. You can't then tell an agent or house finder that you don't like the windows if they went to great lengths to get you everything else on your list.

Wearing my house-finding hat, I find that some buyers are property focused – 'my home needs to be like this' – so I will find what they want and then tell them where it is. Others are area focused – 'it has to be in Hampshire' – so I will show them what they can afford in that county. It is overly ambitious to say, 'I want this and it must be in this place.'

It's unlikely a first-time buyer will get both what they want and in the exact place they fancy. Meeting compromises will be part of the game for most – for example, 'if you venture a bit further out, then I can guarantee you a seat on the train when you commute to work.'

YOUR WANTS AND NEEDS CHECKLIST

- [ ] Work out your 'home triangle': budget, space and location
- [ ] Kick off by looking at a few properties to get an idea of what's out there
- [ ] Draw up 'would like' and 'need' lists
- [ ] Amend the lists as house-hunting proceeds
- [ ] Work out how you might need to compromise (if buying with a partner, family member or friend, both of you should write down what you want)
- [ ] Narrow your search to one area
- [ ] If you can't find anything within your budget in this area, extend your search further

PHIL'S CONTACTS BOOK

Good websites where you can search for property:

- www.findaproperty.com
- www.primelocation.com
- www.rightmove.co.uk
- www.upmystreet.com
- www.zoopla.co.uk
- National Association of Estate Agents – 01926 496800, www.naea.org.uk – the leading professional body for estate agents in the UK that offers advice and advertises its members' properties

CHAPTER FIVE

Getting the Best from Estate Agents

How to get the best out of agents when buying

Nowhere else in the world can you find a market – not just a residential property market – but a marketplace where traditionally all the help and advice is only taken by one side of the deal – the sellers. Forget the mechanics of lawyers and surveyors who obviously work for both sides. I'm talking about the process of finding suitable property and negotiating best terms.

Operating in the market every day, estate agents are the ones who know, and understand to some extent, what goes on. For all but the most experienced purchasers, the inner workings are a complete mystery. With mystery comes confusion, and with confusion comes exploitation.

Love 'em or loathe 'em, estate agents are vital to first-time buyers. It's not crucial when you're selling to get along with a large number of estate agents – after all, you're only going to pick one, or at most a few, to sell your property – but contacting and getting on with many estate agents is terribly important when buying.

'Why?' you might ask. The answer is that you want access to the widest possible amount of information and homes for sale in your chosen area. The only way you will find this out is by talking to every agent operating, despite the fact that some will be good and some bad. You do have to deal with them all, though, certainly to start with.

The role of the estate agent

As a first-time buyer, it's imperative you stop and think of the role of the estate agent. The main thing to remember is that the agent is paid by the seller. A decent agent will try to form a good relationship with the buyers he's trying to sell to, but the buyer is **not** the customer and he's not providing you with a service.

Therefore, there's no point getting annoyed or cross when an agent sends you loads of property particulars (descriptions and pictures of homes for sale) that do not interest you or you believe are unsuitable. The agent's job is to sell as many houses as possible to keep his clients (the vendors) happy. And your job, as a first-time buyer, is to manage the agents.

The irony is that the agent spends more time with the buyer, who is not his client, than with the seller, who is paying his fee. So, there's an interesting relationship between the agent and buyer. The agent is not there to help you as a client, but they do have to help you to make a sale. There's nothing else like it in the sales world.

PHIL'S BIGGEST TRADE SECRET – EVER

Believe me, this is **the biggest trade secret ever**: be very, very nice to estate agents. Until you can learn to love, or at the very least like, estate agents all other advice is at best only 50% effective. I realise this might be a revolutionary concept to first-time buyers but, like all the best ideas, it's simple and it works.

It's worth being polite to an agent, turning up on time and remembering his or her name. Remember, one of these agents will tell you about the place that one day will be your home.

Dealing with an agent

I think a good way of learning how to deal successfully with an agent is to examine and compare how you deal with a salesman in a shop. If you go into a shop and are pleasant to a sales assistant, for instance, I think that generally they'll be more helpful and honest – 'Go for the blue one, it really suits you'.

If you're not amenable and reasonable, a sales assistant won't bother going that extra mile to source an item in a particular size or colour – 'Sorry, we're out of stock'. And they'll take great pleasure in seeing you go out the exit with a purchase that doesn't suit you and emphasises your expanding gut. But, if you're friendly, they may well say, 'Listen, mate, I'm not sure the purple is for you.' Or, 'I'll tell you a secret. The sale starts next week and we have loads of those and they'll be marked down by half.'

The same applies to an estate agent, who essentially is a sales manager or assistant by another name. If you aren't polite, and are brusque and aggressive most of the time, why would an agent choose you over all the other buyers looking for property when something decent comes on his books?

Comments from a sales person might not always be in the best interests of their employer, but you've got the sales assistant on your side. The same applies to agents. If you build up a good working relationship with them, they're less likely to see you walk away with a dud house. Most agents are decent people just trying to keep body and soul together and pay their own mortgages. It's not their fault the products they're selling play such an important part in your life.

Ringing up eight agents (once you've narrowed it down a bit) once a week should become your key objective. It might sound time-consuming, but calling your new best mate Bob (and all your other new best mates once a week) – 'Did you win the football?' 'Did your daughter pass her GCSEs?' – isn't such a big task. You just have to talk to everyone and that's the way it is. It could be the dodgy-looking agent on the corner, or the big-time agent in his shiny office on the park. Don't get sidetracked about judgement at this stage and just get on with it.

Managing an agent

You need agents on side as much as possible to get early information on the best properties – but do be careful how much you let slip. Remember that they are in 'sales' and trained to win your trust. They may try to override your point of view with their own or nudge you into spending more than you want.

While estate agents are **not** in business to look after the interest of buyers, as I've emphasised earlier, good ones are excellent relationship builders. The more they know about you, your property requirements and your finances, the easier it is to sell you a house.

Most agents have viewing targets to meet – and when times are bad, they might even get incentives for each viewing – and will want to show you as many properties as possible. If you read sales particulars and ask plenty of questions before agreeing to a viewing (such as, what is the weakness of the property? – even Buckingham Palace has weaknesses), you should avoid wasting time looking at something totally unsuitable.

Bear in mind that it is a fact that more than 70% of buyers spend 20% more than they ever set out to. This is why agents take you to places you can't really afford, hoping you'll fall in love with one and throw caution to the wind. Equally, don't be so intransigent that you refuse to look at anything a bit outside the box. Friends of mine ending up buying a thatched cottage when they asked to see anything but, because when they got inside they knew it was for them after all.

Agents – the good guys?

Estate agents are a much-maligned breed and the people we all love to hate. But in my experience, the public mess them around far more than they intentionally behave badly.

But what if you are suspicious that you're not being told the truth, or that the agent's hiding something? If there are specific things you're unsure about, ask the agent who shows you the house, ask the vendor, ask your solicitor and ask another agent from the same office. If you're still unsure, ask them all again. If somebody's bluffing, it will come out eventually.

Be a 'hot buyer'

The best properties are always in demand and to find out about them first, you need to be on the agent's 'hot buyers' list. How best to do this? Dozens of variables affect the housing market, some of which we can control and some of which we can't. We have no control over interest rates or employment levels, for example. We cannot foresee disasters or changes in global economic climates either.

We have no accurate method of determining at what stage the market will be at when we come to sell what for the majority of us is our most valuable asset. This means we have to work extra hard to control which-ever variable we are able to – namely, the property we buy and the price we pay.

So, it's worth being highly proactive in order to achieve this. If you get some good estate agents on side, the buying process becomes so much easier.

Supply of quality property is restricted across all price brackets, and to stand a decent chance of learning about good opportunities, you need to work hard at positioning yourself and your requirements towards the top of an estate agent's list of applicants.

I make a living representing the interests of purchasers, and so I spend a great deal of time and energy keeping clients' needs in the minds of agent contacts. The thought process is simple – those at the top of the list get the first bite of the cherry.

There's a common misconception that estate agents should advise **all** their applicants of **every** vaguely suitable property that comes available. In fact, many buyers believe this is central to the role of the estate agent. In slow market, conditions, it probably would be (or should be), but in a faster-paced market it simply does not happen.

Most agents are very busy people paid by volume sales (the more property sold, the more they make) and their living is directly related to the number of deals they put together. It wouldn't matter what the product was, but a busy sales rep won't feel the need to make 50 phone calls if the same result can be achieved by making only five. In general terms, it is these 'best of breed' examples that attract the highest competition and, therefore, require the lowest number of calls, advertisements and viewings to sell. These are obviously the places you, as a buyer, want to be seeing and buying.

PHIL'S TOP TIP

REGISTERING WITH AN AGENT

When first registering your details, try to visit the agent's office in person. As it's easier to recall faces than names, you'll develop a stronger relationship and also get better information about the market by talking face-to-face. First impressions count, so get it right from the outset.

Of course, you need to remember that at the end of the day estate agents are sales people – but also, that they have what you want. Which means, like it or not, unless you're going to retain your own buying agent, you need these people a great deal more than they need you.

Be a swot

If you build up a good working relationship with an agent, they're more likely to want to help. There's nothing in the world agents like more than a well-prepared, decisive purchaser.

Agents love to see people taking notes, which shows they're committed, focused and taking the whole business seriously. Do tell them that the mortgage is agreed in principle and you have a solicitor. Showing them you're not wasting time is a very good move.

PHIL'S TRADE SECRET
By law, sellers and agents don't have to point out any defects or problems with a property. But, they must answer any **direct** questions accurately. If a buyer has been given,

and relied on, false information they may have a claim under the Property Misdescriptions Act of 1991.

For instance, you might ask if there have been any problems with difficult neighbours and the agent or vendor (or both) insist there are no difficulties at all. Then you discover the next-door neighbour has been reported by the seller to the local authority and has been warned for making too much noise and generally making a disturbance – you would have a good claim against the agent and former owner. They might even end up having to pay you compensation.

Get it in writing

When buying and selling, keep in mind that any verbal understanding with an agent that is relevant to the process – whether it relates to price, timescale, chain situations, an exclusive period or the existence of another bid – should be confirmed in writing. If you've laid a paper trail of what's been agreed, there's no room for misunderstanding.

Whether buying or selling, deal only with agents who belong to the Ombudsman scheme (so you have some comeback), or a professional association, such as the National Association of Estate Agents (NAEA) or the Royal Institution of Chartered Surveyors (RICS). Look for a sticker in the window and the association's logo on their letterhead.

PHIL'S TOP TIP

Do ask an estate agent that belongs to an association exactly how many people in the office belong. In order to put the association's logo in the window and on the agent's letterhead and website, only one person need be a member. Sometimes that one member leaves the office and no one is a member at all. So, check out just how qualified the agents in the office actually are.

Who's paying the bill again?

If you're not using a specialist search company to find you a home, then the sales agent is your only avenue to hearing about and gaining access to properties that might be suitable for you. Always keep in mind the person that is paying the agent's bill (the seller) and whose interests the agent serves (the seller).

An agent works in sales – that's what they're paid to do. The majority of complaints about the services of agents come from buyers, who were clearly misguided in the first place, assuming they were about to be provided with a service in the first place. You definitely need them on side, but it is then up to you to manage the agent properly.

Should I hire a property search agent?

If you want to be represented, the best way is to hire a property search agent (also known as a buying agent or property finder). You will have to pay this buying agent a fee for his services, typically a one-off signing fee of several hundred pounds in the first instance and then a percentage of the selling price. This is negotiable, of course, particularly in leaner times.

Pros of hiring a property search agent:
- Someone is looking after **your** interests.
- A search agent often hears about property before it even comes onto the market.
- An estate agent takes a buyer more seriously if they've employed a property finder.
- An experienced property finder can give good advice on how to adapt a property to make it work better for you.
- A search agent has inside knowledge of deals, people and places (such as, a noisy go-kart track is opening up on the edge of a certain village; or a couple are getting a divorce and about to put their home onto the market).

- You can save a great deal of time and angst, as the search agent sifts out inappropriate property and narrows down the right places for viewings.
- The search agent can negotiate the deal for you and sometimes save you money, which justifies his fee.

Cons of hiring a property search agent:
- You do need to pay the search agent a fee, which might be difficult for a cash-strapped first-time buyer.
- There's no guarantee that the search agent will find what you want.
- As the search agent isn't earning much commission for a cheaper first-time buyer property, he might not be as enthusiastic as he would be for clients hunting for a pricier pad.
- He can only do his best with what is on the market, which might not be good enough for you.

Hear, hear – listen to the agent

To get the best from an agent (and all the other agents on his patch), really listen when you're out looking and collect details. If an agent says that a property similar to one you're keen on buying sold for £135,000 six months ago, write this down. It gives you a comparable figure you can use to work out what property you like might be worth.

As I keep saying over and over again (it's that important), the more you bother to build up a rapport with an agent, the more you will learn about the dynamics of the market. There's no point complaining that something is expensive if that's how it is. Reading the local and national press will supply some analysis, too, which can arm you with more information to get the hang of what's going on.

Supply the right information: I'm hooked on you

You'll have more productive viewings and a better chance of locating the right home if you supply all the right information – or 'hooks' – to estate agents. It's all about the detail. Rather than tell an agent that you are keen on outside space, be more specific if you can, explaining that your partner is pregnant and you will need a bit of space for a toddler to play and maybe even kick a ball around when a bit older.

Another example is telling an agent why you want a second bedroom. If it is going to be rented out to help pay the mortgage, then it will need to be a decent size – nearly the same size as the main bedroom – so someone will want to let it. A tiny bedroom the size of Harry Potter's cupboard under the stairs in Privet Drive won't cut the mustard and an agent needs to know this.

Don't become angry with an agent if he can't show you exactly what you want. If it's not for sale at the time you are looking, there isn't much he can do about it. You might need to widen your search to a nearby area that has more property for sale, or where you could get more space or amenities for your money. This isn't a time for postcode snobbery, however. If moving over a boundary gives you more for your money, then certainly consider it.

PHIL'S TRADE SECRET

Property is a people business. You have to ensure you're the buyer agents remember and like. So, be friendly and **don't** be flaky: 'I'm thinking of buying in the Cotswolds, but also maybe in Cornwall or somewhere around Croydon'. This won't wash with agents for obvious reasons.

Instead of being a perceived timewaster, say: 'This is my chosen area and you're the man who'll help me.' And even if you are looking elsewhere at the same time, don't let on.

MAKE YOUR AGENT YOUR FRIEND

Mary Saunders was keen to buy her first home in Leeds, not far from a number of her friends in the city centre. The 32-year-old NHS administrator with £20,000 in savings talked to several lenders and managed to get an agreement for a mortgage of £140,000, in principle. She then registered with six estate agents and waited for suitable property particulars to roll in.

Mary then became annoyed and confused when the property descriptions covered homes in the city centre, as well as in places as far afield as Bradford, west of the city, down south in Dewsbury, and even north of Leeds up in Harrogate.

'I rang up the agents to complain that it was a total waste of time alerting me to these properties that were not even remotely in the heart of Leeds. I want to be close to work, my friends and the nightlife in the city, not stuck out on some moor in the countryside,' she says.

Getting cross with the agents made no difference, however. She was still sent details – in areas she had no interest in whatsoever – through their computerised systems, although she'd protested these were no good to her.

Eventually, a friend and former roommate Mary shared a flat with when at Leeds University recommended she put on a friendly face and go in and talk to the agents in their offices. 'She thought it was worth me taking the time out to tell them what I really wanted and hope they'd think of me when something good came up for sale. My mate did this, and ended up with a lovely flat near the water that an agent spotted.'

Mary said it took her some time to go into the agents' offices after work during the week and on the weekends, but it seems to be paying off. 'Already, I've been sent some good particulars. And, even better, one agent called me to say a really good flat is just about to come onto the market and he'd make sure I'd be one of the first to get inside it to have a look round.'

Mary hasn't yet found what she wants, but she believes that at least now she's going in the right direction. 'Instead of ringing up and getting cross with agents, now I just chat to them to see what's happening. I even took one out for a quick coffee before work the other morning and she said that she'd definitely look hard for the right property for me.'

'It's a bit like when you first start going out with a bloke you fancy and you want to make the right impression,' adds Mary. 'In order for the romance to blossom, you need to be kind, attentive and hopeful. I'm starting to learn that most agents really do want to help, but yelling at them isn't going to make anything better. In fact, it just makes it worse.'

With her new softly, softly approach, Mary is likely to be finding her way onto the agents' hot buyer lists – and one hopes owning her own home in the near future.

YOUR ESTATE-AGENT CHECKLIST

- ☐ Meet agents in their offices while registering
- ☐ Be proactive (a 'hot buyer')
- ☐ Put everything in writing to avoid misunderstandings
- ☐ Check agents are members of professional bodies (NAEA, RICS, The Guild of Professional Estate Agents)
- ☐ Consider hiring a property search agent, if appropriate for you
- ☐ Supply the right information ('hooks') so you get the most from your agent

PHIL'S CONTACTS BOOK
- National Association of Estate Agents (NAEA) –
  01926 417794, www.naea.co.uk
- Royal Institution of Chartered Surveyors (RICS) –
  0870 333 1600, www.rics.org
- The Guild of Professional Estate Agents – 020 7629 4141,
  www.guildplatform.co.uk

CHAPTER SIX

Viewings

You only have a short time to view a property – make sure you make the most of it

You've got your money lined up, in principle, from your lender. You've done your research and honed down your search to one area. You've read a great deal on the Internet, in newspapers and magazines and you've talked exhaustively to friends and families. You've even looked at a couple of properties with some of the agents you've registered with to get a general sense of what's out there.

So far, so good. Now, it's time to start viewing property in earnest and really get going with your quest for the ideal first home.

General viewing advice

As a buying agent and TV presenter making programmes about the best (and worst) homes, I spend all day every day viewing new properties to the market and trying to assess whether or not they'll suit individual client needs.

Useful tools are:

- Notebook
- Measuring tape
- Compass
- Torch
- Map
- Camera

It's always a good idea to have a notebook with you so you can jot down information. You'll sometimes be viewing up to six properties a day (any more isn't very productive, as you'll start to muddle them up) and you'll forget which one is which without anything to remind you.

When it comes to viewings, especially more detailed second and third viewings, which I'll discuss later in the chapter, a measuring tape is a great aid. It isn't always easy visualising what will fit where, and a measuring tape will indicate the sizes of what's there already and give you a better sense of how big various nooks and crannies actually are.

A compass might sound more like the sort of tool you would give a seafaring captain or adventurous explorer. But one of the key factors is which way a building, and also a garden, faces. This will help you work out where the sun rises and sets and how much sunlight you will get at different times of the day.

I always carry a torch (it can be a small one if you're pushed for space in your bag), as often, light bulbs have burnt out or there aren't even any lights at all in certain spaces, such as cellars, storage areas and outside the building if you're viewing at dusk. I think it's quite a good safety measure for viewers to carry a torch anyhow. It can light a path in a mean-looking neighbourhood, although if you feel afraid going out unless you have a torch perhaps this isn't the right area for you.

Despite the fact that we are increasingly able to determine a lot about the position of a property now with Google Maps and other similar Internet tools, a map can give you a strong idea of your surroundings and answer a number of questions, for good or ill. These include:

- Is the property near a post office, shop or church?
- Where is the nearest Tube line or train station?
- How far are you from a main road, motorway or other key artery?
- Is there a park or other green space nearby?
- Is there an airport close by?
- What other amenities are marked on the map, such as a leisure centre, library, hospital, cricket field, museum or even a superstore?
- Are you close to a school?

- Is the property near an exhibition building or town hall, where others might park and possibly block you in or take away residents' parking spaces?
- Is there a stream or river nearby?
- Where's the nearest bridge, particularly if you have to cross one to commute to work?
- Is there a football or rugby ground close by, which could be disruptive when matches are on (unless you're an ardent fan, of course)?

A camera probably isn't necessary for a first viewing, but it can be useful for later viewings. It will help you remember what you've seen, as well as enable you to show a partner, family and friends the properties you like. Getting feedback and discussing pros and cons is always easier if there's something visual to refer to. And don't forget, those viewing from abroad or a long distance away have a visual record to examine when they return home.

Sense and sensibility: use your senses

Engage all your senses when you're on a viewing of a property. From the second you get there, you can get a good idea of the neighbourhood and street and you can gauge a great deal from just the front of the property. The next 10 minutes will be very important, so you need to switch on all your senses and really focus.

Don't be unduly influenced by factors that have nothing to do with the actual viewing, such as the agent arriving late with the wrong set of keys (count to 10 immediately, so you don't have a go at him). Even if you're freezing cold, having waited outside in a biting wind for the agent to actually arrive, put your waiting time to good use.

Neighbours, everybody loves good neighbours

What can you see immediately outside the property and in the street? This can have a huge impact on whether it is worth going any further (when the agent gets there, of course).

- Do the neighbours' houses look smart and like something on Wisteria Lane (think neat and tidy *Desperate Housewives*)?
- Does this look like an up-and-coming place – is building work going on, are basement conversion companies in evidence and are there skips in the road?
- Is the house you're viewing the best on the block, or the worst?
- What's the state of the brickwork, windows, roof, guttering and front garden?
- Is there any parking?
- How noisy is it? Does the neighbour have a yapping dog? Is music blaring out? And, is traffic or train noise drowning out any birdsong?
- Who is lingering in the street – do they look friendly or threatening?
- Are there any nasty smells from a nearby factory, restaurant or pile of uncollected rubbish that doesn't like it's going anywhere in a hurry?

The first viewing

On a first viewing, go inside the property and take a quick look at everything. Know generally how many rooms there are and, once you get your bearings, get to know the essence of the place.

You aren't interested in the intricacies of the heating system, the security alarms or other detailed workings in the property. Focus instead on the layout (the floor plan is very important), the condition of the property, whether or not your stuff will fit in and try to work out if the property will suit you in three years' time.

Life can change quickly, so it is good to look to the medium term at least, particularly in bad economic times with people moving less often. Just because you're frequently going to pubs, playing football on Saturday afternoon and spending several evenings in wine bars now, that doesn't mean this will always be the case.

So, choosing a flat next to your favourite pub might not be the wisest move. It closes down, the landlord (and therefore, the pub's ambience) changes and you get a girlfriend who likes to do other things rather than sit in the pub every night. Suddenly, you wish you hadn't bought a place smack next to the local drinking hole.

Your flexible friend

Because life can change quite rapidly, it's sensible to think about how flexible your options are with a first property. Any opportunity to add value, for instance, should be welcomed, as you might be staying in your property longer than you imagined. A baby might come along, you might start working from home, or you might decide you need to let out the spare bedroom. Being able to convert the loft, or sneak in a compact en suite bathroom into a corner of a bedroom, can make a lot of difference in the future.

The main reason a large number of people end up selling their current homes is simply because they've run out of space. You might have no choice if you can only afford a diminutive studio flat, but any way you can eke out more room and remain longer in your home, if need be, could be a godsend.

Floor plans

Floor plans, which increasingly more agents are supplying with property particulars and on their websites these days, are a fantastic resource for a first-time buyer. Once you get the hang of room proportions, you get a sense right away whether it's worth even bothering to view a property or not.

I find that a floor plan offers a great deal, showing room proportions, any odd angles or crannies that tend to steal space and good and bad layouts. Sometimes, you can turn a bad layout into one that is far superior. But, sometimes it's not worth the bother and you need to know why.

Here are some top tips on layout:

- If you want to add another bathroom and can run plumbing from the next-door room that already has it (another bathroom or a kitchen, for instance), this means the layout is in your favour.
- Is the corridor space sensible, or is it stealing too much space from the main rooms?
- A large, airy reception room is key, as you will spend a good deal of time here.
- If you want to rent the second bedroom, it must be of a decent size.
- The principal rooms (living room, kitchen) should ideally face any outdoor space (a garden or patio).
- Make sure the stairs are in the right place and not dominating a principal room (unless it is very big, of course, which is unlikely for a starter home).

PHIL'S TRADE SECRET

Beware of estate agents including 'dead space' (stairwells, for instance) in their square footage calculations. Also, some round up the square footage (they do have a certain latitude by law, but push it a bit far) and estimate curved areas in the same way they would squared-off spaces. You can tell a lot by a floor plan, though, which will reveal such trickery.

The asking price

I know it can be annoying getting particulars sent out from estate agents for property that is on the market at a price that you can't afford. Most computerised systems put property in price bands, so you might get some property that appears to be beyond your means.

However, you can turn this irritation into an advantage. Remember, the asking price is not set in stone. It is only a guide price that the agent and vendor would like to achieve in an ideal world. It can potentially be negotiated down, especially if you discover the property's been on the market for a long time and evidently isn't shifting. Also, it might be flawed in some way, which explains why no one is biting at the price it is on.

It's best to enquire what the situation is if you are interested in a property that might be priced higher than you like. There's a link between price and time: an estate agent usually prices a property lower if a seller is in a hurry to move.

But, not every seller wants to see his or her property advertised at a lower price. Many are stubborn and believe their homes are worth a great deal more than most people are willing to pay. The estate agent ends up agreeing with the seller simply to get the instruction to sell the property in the first place, knowing full well the property will have to come down in the near future.

The truth is a property is worth what someone is willing to pay for it in a particular market. You can make an offer at a lower level than the advertised price, but it is a good idea to explain how you came to this decision to make your argument more relevant. For instance, you can say the property hasn't been touched over the last decade and you estimate it will cost about £10,000 to upgrade and refurbish it. So, you are offering £10,000 less for that reason.

There are a number of websites (such as www.zoopla.co.uk) where you can see how much a property last sold for, which can give you an indication of if the current owners are overpricing it now.

PHIL'S TOP TIP

Ask the estate agent to show you 'comparables' – examples of other similar properties that have sold recently in the area and their prices. It's his job to do this, so make him earn his money and ask.

What can be changed?

I believe most things about a property can be changed, apart from its position and the amount of natural light a property enjoys (although you might be able to tinker with this second aspect if you are lucky enough to be able to add more windows or skylights). So, always consider these two key factors first.

Other questions you might want to ask are:

- Is the property in a part of the street where you'll feel comfortable?
- Which direction does it face? Facing south or south-west will enable more light to flood in, making your home lighter and brighter.
- What does the property look out on and how noisy is it?
- What is at the back of the property and do you feel secure with what is behind you?
- Can you alter the parking arrangements? You might be able to install a driveway, for instance – and even if you don't drive, you could rent out the parking space for extra income.

These topics should be at the forefront of your mind when you arrive at a viewing. You shouldn't worry about finding out the answers to everything at a first viewing, as this is really just a preliminary visit. If you are interested, you can return and see the home again, and then start asking more questions if you are considering making an offer.

PHIL'S TOP TIP

You aren't buying the previous occupants' lifestyle, so ignore the décor. The soft furnishings might be good, but who cares? Concentrate on what will be left once they move all their belongings out.

Don't get too fixed on fixtures and fittings

Don't be seduced, or indeed put off, by fixtures and fittings. At this stage you're interested in the shell of the home – not in the lifestyle or taste of the current occupiers.

I've noticed that a number of buyers, particularly first-time purchasers, who get side-tracked by superficial aspects when they're renting, get bogged down by new kitchen units, snazzy lights and laminate floors, all of which could be added later, anyhow. It's far more important to check out structural and original features. I believe having the original features, such as large sash windows, and a sound infrastructure (think extremely efficient central heating) is preferable to a quick refit of a bathroom, especially if the makeover is cheap and not very skilfully carried out.

The flip side is those viewers that become totally turned off by overly bold decoration. Okay, so the current owner has a penchant for purple. Try to see past this, because his purple prose phase can be easily painted or papered over. Cosmetic work is something that can always be done later, while structural work to mend dodgy pipe work or patch up a sagging roof is more crucial and, often, more expensive.

PHIL'S TOP TIP

Watch out for unusual or irregular shaped rooms when you tour a property and think about how you'd use each space. A curved or octagonal room might appear funky, but will you be able to fit in a sofa or units? Is there enough room for all of your belongings and will there still be enough space in a year, or three years' time?

Getting on with the vendor

There's no need to be over-friendly to the vendor, but equally, do be polite. You might end up discussing the biggest deal of your life with these people and it won't help if you've upset them at the start.

Sometimes the vendor will be quiet, but present. Other times it will be just you and the agent taking a look around. And you might be in the position where it is just you and the owner, although this is less typical.

Either way, do not become nervous or feel that you have to respond immediately. If asked what you think of the place by the agent or vendor, you can smile and say, it's fine or interesting. Or, you can say you want to have a think and will be in touch later. If you really did love the property, don't get carried away and rave about it to the rafters. Giving away too much information could jeopardise your position later on.

I'm always amazed how rude and candid some potential purchasers can be. Making disparaging remarks about the owner's taste, or announcing loudly that the kitchen has to be ripped out immediately and replaced with something more modern, will not endear you to the vendor. He might even refuse to sell to you, even if you offer the highest price. He has the right to say no, and will direct the agent accordingly. So, keep a good poker face and be as charming as possible.

Don't be too chummy either. Slapping the vendor on the back like you've just met your dearest friend after a long separation isn't *de rigueur* either. You are not there to become the vendor's next best friend. You're there to look at his property.

Feedback

After you've viewed some properties, be sure to give proactive feedback to the estate agent. If something's unsuitable, let him know why. Let him know what you liked and what you didn't.

Having said that, remember whom these people work for and don't give the game away. You won't strengthen your negotiating position at this stage by telling an agent a property is 100% perfect and you can afford to pay the asking price with money to spare.

Questions, questions, questions

If you're reasonably interested, this is the time to start asking questions. You'll be looking for all possible information to assist your decision and subsequent level of offer.

Some post-first-viewing questions could include:

- Who owns the freehold?
- Who manages the property (if it's a leasehold flat)?

- Which direction do the house and garden face?
- How busy is the traffic?
- How much is council tax, and energy (gas, electricity and water) bills?
- What are the transport links like and how far away are they?
- Why is the seller moving, and how quickly do they need to move?
- Has the owner found anywhere to move to yet?
- Is a parking space included in the price?
- How long has the property been on the market?
- Have any offers been made (and turned down)? If so, what were they?
- Is the area safe?
- What are the crime levels like in the area?
- What are the local schools like and are you within the catchment area for good state schools?
- Where is the nearest green space (park, common, walking trail)?
- What work has the owner carried out on the property?
- Are any building works planned for the building in the near future?
- Have there been any insurance claims on the property? And if so, what were they?
- Has the property ever had problems with subsidence (cracking and instability with the foundations)?
- Have prices risen greatly, or fallen sharply, over the last year or so? And by how much?
- Are the neighbours friendly?
- What would you say are the strengths and weaknesses of the property and area?

PHIL'S TOP TIP

When you find something you like, do not be shy. Ask questions about the property and area. If the agent or owner is holding something back, keep asking. By law, they don't have to reveal anything unprompted, but if you ask a specific question it does need to be answered truthfully.

Do **not** ask a ream of questions, however, if you aren't all that keen. It will irritate the seller and agent, and you will get a reputation for being a time-waster.

PHIL'S TOP TIP

The sales market tends to be seasonal, with most people buying in the spring and autumn. So, you could maybe find the odd bargain (and beat the rush) if you look outside peak times (hunt in the summer and winter), when fewer sellers are keen to offload their property. Things slow down just before holiday periods, too, and I've known clever buyers pick something up on Christmas Eve or just before the busy Easter selling season begins.

Do your research

Information is everything, and the more you have, the more confident you can be in your decisions. A great starting point is to have a pint or glass of red in the local pub. Chatting to the pub landlord and the locals can reveal a great deal, including why the vendor is leaving, what the area's like and, even, how prices have been faring of late.

Without appearing cruel, you could discover, for instance, that the vendor is selling because he's lost his job and is getting a divorce. These are two of the three D's: debt, divorce and death; three of the main reasons why people sell their homes. You can casually mention this when talking to the agent, who might supply some information, which gives you some leverage. Or, you can just offer a lower price if you know the owner is desperate and see what happens.

You might not always get the answers you would like, but enough gentle digging round usually uncovers something. It can be something small, like the owner's wife hates the area and misses being near their children. But this gives you information to help formulate an offer and a strategy for buying.

Light up my life

I'm often asked why light and the direction the house faces are so important. Well, it can be pretty grey and dark for most of the year in Britain, so living in a spot that can capture the most of the sunlight is crucial.

Equally, you need to find somewhere that suits how you live. If you want the morning sun because you enjoy breakfast on the terrace, which I love, then facing an easterly direction would be best. Or, you might want to make the best of the sunlight when you come home from work, especially in the summer with longer summer nights. Therefore, facing west or south would be ideal.

Really work out which way the garden, balcony or terrace faces, which is where you'll want to spend time when the weather's clement. It's crazy paying extra for a property with outdoor space that won't be used all that often because it's facing the wrong way – and thus, dark and cold – when you want to sit out there. Sunniest spots face south, while northerly aspects can be relentlessly gloomy.

And yet, don't panic too much if there isn't masses of light. You can do quite a bit to bring more light in, such as installing large glass sliding doors into the garden (pricey, but well worth it) and skylights to bring more natural light into the house. Simple strategies – painting a garden wall white or hanging a mirror on it – can do a great deal to bounce light about and reflect it to boost the ambience.

PHIL'S TRADE SECRET

Repainting in lighter colours; laying pale, natural stone tiles (dark grey can make the property appear even murkier on dark winter days) and cropping any overgrown foliage can add heaps of extra light. You might need to get planning permission from the local authority to prune trees, especially if you're in a conservation zone, so check first before you get out your saw.

The second viewing

After registering a note of interest during or just after the first viewing, don't delay booking the second viewing. There might be other buyers that liked the place too, and you want to be near the front of the queue.

Speedy second viewings

If the market is really roaring, you must carry out the second viewing pronto before someone else snaps up the property. When things are really moving you might be lucky to even squeeze in two viewings, as people do react very quickly in order to get the property they want.

But, don't get caught up in the rush. If you aren't happy about being forced to make up your mind that fast, then walk away. Or, you can still make an offer, and if someone trumps yours an agent or developer will come back to you to see if you want to up yours. Remember, you can always pull out, so you haven't lost anything.

If you do really like something after a promising first viewing and you know there are other buyers on your tail, I would recommend going to see the property for the second time the following day. It's unlikely, even in a crazily over-heated market, that the agent won't delay for a few hours at least. Just say you are very serious, but you want to see the property again with your partner, or in the daylight if you viewed it the previous evening. If it looks as good – or even better – then you can make that offer.

PHIL'S TOP TIP

Take what an agent says with a pinch of salt. In a booming market, he will tell you the whole world wants the same property you want, and if you don't act fast you'll lose it. There might be some truth in what he's saying, but there's bound to be some hyperbole there too. He wants to get a bidding war going, so offers – and his commission – are pushed up. Be sharp, but don't be hijacked by a greedy agent.

Second viewings are when you really do want to engage all your senses and keep your wits about you. This is a more detailed visit than first time round, and should be fairly concentrated.

This doesn't mean you have to spend hours there, but you need to focus clearly on key aspects. I always think knowing what to ignore is as crucial as knowing what to keep an eye out for.

For instance, there's a trend for brewing coffee and baking bread so lovely smells wafting about the property are there to tempt you. This is a selling device – a pleasant and fairly harmless one – but a device all the same. Be careful it isn't masking something bad, such as a sewage plant down at the bottom of the garden.

Damp smells are the ones to sniff out. An unpleasant rotting odour usually means damp problems, and these could be serious – and seriously expensive to sort out.

Equally, I'm always suspicious of vendors who play calming music. Are they just trying to create a pleasing atmosphere, or are they attempting to drown out jumbo jets landing at an airport down the road? Or, perhaps the neighbours' chained-up dog that howls all day and every day when its owners are at work? Noise problems are hard to fix – do you really want endless rows with the students next door that party into the wee hours and play rap music when you've just got the baby to sleep?

Also, the second viewing is when you come along armed with all your tools: your tape measure, to get a better idea of how much space you really do have; and your torch, so you can have a good poke into those dark corners and storage areas.

A friend of mine was very pleased to discover a separate dry and warm cellar space that came with his flat (for the reasonable rental sum of £75 a year) that was far larger than he first realised on the first viewing. Once he waved his torch around, he discovered it could easily store his skis, diving gear, bicycle, suitcases, boxes of books and Christmas decorations. And there was plenty of space left over for a large hanging rail for clothes he wouldn't need every day, and unused space to accommodate more items later on.

PHIL'S TRADE SECRET

Whenever a developer or agent is struggling to make a decision about a property, they often take along a colleague or mate for another visit. A second opinion can be most valuable, offering up ideas and seeing things you might not have come up with, or noticed.

Night and day

Go back and view the property at a different time of day. There might be a mini-rush hour outside your front door at peak times, for instance, and if you don't visit then, you'll never know.

Also, I think it's a good idea to walk past the property at night when your feelings of the road and neighbours will be strengthened. A dimly lit street where you don't feel very secure might not prove a tempting choice, especially for a single woman.

Another example is if the only access to a flat is down a dark back alley; it could be very off-putting for you and your visitors. Yet, remember that some problems or situations can be altered. Clubbing together with the neighbours to install a state-of-the-art automatic lighting system or a burglar alarm could make all the difference.

PHIL'S TOP TIP

Wind direction can change, bringing increased noise and odour levels with it. This is especially noticeable in the country, where traffic noise and nasty smells (silage, pig farms or factory emissions) can be blown through. A peaceful place can suddenly turn into a noisy or whiffy spot.

Important things you might miss

People often miss seemingly small, but crucial, omissions or problems when viewing a home. Here are some you should take sharp notice of:

- Check the **water pressure** by turning taps on. The shower is where people are driven mad by a few sad droplets of water feebly trickling out, when you really want a hard, pumping shower pelting strong torrents of water on you.
- Is the house on **mains services**? If the house isn't hooked up to

mains water, oil or gas supplies, it is likely you will be paying a great deal more money (double in some cases) for your energy supplies. You might not have a choice if mains services do not run up to your door, or village.

- What kind of state is the **boiler** in? And when was it last serviced? This applies to the Aga or Rayburn, too.
- Are there **cracks** or **chunks** of plaster falling from ceilings or walls? This could mean some form of instability, maybe even subsidence, or indicate damp problems in the property.
- Is there **central heating**? **Double glazing**? An agent will add these features to the particulars, praising the fact that they're there, but rather coyly will not mention them if they're absent.
- Are the **windows** and **doors** in good nick? Repairing or replacing them can be costly, so think twice about putting in an offer before you find out when they were last replaced, or at least rejuvenated.
- Are there plenty of **plugs** in each room – and are they in sensible places? Equally, does the property have **broadband** or **wi-fi**? **Satellite** television, or **cable**? Modern communications are becoming pretty much standard these days, and having to drill lots of holes in the walls to run cables round can be disruptive and pricey.

Other suggestions include remembering that if there's a lot of clutter in the property now, it will feel smaller. Once the owner removes his belongings, it should appear lighter and larger. You need to look beyond the large, lumpy armchair and the teetering pile of newspapers crowding the landing.

My colleague Kirstie Allsopp from *Location, Location, Location,* without whom life would be far duller, likes to lie down on the floor and look up at the ceiling before deciding whether a property works or not. It's certainly one way to get a feeling for the place.

PHIL'S TOP TIP

Get out the masking tape and some newspapers. There's no better way to see if the property will accommodate your furniture than measuring items at home, and then measuring the space in the new property, marking the floor with a bit of masking tape. Another good trick is to lay newspapers down on the floor to emulate larger items, such as a sofa or armchair. You can imagine how they will fit within the space.

Before you start snapping pictures left, right and centre, or whipping out a camcorder to make a reality documentary about the property, do always ask the agent and/or the owner politely for permission. They're invariably going to say yes, but it's important to appear pleasant and not too pushy. A photographic record of sorts can be useful – 'Here's the one with the stained glass window in the hall' – and helps you remember which property is which.

While a first viewing is about getting a sense of a place and not getting bogged down by the nitty-gritty, a second viewing is all about short-listing. You should be narrowing down your search to just a few properties so you can make a final decision.

PHIL'S TRADE SECRET

A canny house finder asks a vendor, 'If you were staying, what would you do to your home?' The vendor's answer can be most instructive, because he's lived there and really knows the place. He might answer, 'It would be wonderful to add a conservatory,' or 'I always planned to one day move the bathroom to enlarge the bedroom.'

One friend remembered what the former owner of his Wiltshire cottage said – sentiments that funnily enough were echoed by his house finder. It took 12 years for him to get round to it, but reconfiguring a large bathroom and slicing off a section with a valuable window to make a spare bedroom bigger and lighter has totally transformed that part of the house.

Justify the price

Naturally, you will want to conduct your own research into value, but it's always worth inviting the selling agent to attempt to give a good reason for the asking price. The agent is the one who is selling the property, so it's up to him to convince you of the value.

Remember, the property's value and the asking price are two very different things. Find out whether any alterations have been made to the property. What fixtures and fittings are included? What is the marketing position and have there been any offers? All of this has an impact on the value and could affect the asking price. Yet, some home improvements don't necessarily push up the price, although they might make the house marginally more sellable.

Beware of marketing gimmicks

A word of warning. Be cautious of marketing tricks from desperate sellers. It all sounds very exciting to get the owner's boat or car thrown into the deal, but do you really want a boat? And, what about the proposed automobile? Is it a clapped-out wreck the owner just wants to get shot of?

Unless the supposed 'great' offer is of personal and very good value to you, then don't do it. It's far better, in my opinion, to just get more money knocked off the asking price. Which of course is what they're avoiding doing by offering the car, wife, kids, dog and anything else they have hanging about in order to shift the property.

These sales techniques are usually attached to homes that aren't selling. I think it far better to get to the root of the problem and determine why the place isn't being sold. It could be overpriced, or is the owner hiding something? A few polite, but firm, queries (pretend you're the Detective Columbo of property) should give you the answer.

PHIL'S TRADE SECRET

Giving away 'free' incentives in order to sell a home is a trick developers use if they want to shift new homes in a hurry. Don't get too excited about the free curtains, carpets or landscaping offer, which is usually worth more to the house builder than to you (they do bulk deals on cheaper items, so they don't pay much for them in the first place). Weigh up whether the deal is good for you. If not, don't fall for it.

I find most people end up buying where their friends are buying, or when a colleague heartily recommends an area. Word of mouth is good, of course, but sometimes it's nostalgic ('We had our first flat there and it was wonderful'), which doesn't necessarily mean the area is right for you now. However, it could be terrific still – you just need to check it out.

But as birds of a feather tend to flock together, as they say, you also need to remember to take things with a pinch of salt. Most people don't want to admit they ever made a bad decision or a mistake. How often do you hear people say their house is terrible, and so is their child's school? Normally, people defend their patch so they can justify their decision-making.

CASE STUDY

I BOUGHT WHERE MY BOSS LIVED

Debbie McClaren, who works for a small travel operator, wasn't sure where to look for her first home. She thought initially about buying near where she was brought up in Penn, Oxfordshire, but soon realised there was no way she'd be able to afford anything in the area.

Luckily, her boss came to her rescue. Instead of scolding her for wasting office time looking at brochures and local papers with advertisements about property for sale, she became her saviour.

'I was being a bit naughty one day looking at some possible places I might be able to buy my first place, but my boss didn't tell me off. Instead, she took me for a coffee and tried to help me out. She told me about Wendover in Buckinghamshire, not far from the office. Coincidentally, it was where my boss and her then boyfriend (he's now her husband, which was another good omen for a single girl like me) bought their first place seven years ago,' explains Debbie.

Debbie's boss suggested they go to the town one evening after work, offering to drive her around the area and point out good streets where she might reside. 'We were really lucky, as we spotted a new development that was going up, with starting prices from £177,000 for a one-bedroom apartment, which was within my budget.'

Debbie and her understanding boss went to a pub for a drink and talked to the locals – 'A great way to get to know people and what's going on in the area,' adds Debbie. She found out there are stables nearby where she could ride on the weekends (a favourite pastime), and a good doctor's surgery, village hall, several other pubs and five restaurants nearby.

'I also discovered that the train from Wendover gets into Marylebone station in under an hour, so I would be able to get to London easily to see my sister,' says Debbie. Aylesbury and High Wycombe, with good shopping centres, cinemas and theatres, aren't far away either.

Going to see an area with someone who's had a good experience living there can be really encouraging, according to Debbie. 'My boss jokes that she was just helping me out, because she wanted me to stay in the area so I wouldn't change jobs, but I'm grateful to her for pointing out a place that I didn't even know existed.'

Debbie's now made an offer on a one-bedroom flat and the developer is paying her Stamp Duty and 5% of her deposit.

Best of all, however, is that she feels she's chosen the right location, which we all know is one of the key things to get right in the first place.

The common parts

If you're buying a leasehold flat in a rather decrepit-looking and neglected building, this could suggest that there's a rogue landlord, or freeholders that aren't prepared to pay to keep the place in shape. Before you go any further, get the freeholder's details to find out more. You should also talk to the managing agent (the company looking after the building on behalf of the freeholder), if there is one, and talk to the other residents in the unloved building.

I would personally do as much research as I could before I started forking out a surveyor's or a solicitor's fees. Who cares for the common parts – the communal hallways, stairs and gardens – and how well they're looked after can be a problem. Technically, it is the freeholder's responsibility, but sometimes, residents end up getting involved.

I heard a story about a couple that wanted to buy a fantastic flat in a nineteenth-century building in west London. The communal parts were very shabby, so they simply had their builders tart up the main hallway and the stairs running up to their flat when they were there working on their flat. Their assumption was it wasn't worth the hassle complaining and having endless rows with the freeholder about it. The downside is they were hit with the costs, but when it comes time to sell it makes the access to their home look neat, tidy and inviting.

Signs of a well-managed building:
- Up-to-date notices hang neatly on the notice board.
- The main entrances are secure.
- The intercom system works well.
- The front garden is well tended and looks smart.

- Carpet on the stairs is quite new and nicely hoovered.
- There is no litter or rubbish anywhere.
- The handrail on the stairs is well polished.
- The hallways have been recently painted.
- There is no damp or cracks in any of the communal parts.
- The communal gardens at the back resemble a small friendly park, rather than a threatening jungle.
- It simply feels warm, loved and respected by the residents.

The 10-minute rule

The neighbourhood is a big part of where you live. You won't just be in isolation in your home, unless you've been helicoptered onto Tracey Island as a Thunderbird. So, employ my 10-minute rule, which is very important and hugely helpful.

What you do is walk for 10 minutes in each direction from your proposed new home. Turn off your mobile and really concentrate. Now, what do you see? Is there a friendly shop nearby? How about a park? Somewhere to buy a paper? A coffee? Where's the nearest school? Are there decent streetlights? A bus stop, Tube or train station? A dry cleaners?

Spotting up-and-coming features can occur on your 10-minute jaunts. You might, for instance, find a street with some tired, old shops there. But, what's this? A new delicatessen on the corner – and there's a friendly owner willing to chat to you about the neighbourhood. She points out that the abandoned shop next door is about to be turned into a café and that the new butcher's down the road is doing well, too.

I think it's worth even sketching a little map, showing what you find during your 10-minute stroll. You will learn a lot about the best streets to be in, and if you come across absolutely nothing during your 10-minute stroll, this can be revealing, too. If you're in the countryside and longing for peace and quiet, this is then ideal for you. But, then where do you go if you want a pint (or two), or you've run out of milk? Will you have to drive to get there, which can be a big problem in the country, particularly after you've drunk that pint and don't want to be stopped by the boys in blue in case you're over the limit.

The 10-minute, or pint of milk, rule (what you find within a 10-minute walk, or how far do you have to venture to get a pint of milk) is one of the best ways to learn about your immediate surroundings. You need to think beyond what suits you, too. What about guests who come to stay, or visitors? If they're alarmed about being mugged, or feel vulnerable getting to you from the station, this might not be a great sign that you're in the right spot. There's up and coming, but how long will it be before your patch up and comes?

You might need or want to rent your home at some point, too. If potential tenants feel threatened, or disappointed by the lack of facilities, your property isn't likely to be a successful rental proposition. So, think beyond your immediate needs and put yourself in other people's shoes.

I think being within some form of public transport in 10 minutes in an urban setting is the ideal. You might not quite match this as a first-timer, but if you can come close that will help your enjoyment and others' of your new home when they come to see you or stay.

What you can and can't change

It's good to be realistic and look at the property you're interested in from a pragmatic viewpoint. If you can't change something that is vital to your buying requirements, such as being within the catchment area of a good state school, then perhaps you should stop right here.

Some 'minus' points, however, can be altered and become if not exactly 'plus' points, at least 'not so awful' points. One good example was a female musician who bought a fairly priced one-bedroom flat above a shop and on a busy street (it's difficult to change either of those features, naturally), and even worse, with the entrance to the flat up a dark back alley that didn't look very inviting. The latter 'minus' factor could be changed, though.

With the help of the like-minded upstairs neighbour, a good security light was installed to brighten up the area when anyone approached the building. The two women also cleared all the debris out of the garden, planted some shrubs and flowers and even had the gate mended, so it could be firmly latched to keep out intruders.

Okay, the inexpensive flat was still in a rough area and the access to the building was still up the dark alley. But, the approach was immensely improved by a bit of effort and concentration on what could be changed. These small alterations certainly add to the enjoyment of living there and to the value of the property when it comes time to sell.

VIEWINGS CHECKLIST

- [ ] Gather useful tools (notebook, map, compass, measuring tape)
- [ ] Examine the property's exterior and the street
- [ ] First viewing: take a quick look round
- [ ] Ask agents to show you 'comparables' (prices of similar property in the area)
- [ ] Look out for what you can improve
- [ ] Give feedback to agents
- [ ] Ask post-viewing questions to get more information
- [ ] Do your research on property and areas
- [ ] Check which direction the house faces to get more light
- [ ] Check out crime rates, transport links and whether prices have fallen

- [ ] Second viewing: focus clearly on key aspects
- [ ] Visit at a different time of day
- [ ] Get agents to justify prices
- [ ] Question 'free' incentives (such as a car thrown into the deal)
- [ ] Use the '10-minute rule': what is within a 10-minute walk of the property

PHIL'S CONTACTS BOOK

- www.zoopla.co.uk – a good resource to see how much property has sold over the past few years

CHAPTER SEVEN

Doing the Deal

Putting the wheels in motion –
understanding the conveyancing
process from offer to completion

Well, you've finally got there. Just like when you're desperately seeking a true love, you've managed to complete your amorous hunt and find 'the right one'. The romantic relationship analogy goes a long way here. There are all the fantastic moments to look forward to with Mr or Miss Special, as well as the not-so-good spats and complications you'll have to wade through.

But for now, revel in the good times. Don't panic and start worrying about whether you are doing the right thing. Try not to lie awake at night muttering to yourself, 'Oh, why have I said yes to something I'm not 100% sure I like, and can I afford it at the end of the day?' This is counterproductive and you need to remain optimistic. Some buyers, particularly first-timers, do have an element of 'buyer's remorse' when they start having concerns over the purchase.

My advice is to just stay in the moment and go easy. There are a lot of stages to get through after you make that initial offer and many hurdles to jump. So, in a way, this is just the beginning, although you might feel like you've been trying to find a house forever by now with hours spent researching and viewing countless properties.

Equally, don't be like a star-struck lover and begin imagining how sensational it will all be with your sofa cosily tucked into the corner of the living room, your cutlery set from Aunt Mary lined up in the kitchen drawers and your books lining the new shelves you'll install in the hallway.

And as cruel as this sounds coming from an outsider who hasn't had Cupid fire an arrow into his heart recently, no property is a one-off. There are thousands of places out there. Just as a lover can rapidly be replaced by a new flame, if you lose this home another will come along. Look at making an offer in the same way as asking a girl you fancy to go out to the pub with you. You'll be upset for a week or two if she declines your offer, but someone else will come along who will be happy to join you for that glass of wine.

Getting the ball rolling

You don't want to lose your new beloved, but if you're thinking of making an offer, now is the time to ask the agent a number of questions, so you'll be ready to proceed quickly when the starting gun goes off.

What to ask before you make an offer:
- Is it in a quiet street?
- Ask to see the Energy Performance Certificate (EPC) – for more information, see page 156.
- How often do the rubbish collectors come to take away the trash?
- Is the council good at cleaning the streets, clearing away snow in the winter and maintaining the road?
- Are there any plans for any major development or building work in the area?
- How close are amenities, such as a local leisure centre, a farmer's market, a post office or a library?
- Is there a good state school nearby? Although you might not be producing a family in a hurry, living in the catchment area of a popular school will push the price of your property up and make it easier to sell.
- Are there any green spaces within walking distance?
- How far away is the nearest bus stop, Tube or train station?

If the place you want to buy is leasehold, there are some additional questions that you need to ask.

What to ask if you're buying a leasehold flat:
- Who is the freeholder?
- How long is the lease?
- If it's a short lease, what would it cost to extend it?
- What does the managing agent of the building charge per year?
- Ask if there is a 'sinking fund' (a pool of cash to go towards larger repairs, such as mending the roof) and how much are you expected to contribute annually.
- How much are the ground fees?
- Is there a porter or concierge, and how does he operate?
- How is the rubbish collected in the building?
- Are there any rules about keeping pets?
- What happens in emergencies – who do you contact and is there a 24-hour number to call?
- Is your heating included in management charges? This is sometimes the case in large mansion blocks.
- Do you need to pay separately for a parking spot, and can you buy or rent it?
- Is there any extra storage space you can rent?
- Are any building works planned in the future, what are they and what is the anticipated cost?

It's good to make a start at gathering up some of this information now, as it will need to be dealt with in more detail by your solicitor if your offer is accepted (see page 154 for advice on choosing the solicitor who's right for you). And if you discover the agent and vendor aren't very good at coming back with information, this could indicate they're not very well organised or enthused about doing much at this point. This shouldn't be a problem in the long run, but you won't be surprised if it takes time for your solicitor to get all the data he needs.

The asking price

Remember, the asking price is just that – an asking price. It's not set in stone and you don't have to buy exactly that amount in order to get the property. An asking price is a valuation essentially, with what the agent and owner hope to ultimately get tacked on top.

You can always challenge the agent about how he came about formulating the asking price. It will be interesting hearing how he justifies it, and if it doesn't remotely match the value of other similar properties (agents call these 'comparables', as mentioned before), then ask why.

Sometimes, if someone isn't in a rush to sell, they just try it on. Asking an inflated price in the hope that someone might pay it generally doesn't get the owner anywhere. Somebody might walk in and pay the figure they want, but then again, they probably won't. As soon as a property starts to languish on the market, it will look tainted even if there isn't anything particularly wrong with it. And when the price is slashed it's a good time for you to make a move.

Asking prices in Scotland

Do note that the above applies to England and Wales, but not to Scotland. If the property is offered at a fixed price in Scotland, this means the seller is willing to accept the first firm offer at the price specified. However, if the property is advertised as an upset, or 'offers over' price, the figure specified is the minimum amount the seller would be willing to accept. Once a binding contract is in place, the buyer can't withdraw without becoming liable for compensation. For more information on the Scottish buying and selling process, visit www.adviceguide.org.uk.

When prices mean different things to different people

The asking price can be confused with a 'guide price', or even the lowest price someone will accept. A guide price generally suggests a band of values (from £165,000–185,000, for instance). This means the seller would ideally like a minimum of £165,000, going up to £185,000 for the home. This isn't set in stone and is still a suggestion, like the asking price, but the agent is guiding you as to the range within the seller is likely to accept.

In some places, sellers like to say this is the lowest price I would accept (almost like the reserve price at an auction, which I'll explain more later in the book). Yet, everything is still negotiable, so don't be frightened by any figures that appear rigid. At the end of the day, a property is worth what a buyer will pay for it at that time.

Making your first offer

It's a big call to make. How do you know when is the right time to step up to the line and make an offer? How do you choose between what you've seen, and how do you know that something better won't come along?

Well, you'll never really know, will you? The best you can do is to think something's worth making an offer on, then go for it. The good bit is that you don't have to go through with the actual purchase. You, as a buyer, are under no commitment whatsoever to go through with buying the property just because you made an offer. No one has agreed to anything yet, so you're in a holding pattern until the agent talks to the vendor and comes back and either:

- Accepts your offer at the price you've suggested
- Says he likes the idea of your offer, but wants to talk about price (in other words, your offer is too low and can you bump it up a bit)
- Turns your offer down outright
- Says there's been another slightly higher offer and can you match or exceed it
- Takes the property off the market

The poker player

If you're good at playing poker, then you'll make a good purchaser. Usually, it's best to make a first offer and see what comes back without revealing your hand. Keeping your best card to play later makes good sense. After you've played your opening card, you wait to see what counter-offer the agent/vendor plays.

Money isn't the only chip on the table. There are several other factors up for negotiation, too. Working these into the deal complicates the rules of the game, but helps both sides save face when they have to compromise to a degree on something.

Here are some bargaining devices worth considering when emotions run high. The last thing you want is to lose your cool, so leaving the other side with dignity is crucial. Remember, you have to live next to the owner's neighbours, and maybe even friends, so take a deep breath and count to 10. Be firm and strong, but also pleasant and fair if the game gets out of hand.

Phil's bargaining devices:

- **Exclusivity**

  If you offer near or at the asking price, it's only fair to ask the owner to take the property off the market for an agreed exclusive period of time during which the home will not be shown to anyone else. This allows you time to get your solicitor to carry out searches and surveys (more on this soon), and for you to get a surveyor in if you want to check out the property in more depth, which the lender could well request.

  Although the vendor could agree to this exclusivity period and the property is said to be 'under offer', you are relying on the goodwill of the agent and vendor. Some play a straighter bat than others, with the more devious still showing the property around in the hope that someone might still make a higher bid. It's worth keeping an eye on the agent's website to make sure there's an 'under offer' tag on the property, or that it has been removed altogether.

PHIL'S TOP TIP

If you're suspicious that the agent is still showing the property to other prospective buyers after agreeing to an exclusivity period, do ask him what is going on. A good way to check out the agent is to simply get a friend to ring up and ask if the property is still for sale. If the agent readily agrees to show your mate the property, then you have proof he's not sticking to the agreement. And don't forget the vendor might be prompting the agent to keep showing people around his home. Either way, you need to stand up to them.

- **Timescale**
  What will happen time-wise with the sale? You need to mutually agree a date when the owner will move out and when you will move in. To help the owner, who might need time to find somewhere new to live, you could agree to a 'delayed completion' (exchanging contracts but not actually taking ownership of the property right away; see page 169 for more on exchange and completion). This could benefit you if you're not in a rush, and get you into the owner's good books.
- **Fixtures and fittings**
  You shouldn't feel dragooned into buying the owner's brown armchair (hmm, nice) if you don't really want it, but equally, buying a few items because you really want them could smooth ruffled feathers on the other side. And yet, if you feel the price is a bit high, getting the owner to throw in some decent appliances and furniture that you are keen on having (make sure you really do want them, though) can be a good way to clinch the deal. Equally, be careful about falling out over a set of curtains or a side table that you want and the owner's reluctant to part with. Quibbling over small items is mad, in my opinion, and I've known many a good agent who's simply gone out and

bought a replacement just to keep the deal on track and end the crazy bickering.

- **Flexibility**

  If you're in a position to show any flexibility, this could help the vendor and make him more likely to agree to your offer. A delayed completion (as mentioned previously), and even letting the vendor take some much-loved plants from the garden when he moves out can keep the peace. Remember, you are a very desirable buyer as you are not in a chain and do not have to sell anything first. Emphasise this position to make the vendor realise how lucky he is to have you as a buyer.

Careless talk costs homes

At this point, it's probably best not to talk too much to many people about the property. As crazy as it sounds, people who know each other tend to make changes, such as having children, buying a home and starting a new job, during similar periods in their lives. If someone you know is also house hunting at the same time, they might be tempted to look at your property – and who knows? It could be stolen from right under your nose.

Also, it could be discouraging to say how you've found the perfect place and can't wait to get everyone round to dinner, etc, and then you lose the property. Maybe it's best to just stay calm and wait until the deal actually goes through.

PHIL'S TOP TIP

Now's the time to dig out your original 'wish list' to look at what you said you wanted when you first set out on your quest. You'll probably be amazed at how what you've selected doesn't match your earlier brief.

I've witnessed everything from people demanding an easy-care modern home ending up in an ancient period cottage, to those refusing to even consider a terraced house (they wouldn't be caught dead in anything other than detached) ending up in a charming row of adjoining homes.

This could be quite instructive and show what you've come to accept, what you refuse to compromise on and how one learns to get a balance of sorts between desires and what's out there within your budget. Shifting from one area to another to accommodate your tastes and wishes is another quite common event.

Making a formal offer

While you are likely to make a verbal offer first to an agent, you show how serious you are when you make your offer in writing. You send it to the agent by email or post with the phrase 'subject to contract and survey' included. This means that nothing is set in stone until you receive a contract you and your solicitor approve, and you've had a survey carried out.

If something bad comes up on the survey, you can always duck out of the deal entirely or go back to the agent and say you want to revise your bid after discovering that the roof needs to be totally retiled, or the surveyor believes the house has subsidence, which could cost a great deal to rectify. Getting an approximate quote for work that needs to be carried out and deducting that from your original quote gives a solid reason for the price reduction.

You will be expected to offer proof at this stage that you can get a mortgage if you need to borrow money. You do this by getting an agreement in principle from your mortgage provider, showing how much the lender is willing to give you. If you don't need to borrow all, or any, of the money, you will need to send proof that the money is in an account somewhere and waiting to be transferred if the deal goes ahead.

The deposit

Typically, you'll be asked to pay a deposit to the seller or estate agent, demonstrating your intention or commitment to buying the property. The deposit could range from anything from about £500 to several thousand pounds, and can be repaid if the deal falls through. Some tough-talking sellers and agents might ask for a non-refundable deposit to show just how serious you are – this gets rid of time-wasters – but this is generally only at the top end of the market.

PHIL'S TOP TIP

If you've made an offer on a leasehold property, once you get the name of the freeholder and managing agent for the building where you hope to buy a leasehold property, you can look both of them up on the Internet. This can reveal what other businesses they own, what kind of condition they're in and whether there's anything alarming about any of their property or business dealings.

Negotiating

Negotiating on the purchase of a home is something that some people love. Yet, others are very afraid of taking part in any kind of negotiation process.

As a house finder, for me this is where the fun begins. I find trying to reach a compromise, the discussions and all of the bargaining to be one of the most interesting parts of the job. Putting the whole deal together gives me a buzz, but I can understand why some would shy away from it.

At the end of the day, negotiating comes down to a dialogue between two people, or parties, where you are driving a bargain. Each person is trying to gain the biggest advantage for himself at the end of the process.

The big question facing purchasers is always, 'What's it worth?' The more information you have, the more confident you can be when you make the offer (as I've said time and time again).

When gathering information, the Internet is now a very useful tool to learn about market conditions and historic sale prices. An important part of a surveyor's work is to ring agents for recent sale prices of 'comparable' properties (agents will bang on about 'comparables' all the time, which can be helpful, but they must be analysed in context), so, try doing this for yourself. Find out when they sold and in what condition. Although only to offer a rule of thumb, it can also be useful to calculate a pounds per square foot price for each 'comparable'.

Keep an eye out for overvaluing. It can be tempting for agents to overvalue a property in order to win the instruction from the seller in the first place, and then they wait for the market to catch up. The rather feeble argument being that by the time the mortgage company's surveyor or valuer arrives to value the place, what may have started life as an inflated asking price has in fact become established value. This is potentially very dangerous ground for buyers who are panicked or ill-informed.

Another key question to ask is, 'How long has the home been on the market?' If it has been on for some time, and you can establish why the vendor's selling (maybe a new baby is about to arrive and more space is a priority), you'll know whether he's in a great hurry to sell. This could make it easier for you to negotiate the price down somewhat.

But, if the house has just come onto the market, it's unlikely the owner will accept anything much below the asking price (unless he's eager to get on with it – maybe he doesn't want to lose the property he hopes to buy). I do think you can be a bit mischievous if the property's been lingering and not selling – the beleaguered owner might think a lower offer is better than no offer at all.

Every situation, and therefore every deal, is different, so there are no hard and fast rules about how to negotiate and make the deal come together. A variety of purchasing tactics can be employed. Whatever happens, emotions and worries about money ('Are we getting enough' from the seller's point of view, and 'Do we have enough' from the buyer's) generally run through the whole process.

It might sound silly to say you should show a certain amount of enthusiasm for the property if you're going for it, but without overplaying your hand and jumping up and down. The owners might say only money matters, but most feel nostalgic about their home – even before they have actually sold or left it.

And at the end of the day, market forces dictate value, not surveyors, not pounds per square foot calculations and not even comparable evidence. The amount you are willing to pay will be a reflection of what you can afford and how much you like, love or need that specific home, as well as what is happening with the property market as a whole.

When the property market is skyrocketing, creating an atmosphere of frenzied bidding and almost manic turnover, buyers can end up paying well over the odds for 'good' or even 'average' properties. A seller's market like this does not go on forever, and can become completely unsustainable. When the market slows down, a small level of uncertainty and sensible level of caution returns, making it much more of a buyer's market.

PHIL'S TOP TIP

There's plenty of money at stake here, and you must keep reminding yourself that the estate agent is working on behalf of the seller. They're also handling property negotiations every day of every week – so it's not exactly a level playing field. Tread carefully.

Sealed bids

In a competitive market, sealed bids (or 'best and final offers') can become commonplace. Usually, a sealed bid situation arises when more than one offer has been made and the agent wants to get the best price possible for the property.

Yet many first-time buyers don't realise that sealed bids aren't always all about who has the most cash. Sometimes, the home does not go to the person that made the top bid, but to the buyer thought to be the most suitable by the agent, seller or even the seller's solicitor.

An attractive buyer in a sealed bid situation could be one that:

- Has nothing to sell and, therefore, won't delay the process (this can make first-time buyers very attractive)
- Has cash to buy and doesn't need to wait to raise the money
- Is flexible and will move at a date that suits the owner

When putting your bid in writing, you should make sure you include the amount you are willing to pay in words and numbers.

PHIL'S TOP TIP

Make your bid an odd number. Most people bid in even figures and this might mean you'll beat someone else by only a few pounds.

Also, include the name and address of your solicitor to show you're prepared and ready to go, a letter from your lender that says what you're borrowing is in place, a letter from your bank confirming they have your deposit and a personal note. You should say why you like the property and how much you want to live there. As corny as this might sound, often the heartfelt personal plea of a prospective buyer can swing it for a vendor.

A sealed bid is a one-shot wonder, so you need to determine in advance how much you'll offer. You don't want to pay massively over the odds, but equally, how would you feel if you found out you lost the home you fell in love with by just a few hundred pounds?

The seller's agent will give a final date and time by which all the bids must be delivered to his office. Ask when the vendor is likely to reply to the bids, so you get some indication of when you will know the answer. So let's say that you have undergone some negotiations, or your sealed bid has been successful, and your offer has been accepted. What now? You're going to start the process known as conveyancing.

What is conveyancing?

Conveyancing is simply the process that transfers the ownership of property (land or buildings) from one person to another. It refers to all the legal and administrative work associated with transferring the ownership, starting after an offer has been made and accepted for a property and solicitors' details have been exchanged by the two parties.

Traditionally, solicitors took on all conveyancing work, but now there are also licensed conveyancers to do the work as well. It's illegal for conveyancers who are not licensed to charge a fee for any conveyancing work. Check with the Council for Licensed Conveyancers (www. conveyancer.org.uk) to ensure a named conveyancer is licensed.

You can choose a solicitor or a licensed conveyancer. I think the key factor is whether the person carrying out the conveyancing is experienced and can do the work promptly and efficiently.

Finding a solicitor

One of the best ways to choose someone is by personal recommendation. If you know someone who was happy with a solicitor's services, this is one of the best ways to determine his quality. Otherwise, you can consult the Law Society's regional directory for solicitors in your area (www.lawsociety.org.uk and look at the 'find a solicitor' section). Or, check out the Yellow Pages or local newspapers for adverts.

If you have already used a good solicitor for other matters, you could contact the firm to see if they have a conveyancing solicitor, or get recommendations for other firms. The same solicitor cannot act for both the buyer and seller of a property, but two solicitors from the same firm may do so, as long as there's no clash of interests between the buyer and seller.

What to think about when choosing a solicitor

- **Price**
  Solicitors' charges can vary, but beware of the very cheapest services, which could indicate a lack of experience and poor quality. It might be worth paying a bit more for good service. On the other hand, the most expensive quote isn't necessarily the best.
- **Experience**
  Look for a solicitor who has had previous experience of conveyancing, so important details aren't missed. Anyone who rushes the job could miss a vital clue to a problem, while a slow moving picky solicitor could halt the whole process, threatening to break the chain.
- **Trust**
  Buying a property is a stressful business and your house is likely to be your principal asset. It's important you get on with your solicitor and have faith in him.

Make sure you hire a solicitor or conveyancer at the start of the home-buying process, so they'll be ready to spring into action as soon as you have had an offer accepted, or even earlier when you know you're likely to make an offer. The faster things move, the better the chances that everything will go smoothly.

Can't I just do the conveyancing myself?

It's possible to do the conveyancing yourself, but it's time-consuming and could be risky if you don't have the expertise. Although professional services are expensive, they have become cheaper in recent years and it is worth the cost to successfully complete the purchase and to resolve any possible problems. This part of the process is crucial.

DIY conveyancing: the pros and cons

If you are bright, able to cope with legal jargon and have the time to do the work (there are large amounts of paperwork involved, so you've been warned) you can be a DIY-conveyancer.

However, if you don't handle all the conveyancing properly, you could find yourself involved in costly disputes over boundaries, discover (too late) there's a new road to be built opposite your home or that the seller isn't even the legal owner of the property.

I don't know many homebuyers, particularly first-timers, who like to do the conveyancing themselves, for three good reasons:

- Most lenders insist on a solicitor doing the conveyancing to protect their interests.
- There's a higher risk of things going wrong.
- Others involved in the process (the vendor and his solicitor, for instance) might not be thrilled with you doing your own conveyancing, and may even reject your offer on this basis.

I would argue that DIY-conveyancing is totally inadvisable if:

- The property is being sold by a divorcing or separating couple (this requires specialist knowledge).
- The property is not freehold.
- The property isn't registered at the Land Registry.
- The property is not a house (leasehold flats are usually more complicated to deal with).

The Energy Performance Certificate

When a property is being sold, an Energy Performance Certificate (EPC) will need to be ordered before the marketing of the property commences. It must be made available to potential buyers as soon as possible, and certainly before the exchange of contracts. In Scotland, different rules apply where the EPC is part of the Home Pack, or Home Report.

An agent can sort this out for the vendor, or the vendor can order it himself. There are a number of firms that can provide the Energy Performance Certificate from as low as £30.

The certificate indicates how energy efficient the home is, and suggests ways it could be improved. If you aren't shown the certificate by the vendor or his agent, you are within your rights to ask to see it, and your solicitor will certainly want to see it as part of the conveyancing.

Chasing your solicitor

If you've hired a good, reputable solicitor, you should have no problems. And yet, some solicitors do drag their feet, which can hold up and could even scupper a sale. Do nag, cajole, encourage and coax a reluctant (probably overworked) solicitor. You should email and telephone your solicitor frequently to make sure he's on top of everything.

Co-owning

If you are buying with a partner, friend or family member, you will need to consider what type of ownership to choose. You will have to choose one early on, so your lender and solicitor can proceed with the agreement and contract.

Joint tenants

A joint tenant agreement says that each person has equal ownership of the property, rather than a specific share. If one owner dies, the whole property would legally belong to the other owner, regardless of any specifications made in a will. This agreement is usually chosen by co-owners who don't see themselves living separately in the future, and would want their property to pass on to the other owner if they died.

Tenants in common

The co-owners specify how much of the property each person owns. If one person were to die, their share of the property would go to whoever was specified in their will, rather than being passed automatically on to the other owner. Having ownership of a particular share of the home also means it's easier to determine how much of the equity should go to each person when it's time to sell. A tenants in common agreement is, therefore, usually selected by co-owners who are friends, relations or, possibly, business partners.

Co-habitation agreement

No matter how good the friendship or how much you love your brother or sister, I think it is always worth paying a solicitor to draw up a co-habitation agreement to insure against possible disputes. This agreement will help the two parties resolve any disputes that might not have been considered at the time of the purchase. But, it's not intended to allow one party to gain an advantage over the other.

To come up with a suitable agreement, I'd suggest the co-owners first draw up a draft agreement together and then give it to a solicitor, or other legal advisor, who can put it into an appropriate format. The solicitor could act as arbiter if a disagreement arose, and his decision would be binding.

A co-habitation agreement should contain the following:

- Deposit paid by each person
- Purchasing costs and solicitor's fees paid by each party
- How much of the mortgage repayment will be paid by each person
- How and when mortgage payments will be made
- How the cost of home and contents insurance will be shared

- How the day-to-day running costs of the home will be shared
- Furniture, shared items and any other costs when they are purchased or incurred
- House rules, including unacceptable behaviour
- Agreed policy for keeping up payments
- Agreed policy for the event of one person going into deliberate default
- Agreed policy for another mortgage payee joining the arrangement
- Agreed policy for breaching any of the co-habitation clauses
- Agreed policy were one person to die

Trust deed

A trust deed works in a fairly similar way to a co-habitation agreement, helping owners avoid possible conflicts. The deed is drawn up detailing how much of the equity in the property each party is entitled to when the place is sold. There is no set way to work this out, as it could depend on contributions to the deposit, who pays which bills or maintenance costs, as well as who pays what portion of the mortgage.

Buying out a partner, friend or family member

Buying out a partner, the legal joint owner of your property, can sometimes be a little tricky, but it needn't be a massive problem. Owners, who are each named on house deeds, each have the same legal right to live in the home, and under very few circumstances can be forced to sell the home.

Unfortunately, not all co-owners are happy to sell at the same time, so joint owners finding themselves at an impasse might want to consider attending mediation sessions to work through their disagreements, or even each hiring a separate solicitor to sort something out. I'd advise trying to resolve things yourself first though, as hiring legal expertise can be expensive and combative.

Once you both agree to sell, you'll need to decide what kind of offers you'll accept. If both owners are named on the deed, then you must both agree to a sale in order for it to legally go through.

Sometimes, things go wrong, however, and in some cases you could end up going to county court for an order that forces, or postpones, the sale of the home. Orders are usually only issued, however, if it's believed that one owner is trying to accept an inappropriate offer. However, this is not usually the norm for joint owners who are in a situation in which one owner would like to buy out the other.

Ownership percentages

If one owner wants to buy the other out, both co-owners will need to be clear about how much of the home each one owns. This strict percentage should have been worked out already in previous legal documents, such as the trust deed, and is often in line with what percentage of the deposit and mortgage each paid.

If there's no dispute over this split, then determining how much the partner interested in buying out the other should pay should be as simple as working out the fair market price of the home, and what the other owner's percentage of that price would be. Interest, fees, Stamp Duty Land Tax and other costs will have to be taken into account as well.

Timeline for a buy-out

Buying out a joint owner is not usually a fast process, even if both owners are perfectly happy with the future sale. Typically, the partner making the purchase will need to come up with the lump sum required, either by selling some assets or getting a loan. Then the sale will be completed, with both parties signing on the dotted line.

If the owner who is being bought out will remain in the home as a tenant, then further legal issues may arise. I'd recommend getting a solicitor to help to make sure everything goes through smoothly. Falling out with family or friends at this point would be a terrible shame, so paying for legal help could be worth every penny to save the relationship.

Surveys

Once your offer has been accepted (subject to survey), it's then important you carry out a survey on the property. Even if you think it's in fairly good nick, you should at least consider a less pricey 'walk round' survey if you don't think it needs a more detailed one.

A mortgage lender will want to carry out a valuation, a simpler version of a survey, to determine whether the property is worth the asking price. If you want a more detailed structural survey, which is advisable, it is a good idea to get one carried out.

As I mentioned, with new homes you don't need a survey, as it should have an NHBC (or similar) certificate, giving you a 10-year guarantee against any major faults.

What's the difference between a survey and a valuation?

A lot of first-time buyers mix up a survey and a valuation – an easy mistake to make.

- **Valuation**
  A valuation is an inspection that checks the value of a property to see how much it is worth and whether it is worth the asking

price. Usually carried out by a surveyor, a valuation is used by lenders to decide how much money they're willing to lend you (also known as a land valuation, or a real estate appraisal). The lender will organise the valuation, but you will have to pay for it. It costs from about £125.

- **Survey**

  A survey is a surveyor's report detailing the results of a property inspection. A lender might ask for a detailed survey, particularly for an older property in need of a good deal of repair, but normally, a buyer has a survey done to assess for himself whether the property is worth the price and whether it is worth buying.

  It also gives a good indication of the work that will need to be carried out. A survey can be used in the negotiation process, where a buyer can ask for the price of the property to be dropped if there's a lot of work to be done.

  There are various surveys that can be carried out, including a full structural survey. A quick 'walk round' or 'walk through' survey might be sufficient for a property that appears to be in good shape and doesn't require a full-blown survey.

  A survey can cost anything from a few hundred to many thousands of pounds. I would recommend getting a survey carried out, particularly if there are any indications of structural problems or severe damp problems.

How to find a good surveyor

You can ask a good local estate agent or your mortgage lender to recommend someone. Your conveyancing solicitor might also have some good suggestions.

I think it's important hiring someone qualified who is a member of the Royal Institution of Chartered Surveyors (www.rics.org). You can identify a surveyor with qualifications from the letters that come after his name: MRICS or FRICS, or TechRICS for technical surveyors.

Do discuss what you want from the survey with your surveyor. You can come up with a bespoke package: get the surveyor to do as much, or as little, as you want. If you have any particular concerns from the viewings, do tell the surveyor.

A full structural surveyor is a good idea for:

- Listed buildings
- Older homes built before the twentieth century
- Any building that has been erected in an unusual way, no matter how old it is
- Anything you are considering altering drastically
- A property that has had a number of additions and alterations already made to it

What to look for in a survey

Some of the phrases used in a survey might scare a first-time buyer, but don't be unduly alarmed. A surveyor might not always be stating that there's a major problem with the property, but he's trying to point out that there might be difficulties in the future if something isn't sorted. Most problems are easily sortable and you should discuss the survey with the surveyor, asking him outright if anything was downright disturbing.

Some of the things you should look for in the survey are:

- Is there a damp-proof course (a layer of waterproof material in the wall of a building near the ground to prevent rising damp)?
- Is the flashing (weather-proofing strips of lead around the chimney stack to prevent water from getting in) in a good state?
- Did the surveyor spot any major cracks that might indicate subsidence (this can be expensive to sort)?
- How efficient is the guttering?
- Is the roof in good condition (does it sag, or are there any slipped tiles)?
- Is a tree with a large root mass close to the house (it could affect the drainage and foundations of the building)?
- Is there any sign of woodworm, dry or wet rot in the timbers?
- What state is the electrical wiring in?
- How old is the heating system and how efficient does it look?

Don't become too concerned if the survey points out some problems. A surveyor plays it safe generally (he wants to know he's covered himself if something untoward does crop up) and errs on the cautious side. If an old building is still standing after 300 years, it will probably remain standing for a few more.

I'd ask his personal opinion ('Would you buy this property?') and have a chat with him. A good surveyor is usually sensible and will reassure and advise you accordingly.

Survey shambles

If you are very worried about something negative that comes up in a survey and are considering abandoning your new home, do ask yourself the following questions to make sure you're making the right decision:

- Have you overreacted to the survey?
- Have you thought of getting a second opinion that could perhaps allay fears?
- Have you taken a builder to look at the property?
- Have you reminded yourself that no property is perfect?
- Have you been too risk-averse?
- Has your solicitor been too conservative?

Buildings and contents insurance

A number of first-time buyers forget about the added cost of insurance, but you will need to look into getting buildings and contents insurance to protect your home and your belongings.

Buildings insurance

This covers you for any damage to the building from fire, flood or wind damage. When you look at the cost of an insurance policy, check to see what it covers. One company might offer a lower quote, but perhaps it is not offering as much cover as a rival company. The policy should cover the cost to rebuild your home (in the most dire case), and not just what you paid for it. Most lenders will want to see this insurance is in place before completion on the property.

Contents insurance

Contents insurance is vital too, as it covers the cost of having to replace everything in your home if it is damaged by floods, fire or theft. Being underinsured is foolhardy, and it's not worth saving a few pounds if you then have to replace expensive jewellery, electrical equipment or appliances and the insurance company won't cough up. Remember that there usually is a certain amount of money that the insurance company won't pay. For example, if you make a claim the company might stipulate that the first £200 to replace or fix items has to be paid by you.

PHIL'S TOP TIP

Often, you can make a saving by getting buildings and contents insurance together. The costs are usually reduced if you take out both policies from the same company.

Personal insurance

It's all very sensible to cover your property and the contents, but what about insuring yourself? How would you (and your partner) manage to pay the mortgage if you lost your job, became ill, were injured or even died? There are several types of insurance you should consider, including:

- **Critical illness** – gives you cash if you become seriously ill
- **Life assurance** – gives cash to your next of kin if you become terminally ill or die

- **Income protection** – can provide a monthly income if you can't work, because of an accident or illness
- **Mortgage payment protection** – covers mortgage payments if you can't work because you've lost your job, or you've had an accident or become ill

Managing the chain

Chances are you'll be at the bottom of a chain as a first-time buyer. The good news is that at least you're not in the middle where there's more potential for the chain to fall apart.

But, even tucked away at the bottom of the chain, you'll need to get to grips with what's going on. Find out the length of the chain, the people involved and to what stage each purchase has reached. Only if you can really understand what is happening can you make informed decisions and talk to the agents involved. A good agent should do this for you, but you might have to become more proactive if things are not moving fast enough.

Unfortunately, people are not always straightforward about where they've reached when asked the question. Obviously, being a link in a shorter chain is preferable, but the good news is you're the most favoured person in the chain. Last in is most popular in this case, because they need you to make the whole process move along.

Try to determine the timing of the offer and whether the person you're buying from has actually started looking for a property. Have they made an offer on something? If so, has the offer been accepted? It can be incredibly frustrating not hearing anything for six months. You need to maintain the situation and look after your interests – and all with a cool head. Losing your temper won't get you anywhere, so take deep breaths whenever possible.

Without appearing negative, I think you should consider losing the property. Ask how much you really like it, and if everything did go pear-shaped, how hard would it be to find a replacement? Could you find something else within a week? I'm a great believer in assuming that until contracts have actually exchanged no one is legally bound, so anything could happen.

But, if your relationship with the vendor, agent, solicitor and anyone else involved is good, they should look after you the best they can. The more morally and fully engaged they are with you, the better are your chances for being treated properly.

However, things can alter – jobs change, people have babies – and if everything collapses, it can be rebuilt. Say you agree a deal back in January when the market is in the doldrums, for example, but you don't actually exchange contracts until June. Don't be surprised if it's suggested you should be paying the price in the market at the time.

Equally, over a four-month period, the market can be in a very different place that goes in your direction and favour. You can say, 'This means my offer is now *this.*' This is an area where people get all principled and upset, but you do have to pay the right price at the time – and this works both ways.

Troubleshooting: gazumping and gazundering

Not the names of a new comedy stand-up duo, but two unpopular practices, which might occur once an offer has been accepted.

Gazumping is when a seller accepts your offer and you start getting searches and surveys, etc, carried out on the property (which all cost money), but then later on the seller accepts a higher offer from another buyer – thus, gazumping you.

It sounds like a dastardly and deeply unfair thing to do to a buyer, but unless you are the victim of gazundering, it's not really your problem. If you are shown a property that is 'under offer' by an agent, this generally means that the seller is still showing the property despite accepting an offer and could well gazump.

Is it unprincipled for the agent to keep showing people the property if the seller has accepted an offer? Not really. People blame the agent, but the agent only acts for the seller. The agent does what the seller instructs him to do. Most agents simply want to make a sale and avoid any complications, which can be time-consuming and annoying.

The best way to avoid being gazumped is to have everything in place, or as much as you can conceivably have in place, so you're seen as prepared and reliable. Then, there's no reason to bother with finding another buyer. I can't emphasise strongly enough how crucial it is to have your deposit, solicitor and mortgage sorted, which means you're less likely to be gazumped.

Believe me, a good seller and a good agent don't want to get involved with gazumping, and most are quite honourable to sound and ready buyers. It happens rarely, and if it does, you can offer more money if you really have your heart set on the property. Or, you can simply walk away and play again another day.

Gazundering is at the opposite end of the spectrum from gazumping. This involves the buyer wanting a price reduction at the last minute before the sale goes through. Agents, not surprisingly, call gazundering an evil practice – perhaps even more so as gazumping, as it affects their clients having to take a bit of a hit.

Is it ethical? Well, like gazumping, it isn't against the law, and if you feel prices have declined in the area since you made the offer then you might well have a point that you should get a reduction. In a slower market, and after a calamity that rocks the markets and economy, your gazundering might appear logical and even above board in some quarters.

The deal's not done until the contract's signed. It isn't always a dirty game, but you might have to play hard at times to stay at the table – and ultimately win. If you do choose to go down the gazundering route, it's best to have a reason for the new last-minute figure you are offering. Simply doing it to bully the vendor and save a few thousand pounds could engender more grief than it's worth, but if the vendor is playing hardball you might have to stand up for yourself.

The conveyancing process

Buying or selling a home can be complex legally and administratively. The exact order of events varies, but there are three main stages.

Stage one: before the exchange of contracts

1. **Your solicitor contacts the seller's solicitor**
   Once the seller has accepted your offer, the buyer and seller exchange solicitors' details. Your solicitor will then contact the seller's solicitor and receive the draft contract.
2. **Your solicitor receives and negotiates the draft contract**
   The draft contract contains details of prices, the two parties, other information about the transaction, such as deposits, and information from the seller's title deeds.
3. **Your solicitor makes pre-contract enquiries**
4. **Your solicitor sends you a property information form, or a copy of the draft contract, for you to check**
   A property information form might be included if the solicitors are operating the TransAction Protocol. This is a Law Society scheme used by many solicitors in the conveyancing process. If your solicitor is operating this scheme, the seller's solicitor provides a package at the beginning of the process which includes:
   a. The draft contract
   b. Copies of previous title deeds (registered or unregistered)
   c. A property information form, giving key property information (this saves the solicitor from some of the preliminary enquiries)

d. A fixtures, fittings and contents form, telling you which fixtures, fittings and other items are included in the price, and which ones will be removed. You should agree with the seller what is to be included, and make sure everything is on the form. Your solicitor will check the details of the draft contract and negotiate it with the seller's solicitor. It's a good idea to check through the draft contract yourself in case anything has been missed out, such as any agreements you've made with the seller, so ask your solicitor for a copy if you have not been sent one.

5. **Your solicitor applies to the local council for local searches, checks the title of the property, contract and papers and raises any queries with the seller's solicitor**

It's your solicitor's or conveyancer's job to make all the necessary enquiries to ensure that there's no reason why you might want to change your mind about buying the property. For example, it's vital to guarantee that the seller really owns the property and has the right to sell it.

The main standard searches are:

- **Local authority searches**

Enquiries are sent to the local authority, including whether there are any plans for a major road to be built nearby, or whether there are any problems with the property which you would need to rectify. Your solicitor should also get checks done on nearby buildings or empty land. Do they have planning permission for more buildings or for any development?

- **Enquiries to the seller's solicitor (the 'preliminary enquiries')**

Your solicitor will send a standard set of enquiries to the seller's solicitor, including: ○

○ **Disputes:** whether there are any disputes relating to the property, such as disputes with neighbours

○ **Boundaries:** what exactly are the boundaries of the

property and who has responsibility for the maintenance of hedges and fences. Arguments over boundaries between neighbours sometimes end up in court, so it's important to establish this now.

- ○ **Planning constraints and permissions:** whether any additions or alterations that have been made to the property have met local planning requirements and that building regulation consent was received.
- ○ **Rights of way:** checking there is no right of way or footpath through the property, and on shared rights of access with a neighbour such as a garden or driveway.
- ○ **Restrictive covenants:** whether the deeds specify that certain things are forbidden (for example, keeping pets, or specifying that the house cannot be painted a different colour from other houses on the street).
- ○ **Guarantees or insurance policies:** whether the property is covered by the NHBC guarantee, or a wood rot treatment guarantee, for instance.
- ○ **Services:** whether the property's utilities (gas, water, electricity) reach it via a neighbour's property, or are shared with a neighbour.
- ○ **List of contents included in the sale:** you must make sure you have reached an understanding with the seller about what is and what is not to be included and ensure it is listed clearly.
- ○ If it is a **leasehold** property, who is the managing agent, who is the freeholder and whether the seller is up to date with ground rent and service charges.
- ○ You might want to make **additional enquiries** through your solicitor, including whether the property has been burgled, more information about the neighbours or any known building works.

- • **Other searches**

  A set of standard questions is also sent to the water authority. There are additional searches that may be carried out if necessary (for example, commons searches, coal mining searches and so on).

If you are buying a newly built house there are particular checks that must be carried out by your solicitor. Your solicitor will then check the draft contract and send anything that needs changing back to the seller's solicitor.

6. **The contract is negotiated and agreed. A completion date is agreed**

There is often a certain amount of correspondence that goes on between the two solicitors, so finalising the draft contract can take some time (four to six weeks is typical, although it can be faster). Make sure your solicitor knows about any agreements you have made with the seller.

The day for the completion of the transaction (the day when the deal is finalised) must be agreed upon before contracts are exchanged. It normally takes about two weeks from the exchange of contracts to completion day, although it can be shorter, or lengthier. Some people arrange for the exchange of contracts and completion to take place on the same day, but this is not always possible. Note that if you are part of a chain (a line of people all buying and selling properties to or from each other, and are therefore, linked together), the completion date will probably need to be agreed with more than two parties.

7. **You get a formal mortgage offer (if you are getting a mortgage) on the property, not just an agreement in principle. Your solicitor will send you a mortgage deed to sign**

The formal mortgage offer for the property that you obtain at this stage is distinct from an agreement in principle (which you should have obtained earlier). At this stage, you also need the results of your survey if you are having one done, and to have accepted these results. If you are not satisfied with the results of the survey, you need to address any problems at this stage, not after the exchange of contracts when you are legally bound to buy the house. Make sure the two parties have agreed all the terms of the contract and that any disagreements or any matters that are unclear have been resolved.

Pre-stage-two checklist

Before exchanging contracts, check that:

- You have received and are satisfied with the survey report.
- You have received your formal mortgage offer, and are happy with it.
- The deposit sum has been agreed and you have the money available.
- You have arranged life and property insurance and they are ready to begin on completion.
- The completion date has been agreed with all parties.
- The terms of the contract have been checked and finalised by all involved.

Stage two: exchange of contracts

1. **Contracts are exchanged**

   Once you and your solicitor are satisfied that everything is in order, the contracts can be exchanged. You sign a copy of the contract that is passed to the seller, and the seller signs a copy of the same contract that you receive. Once contracts have been exchanged (normally by the two solicitors), both parties are legally bound to follow through with the transaction. You can no longer change your mind – if you pull out it's likely you will lose your deposit and could be sued for breach of contract. You also now have no need to worry about gazumping.

   At this point you hand over a non-refundable deposit as security to the seller in case the contract is not carried out. This is normally 10% of the purchase price, but is usually negotiable.

2. **Your solicitor draws up a transfer document and sends it to the seller's solicitor**

   Once contracts have been exchanged, your solicitor prepares the draft transfer document (if the land is not registered it will require a special kind of transfer or 'conveyance'). This document transfers the title of the property from the seller to the buyer. Once both parties have agreed on the draft, it's signed by both buyer and seller.

3. **Your solicitor arranges the finalisation and signing of your mortgage documents** and arranges for the money to be available on completion of the sale.

4. **Your solicitor carries out any final searches and enquiries,** including Land Registry checks to make sure nothing is registered against the seller (or at the Land Charges Registry if the property is not registered). Problems, such as undisclosed mortgages or disputes, could be uncovered at this stage.

There will be various matters for you to deal with in the run-up to completion. There will be some documents to be signed and payments to be made: you must pay Land Registry fees (from £40 and up to £800, depending on the price of your property) and Stamp Duty.

Before completion, the vendor has to make sure that all the terms of the contract have been fulfilled, such as any repairs.

You also need to be arranging all the practical matters related to moving house.

Stage three: completion

1. On the day of completion you receive the keys and the seller is obliged to move out.

2. You pay the seller the balance of the price of the house (the agreed price minus the deposit that you've already paid), usually through your solicitor or conveyancer.

3. You receive the transfer document and the title deeds. The seller's deeds are now handed over to you, and arrangements are made for any outstanding mortgages on the property to be paid off.

4. You pay any extra costs: Stamp Duty, Land Registry and solicitor's fees.

5. Your solicitor ties up final details, including:
   • Informing your mortgage lender, life insurance company and the freeholder that the sale has been completed.

- Registering the transfer of ownership at the Land Registry. The Land Registry will then send the deeds to your mortgage lender, who will keep them until you either sell the property or pay off your mortgage.
- Paying the Stamp Duty.
- Sending you a statement of completion, including a summary of the financial transactions. If you have not already paid the solicitor's fees, he will ask for these now.

Completion usually takes place a few weeks after contracts have been exchanged, but the time period should be stated in the contract. In some cases, a buyer might have agreed to a 'delayed completion'.

What's a delayed completion?

A delayed completion is when both sides agree to a longer completion date. A typical reason is that a delayed completion gives the seller more time to find somewhere to move. This can be a good bargaining chip for a buyer, who can be seen to be helping out the seller.

Your solicitor will be doing the following leading up to completion:

- Sends a copy of the title deeds to the buyer's solicitor, or a summary of the contents (called an 'abstract of title')
- Checks that the final conveyance document is correct and gets you to sign it
- Makes sure the balance of the purchase money (usually the rest of the money after taking into account the amount of the deposit) is handed over by the buyer
- If you have a mortgage, the remainder of the mortgage is paid over to the lender from the sale money, along with any fees or penalties owed to the lender (known as 'discharged in full')

PHIL'S TOP TIPS

TO HELP THE OFFER SAIL THROUGH THE CONVEYANCING PROCESS

- Micro-manage the deal. No news is usually not good news.
- It's all about psychological game playing, so go with your gut feelings.
- If you don't think you're being told the right thing by an agent, talk to another agent in the office, the secretary and/or your solicitor.
- Keep a paper trail on everything said or agreed.
- A lot of communications are carried out by phone where there's room for misunderstanding. So, confirm what was said in an email: 'You said this and therefore, we're now doing that'.
- Be careful of your reputation (agents do talk to one another). If you keep changing your mind, it won't help your cause.

CASE STUDY

ASK AND ALL WILL BE REVEALED

Landscape designer Martha Burrell was nervous about following the process when she bought her first home, a £173,000, two-bedroom flat in Newcastle. As she had never borrowed money before and had no idea how a solicitor works, she was scared she wouldn't be able to understand what was going on with the purchase of her property.

'I really didn't have a clue and I was very scared I'd misunderstand something or miss an important detail,' Martha explains.

To help her comprehend the exchange and completion procedure, Martha looked on the Internet and discovered her building society had a useful guide, which she printed out and referred to at various stages. 'My brother suggested the idea, because he'd bought his place three years earlier and was just as vague about the methods and process as I was. It really worked for him, so I did the same.'

Even if Martha didn't fathom absolutely everything, she says it meant that at least she knew the sorts of questions to ask her lender and solicitor. 'For instance, I couldn't get my head around some of the terms and phrases that were being used by everyone. By doing my research and reading about it, I could try to work out what things meant – and if I still wasn't sure, I could ask the solicitor.'

Martha said she was a bit embarrassed displaying her low level of knowledge, yet she found everyone was really helpful and didn't mind being asked questions, sometimes repeatedly. 'My solicitor, who I found through the Law Society, was really terrific. He was so patient with me and was happy to explain confusing things over and over again. I thought he should have been awarded some kind of medal at the end of it all for his calm and pleasant demeanour.'

Advice Martha would pass on to other first-time buyers includes making a list of questions when you think of things, so you don't forget what you want to ask. 'Then, the next time you speak to your solicitor you can mention them.'

Also, she says you should get everything in writing. 'My solicitor was happy to send me brief, but helpful, emails regularly that explained what he was doing and outlining any information or paperwork he needed from me. I would respond accordingly, and I found this paper trail incredibly important to get through the entire process.'

And a small final tip: 'Do thank any of the people you deal with who've done a good job. I gave my solicitor and the estate agent I dealt with each a bottle of wine. It can make all the difference to the service people receive if you acknowledge excellence.'

CONVEYANCING CHECKLIST

- [ ] Choose a solicitor
- [ ] If buying with a friend or partner, get a co-ownership agreement drawn up
- [ ] Ask to see the Energy Performance Certificate for the property
- [ ] Make enquiries if buying a leasehold flat (who's the managing agent, can you keep pets and how much are ground fees?)
- [ ] Check out the freeholder and managing company for a leasehold property
- [ ] Make an offer in writing
- [ ] Ask for an exclusivity period (so the seller doesn't show the property to anyone else)
- [ ] Mutually agree a date when the seller moves out and you move in
- [ ] Show proof that the lender will give you money (if getting a mortgage)
- [ ] Check the solicitor is making enquiries and getting the title deed information
- [ ] Choose a surveyor
- [ ] Organise a survey, if required
- [ ] Set the completion date
- [ ] Get the mortgage deed from the solicitor to sign
- [ ] Sign the contracts for exchange
- [ ] Pay the balance of the property's price
- [ ] Get the transfer document and title deeds
- [ ] Take out building and contents insurance
- [ ] Pay Stamp Duty, Land Registry and solicitor's fees
- [ ] Get the keys to the property

PHIL'S CONTACTS BOOK

- Law Society of England and Wales – www.lawsociety.org.
  uk – consult the regional directory to see if your solicitor
  belongs to the Law Society
- Yellow Pages – www.yell.com

CHAPTER EIGHT

What to Do if Things Go Wrong

The deal goes south: now what?

I can certainly sympathise how you feel when the whole pack of cards collapses and you lose the home you thought was yours, and yours alone. It's happened to me professionally and personally, and it isn't much fun when the sale of a property falls through. Keep in mind, however, that no matter how organised, professional or sensible you are, sometimes things just don't work out.

This chapter is all about how to cope, pick yourself up, dust yourself off and get on with it. Losing the home that you had set your heart on reminds me of a film where every impediment seems to be placed in the hero's path – from threats by a bad guy, being double-crossed by his best mate and then, to top it all off, the loss of his beloved. But, our hero does survive and goes on to win the day. I know it's fiction, but in real life, we have to face disappointments like this – even if they're a bit less dramatic – and carry on.

Remember, the deal's not done until the deal's done, and in an emotionally charged atmosphere everything can appear worse than it might really be. Whatever you do, please don't start choosing the curtains for the new flat before contracts have been exchanged, or you will be doubly disappointed. On the flip side, doing nothing at all in a dejected state where you can't be bothered isn't particularly helpful either.

My best advice is when you fall off your horse get back in the saddle as quickly as you can. Your contacts are still live, you know what you want, you have up-to-date prices and you're known to all of the agents, so this is the best time to try again. If you take two or three months out to lick your wounds, you'll lose the momentum.

You have to keep telling yourself not having your offer accepted, or losing that home at the last minute, wasn't your fault. There could be some goodwill about, because of what you've just gone through, so the estate agent may see you right. He might feel he owes you one.

PHIL'S TOP TIP

It sounds tough if you have been gazumped, for instance (see page 167 for definitions of gazumping and gazundering), but the time to crack open the champagne is not until contracts have finally been exchanged, so don't get ahead of yourself.

If you feel you've been really badly treated, you can contact The Property Ombudsman (tpos.co.uk). But, you can only do this if you can prove something has gone badly wrong and you have a paper trail (copies of emails, letters and notes), and that you've already tried to solve your problem with the agent.

What to do if you have a complaint

I would start by talking to the manager of the estate agency office, or the area manager. The higher up, the better, I think. You can address it to the manager and then copy in the area manager and managing director of the entire company.

If you are very unhappy about something that has occurred, then you must say something. But equally, it will not help matters if you really annoy an agent for something small. Word gets around and other agents will know quickly about your complaints.

You can complain formally, however, if you're still not happy with the response you've had, or not had, from the senior figures in the company. All estate agents in the UK engaged in residential estate agency work have to belong to an approved redress scheme. Redress schemes deal with complaints about the buying and selling of residential property.

Do consult the appendix on page 286 for more information on approved redress schemes if you do have a substantial complaint.

Never give up

No matter how disillusioned you might become, never give up. You might think your dream home has disappeared forever, but sometimes funny things happen.

For instance, a friend of mine buying a small cottage in Wiltshire thought it had gone completely when the seller rang in tears to say he and his family were staying put, as the home they wanted to buy in the next village had come off the market. The agony of being in the chain meant my friend would lose out, too.

But he stayed in touch with the owner of the cottage he so admired, and sure enough, several months later the owner rang to say he'd found another property, and was my friend still interested in buying his place? The good news was my friend had everything in place – the finance, the surveys and searches, even the number of the removal company he wanted to use – so he got his dream cottage after all. The seller was pleased, too, because he didn't have to remarket the property, saving time and money.

Not all tales end quite so happily, but remaining calm and pleasant can have its pluses. If my friend had become angry, although the delay wasn't really the seller's fault, he probably wouldn't have been contacted and he wouldn't have got the cottage at the end of the day.

> ### PHIL'S TOP TIP
>
> *Remember, even if you think you've lost a property, your dream home is not 'sold' to someone else until the contracts have been exchanged. This process can take time and things can go wrong, so be patient.*
>
> *So, do go ahead and badger the agent about your lost gem, while continuing to look at other property. Even if the property might not be perfect, you can still make an offer if it is nearly there. Something better might come along within your timeframe, but then maybe this will be as good as it gets. You'll end up kicking yourself later on if you pass on something that perhaps you should have made an attempt to get.*

Sealed bids

As I mentioned earlier in the book (see page 152), sealed bids can be high pressure, and there's only one victor. Again, don't just walk away. The highest bidder might not be able to stump up the cash – people do get carried away sometimes when bidding, just like at an auction – and if they drop out, you might be considered the next best option.

If the winning bidder discovers how much more he's paid than the other bids, he might become fussy, picking holes in the property and trying to either knock off money, or even back out of the deal altogether. So, keep smiling and be friendly to the agent, who could recommend your lower bid to the vendor.

The vanishing vendor

If the vendor suddenly takes his property off the market for no apparent reason, just walk away from the whole deal. Sometimes, when you're dumped it's better to leave with dignity, rather than grovel and whinge. Your agent, if he's good at his job that is, should be able to read between the lines and advise you whether you're wasting your time still pursuing this property or not. But, my personal judgement is that sometimes it's best to leave well enough alone.

The flip side is your departing vendor might become a bit less cocky, once assuming he can sell to anyone at anytime he wants, when he sees how quickly you've moved on. This burst of action on your part could change his mind. And if it doesn't, you're out there hunting for property again, which is a positive thing to do.

The blame game

Another barrier might be that you're playing the dangerous blame game where ultimately, no one's a winner. I think there can be a tendency when someone's upset to blame the estate agent, solicitor, vendor, property finder, mortgage lender, surveyor, co-purchaser (if you're buying with someone else), postman and even your father, who maybe didn't think that buying that particular property was such a good idea, anyhow.

One of the disastrous consequences of playing the blame game is that in order to make yourself feel better, or even less of a failure in your eyes, you can lessen the blow by blaming someone else. This is pointless and very unhelpful. It will get you nowhere and by displaying anger towards those most likely to help you, you're putting yourself back months (or even years) in the search for a new home.

Instead of blaming whomever you have in the firing line, why not examine what's happened, what went wrong (if anything) and how you can make things better next time round. A list of positive ongoing thoughts or ideas (sort of the property equivalent to New Year's resolutions) could include:

- Focus on ringing up three helpful agents almost daily, so they will ring you first when a good property comes up for sale.
- Spread your search slightly wider into the next-door borough or town to make it easier to find something.
- Communicate better with your solicitor.
- Make sure that estate agents know exactly what you're looking for.

- Consider other avenues of home-buying, such as auctions or rent-to-buy.
- Read all the property sections in the local and national newspapers, magazines and on the Internet.
- Refine your 'must have', 'would like to have' and 'won't accept' lists.
- Being overly fussy can make life difficult, so try to think about possible compromises you could make.
- Teach yourself to keep calm and leave some time before replying to a message that has angered or upset you.
- Never reply in writing when you are angry – sleep on it and do it the next morning when you're in a better mood.

Live to fight another day

Sometimes, your dream property is unlikely to reappear and it's back to the drawing board. Do not be daunted or depressed. You know what to do this time, so go back to basics with your expanded knowledge.

PHIL'S TRADE SECRET
Just as good estate agents who've gone through a bad patch go back to basics – they drag out their contacts' database and start ringing potential sellers and buyers up – so should you get out your own mini-database or lists of agents. Get on the phone and tell them you're still looking for a home, are as keen as ever, and would be hugely grateful for their assistance. The more proactive you are, the better will be the results.

Be professional: no amateur dramatics

Whatever you do, don't bore agents with your lengthy, sorry story of what went wrong and how dreadful it was. Just as no one really wants to hear the epic tale of why your boyfriend or girlfriend dumped you, believe me, no one wants to hear about how you lost your beloved potential first home either.

When talking to estate agents or other property professionals, be brief, polite and professional, as you would expect them to be when speaking to you. An edited version of the mishap or loss is enough to convey that you were not at fault, and that you're still in the running for a property.

Since the disaster, your needs and wishes might have changed, so do tell the agents what you now require. You might have learned something from your first offer being declined, so tell agents how your thinking has altered and what this means for them when they're hunting for a home on your behalf.

For example, maybe you made an offer under the asking price for a two-bedroom flat with a short lease that was turned down. But after some thought, you realise the second bedroom wasn't big enough (you're letting it out to a friend and you were kidding yourself it would be large enough to attract a decent rent), and the thought of borrowing extra money to extend the lease really wasn't a good idea after all. So, maybe you lost the flat, but you gained some knowledge in the process and have honed down what you really think is suitable for you.

Tell agents what you lost: what you really, really wanted

Do tell agents which property you had hoped to buy. This will help them establish what kind of property it is that you fancy, which street or area appeals and roughly your price bracket.

Be open-minded, however. If an agent thinks you only want to live in one street it could take awhile for another property to come up for sale there. Emphasise that you have an open mind, and if he can come up with any new ideas to get you onto the property ladder, you'll at least consider them. Something might come out of left field that you'd never even thought of before, and who knows, it might fit the bill.

Always look on the bright side

I know it can be hard at this stage to be perky and positive, but wallowing in your own misery will be very counter-productive. Even if you can't see the sunny side of the situation quite yet, you will eventually find something positive that will help you move ahead. And hopefully, one day you'll say, 'I'm so glad we didn't go for that first place, which we made an offer on.' You will appreciate the home you eventually buy with no regrets, knowing it is better.

CASE STUDY

PICKING UP THE PIECES PAYS OFF

George Murray was heartbroken when he lost a two-bedroom cottage near Ludlow in Shropshire. It had taken eight months to find his ideal first home, and then it was wrenched from him.

'I hunted for ages, talked to dozens of estate agents and spent many hours viewing property to get what I wanted, and then in a second, it was all lost,' points out George, who not surprisingly, was hugely disappointed when the owner of the pretty cottage pulled it off the market.

Although his instinct was to blame the owner and estate agent for what happened, he says he took a deep breath (or two) and tried to remain calm. 'My first instinct was to accuse everyone of not doing their job properly, or of treating me badly, but at the end of the day, what happened wasn't really anyone's fault.'

George asked his solicitor to find out why the seller had pulled out of the sale at the last minute (just a few days before the exchange of contracts was about to take place). It transpired that the owner had just been given notice by her company that she wouldn't be transferred after all to another branch in Manchester, so she didn't need to move.

To keep the peace, George's solicitor suggested the seller contribute some money towards George's costs so far (solicitor's fees, survey and valuation costs), and even though the seller wasn't bound by law to do so, she graciously offered £300 to help cover some of the deficit.

'It was really good of the seller to be so generous,' admits George, who wrote her a note thanking her for being so considerate and wishing her well in the future. His polite behaviour paid off, however, when the seller's company informed her six weeks later that she would be sent to Manchester the following year. She rang up George and he decided to go ahead with the purchase right away. The solicitors negotiated on a delayed completion date that suited the seller, with George knowing he would finally get the property he'd set his heart on.

'I know I was lucky, as things don't always end so happily, but I'm also aware that if I'd behaved badly and fallen out with the seller, she wouldn't have got back in touch with me,' he adds.

PICKING-UP-THE-PIECES CHECKLIST

- [ ] Make a complaint to the manager of the estate agency or Property Ombudsman if you feel you've been treated badly
- [ ] Chase up the agent to keep track of the property you lost (it might come back)
- [ ] Keep looking and ring agents frequently to show you're serious
- [ ] Spread your search wider for more choice
- [ ] Consider other avenues: auctions or rent-to-buy, for instance
- [ ] Refine your search lists
- [ ] Don't give up

PHIL'S CONTACTS BOOK
- The Property Ombudsman – tpos.co.uk

CHAPTER NINE

Moving in

Moving day can be fraught with problems, so here are some tips to minimise the pain

Moving house is one of the top three stressful life events – it's just behind death and divorce – although I don't think it has to be such a horrendous or, frankly, expensive experience. You just have to plan ahead, be organised and stay calm to have a moving day that isn't in the first circle of hell. Getting an extra pair of hands (or several pairs of hands) will lighten the load, too.

Run-up to moving day

Before you book the removal men, talk to your agent and get him to be as precise and honest as he can about when everything will join up so you can determine what day contracts will be exchanged. Then, you can set a moving day.

You want to get this right, as it costs money to cancel the hire of a van, or several removals men and a truck, depending on how big your team will be, after you've booked them in on a particular day. You could lose your deposit, which could be anything from £50 up to several hundred pounds.

Moving might be a leisurely affair, especially if you are still living at home, or with friends. Equally, you might be renting a property and have several weeks clear before the contract ends.

Yet, it could also be a quick move if you go through a rapid exchange and completion. This tends to happen when you're stuck in a chain that goes beyond the suggested exchange date, but everyone is still aiming for the same completion date. Planning ahead to move house without any guarantee that the purchase will actually go ahead is not only tricky, but can be incredibly nerve-racking.

Don't rush: slow movers

Discovering that you don't have to rush the move is a very good position to find yourself in. You can toddle round to your new home when you feel like it with a few plants or your more precious items, if you don't live too far away. Not having to stuff the entire move into one day – or even worse, into a few hours – is a rare blessing.

You could even settle in pets or children gradually, if this helps achieve a peaceful and orderly relocation. Who knows, you might be lucky enough to clean the entire place, or even decorate it, depending on how large the gap is when the previous owners leave and you arrive.

See your new home with fresh eyes

I find many new owners of a property are a bit shocked when they first waltz back into their new home. Often, when the deal has been struck, vendors tend to become slack and stop looking after the property quite as well as they did when viewers were coming around regularly. Don't be surprised then when you find a jungle for a garden, scuffed walls and fresh stains on the carpet.

Even if the outgoing owners have tended the property fairly well, you do see things in a whole new light when you've exchanged contracts and see your soon-to-be new home in a different way. You're about to pay a great deal of money for this place, and did it really look that tired when you did that second viewing?

On the other hand, things might look better – you hadn't really taken on board just how well tended the communal gardens are, or properly noted the gorgeous river flowing just behind your property on the edge of the village. For instance, I know one friend who saw a flat at night. It had just come on the market and she was only the second person to set foot over the threshold. She loved it, and bravely made an offer there and then. She asked to make a second viewing the next day and saw how the daylight flooded through the floor-to-ceiling windows and that the vendor had laid down decent laminate flooring and installed good sinks and taps.

Equally, some sellers are good people who do look after a home. Just because they've accepted your offer and contracts have been exchanged doesn't mean they're going to let the place run into wrack and ruin. Considerate folk such as this are likely to give the lawn one last mow before you arrive, hoover the carpets and clean the kitchen and bathrooms. You could even find a bottle of wine waiting for you so you can toast your new premises, along with a welcome note and a list of the best local shops and restaurants. Vendors like this are worth their weight in gold – and sadly, there aren't enough of them.

Moving checklist

The good news is that not only do most estate agents have pretty good removals checklists they can provide you for free, but there are a number of websites that have sprung up to help with who to contact when you move and reminders of what you need to do before moving house, and on the day. My Contacts Book at the end of the chapter lists a number of these sites.

Royal redirection

To start with, you can use the Royal Mail's very handy post forwarding service. You will still need to write to everyone, giving them your new address, but at least the Royal Mail will redirect post from your old address for a stated period of time.

To apply for the Royal Mail's redirection service, go to www.royalmail.com, or call 08457 740740 if you're calling from inside the UK. If you are calling from abroad, ring +44 1752 387 116.

The Royal Mail will redirect your post from your old address in the UK (but not from an address abroad) for a set fee from one month and up to two years. The prices at the time of going to press were £7.62 per surname for one month, £16.82 for three months, £25.96 for six months and one year for £38.99 per surname.

The Royal Mail will write to you two to four weeks before the redirection period runs out and you can renew again online, or by telephone. You can cancel the redirection at any time, although you will not get a refund if the service has already started. You need to allow at least five working days before the service will kick off.

Meanwhile, here's my **checklist of whom you need to inform of your new address**:

- Bank
- Building society
- Pension provider
- Any other financial providers (shares, premium bonds, ISAs, etc)
- Credit card and store card companies
- Mobile phone and landline phone companies
- TV cable or satellite company
- Email service provider
- Gas, electricity and water companies
- Local authority for council tax
- Post office to redirect any post (remember, there's a charge to redirect post)
- General practitioner
- Insurance companies
- Inland Revenue
- DVLA (to get your new address on your driving licence)
- DSS office
- Electoral Roll
- Employer
- Dentist
- Friends and family (you can get change of address cards printed inexpensively at your local printers, and you might want to get small, sticky labels with your new address printed to put on your Christmas cards to mop up anyone who's missed getting your new details)

PHIL'S TOP TIP

It can take time to get your telephone and Internet connections reconnected at a new address, so book ahead and chase them up a few days before you move so they can't complain they have forgotten to book you in.

Timeline for moving house

- Plan your moving-in date and book time off work.
- Book the removal company after getting at least three different quotes from different firms.
- Check with the firm you choose whether you're insured if you pack the boxes yourself and something gets damaged.
- Consider packing yourself, so you force yourself to de-clutter and you will know what has been packed where.
- If you are renting:
  - Give notice to your landlord.
  - Tell your utilities and telephone companies you are moving out of your current home.
- Confirm your moving date, your new address (make sure the postcode is correct) and get new agreements with:
  - Gas, electricity, water and telephone companies
  - Your local authority for council tax
  - The post office to redirect post (there is a charge for this service)
- Start to sort out all of your belongings. Clear out, sell on (eBay, Amazon or a similar website is a good way to make a bit of cash from all those things you want to get rid of) or donate what you don't need to charity shops. Some local councils operate services where they will remove sofas, chairs and beds for you for a small charge.

PHIL'S TOP TIP

Remember, a removal company charges you by the number of items you own. If you get rid of a large number of things before they come round to make an estimate, you will save a great deal of money.

- Book a van, removal company or arrange for family and friends to help move you and your things. Always use a reputable removal firm (check they belong to the British Association of Removers), and always get quotes in advance.
- Check that your home insurance covers you for any damage during the move, and ask the removal company what compensation they offer if there's any damage. Check the fine print, as you might have to make any claim by a certain date after the move.

Just before the move

I think it's crucial to double-check a number of important details prior to the move. It will make the day go smoothly and save a lot of angst.

Phil's pre-move checklist
- Check what time you can actually move into your new home and plan everything around that hour.
- Confirm all of the details with the removal company or the friends and family that are helping you.
- If you are hiring a van, find out what time you can collect it and when it needs to be returned.
- Speak to your neighbours at both your old home and your new one to see if you can get access to park the removal van.
- Tell the removal company about any narrow roads or drives, so they are warned about how tricky it might be manoeuvring a large vehicle around the corners.

- You might need to contact your local authority (this can take up to a week in some places) and get a parking bay, or two, suspended to make room for the removal van. There are different regulations about whether you need to do this or not, depending on where you live, and you might have to pay a small fee, too.
- Pack up everything, except for those items you will need just before the removal day.
- Label each box with the contents and the room they should go in. Do not put 'miscellaneous' on virtually every box, which a 'helpful' removal man did for a friend of mine. It took her months to find everything again.

PHIL'S TRADE SECRET
A clever trick that the professional movers use is to number each room (for instance, '1' for kitchen, and '2' for living room) and then write the number on the corresponding boxes. You can also put sticky labels on beds and furniture with the room numbers. The removal men will love you if you do this, as it makes their job easier.

- Place all valuable or important items somewhere safe.
- If you are worried about valuable or precious things being damaged or broken, you might consider getting the removal men to pack those items for you. This service costs extra, but it might be worth the extra money.
- Visit the owners of your new home to make sure that:
  - They've shown you where water cocks, fuse boxes and gas and electricity meters are.
  - You've looked into and sorted out a parking permit (if needed).
  - All window, garage, shed, internal door and front and back door keys are all left labelled and in one place so you can find them.

- ○ All relevant manuals, leaflets, guarantees and instruction booklets for the boiler and appliances are left in the property.
- Pay all the bills for your old property.

Moving day: a moving experience

On moving day itself, make sure you have a 'moving box' of essentials. I look at this box in the same way as a woman about to have a baby packs a bag for when she has to go to hospital. It needs to hold certain crucial items to keep everyone happy.

And don't do what a friend of mine did and leave the essentials box out so the removal men can get hold of it. They packed it onto the van and my friend didn't find the box – or the kettle inside – for a number of weeks. Lock it into your car, or similar, so you personally know where it is.

Here's what the 'moving box' should contain:

- Kettle, mugs, tea, coffee, milk, sugar and biscuits
- A few bowls, plates and some cutlery to get you through the first day in your new home
- Some cereal, bread, butter and fruit for snacking and your first breakfast in your home
- Cleaning items, including cloths, washing-up liquid, detergents, dustpan and brush, hoover, rubbish bags and brooms
- Toilet paper, tissues, soap, towels and tissues
- Pens, paper and Post-it notes
- Torches, candles, matches, light bulbs, pliers, sharp knife and screwdrivers
- A bottle of wine or bubbly to toast your first evening in your new home (besides, you'll probably need a drink by then)
- List of important contact numbers and a Yellow Pages, or similar directory
- Keys

Get every member of the household to pack a small bag or case with a toothbrush, pyjamas, dressing gown, slippers and clothes for the first couple of days in the new house. I would also put personal valuables, such as passports, insurance documents and any other key paperwork, in a case and keep it with me (or give it to a friend to mind). And, don't laugh at this, but keep the files with all the removal and moving house documentation close at hand, too. Things can get swallowed up all too easily when a number of people are milling about and helping you pack up.

Also, it is key to make sure all services – gas, electricity, water and phone – are connected and working properly. Having hot water will cheer everyone up at the end of a long and tiring day, so check it is working as soon as you arrive at the new property.

Recheck your insurance to make sure the insurance on the new property is in effect as soon as you move in.

Put each box into the room where you intend things to be in and don't worry about unpacking everything at once. Start with the kitchen and foodstuffs.

Just as important are the bedrooms, so you have somewhere to sleep even if you don't finish unpacking everything in one day. I'd also put duvets, blankets, pillows, sheets and pillowcases in a well-labelled box and make sure these go onto the van last (or put them in your car, if you'd feel happier knowing where they are). Get the beds put up (have a screwdriver or two to hand to put the beds together) and make them up with the bedding, so you don't need to worry about this when you're exhausted and about ready to collapse.

Moving with children and pets

If you're moving with children, pack up a few of their favourite toys to make them feel at home right away. It can be quite disconcerting and confusing for small children, so you might be better off getting a friend or grandparent to look after them for the day, so you can concentrate on moving in. The child will probably be happier away from all the chaos anyhow.

The same applies to pets. Securing them in a pet-carrying basket, or similar, would make sense, and perhaps you can get a friend to mind them. Then, you can collect them later on when all the excitement has died down. They could go missing with all the to-ing and fro-ing, so be cautious. Or, you could put them in one room and close the door, although there's always the possibility that someone might mistakenly enter the room and let the animal out.

PHIL'S MOVING TIPS

- Communicate with your mortgage company, broker, solicitor and the chain ahead to make sure everything's going through.
- Get your solicitor to check the money's gone through for the property and that you will get the keys immediately after this happens.
- Confirm the time you can get into your home, and don't be shaken if there's a small delay.
- A small detail, but an important one: buy tea, cold drinks and biscuits (and maybe even sandwiches if it's a long process) for the removal men. Like armies, they march on their stomachs and a bit of friendly goodwill could go a long way. And, tip them at the end if they've been particularly helpful and supply some cold beer to christen the move and the new house.
- If you can afford it, why not escape all the hassle and hire a really good firm that will do absolutely everything for you. Then go on holiday for a week, and you can come back to a new home with all your possessions unpacked and neatly put away. If you're really brave, you can even engage decorators to spruce the place up for you. However, it might be wise to get someone to oversee the move and the work.

If you have taken the day off to pack and you don't get the keys until four o'clock in the afternoon, you will probably feel incredibly excited and quite emotional by the time you can pick up the keys and open the front door. This is a real moment to savour.

But, prepare yourself. You might not have seen the property for six months and it might not look as nice as your remembered, even if the owners have looked after it well. There are bound to be marks on the wall where furniture and pictures have been removed, which can look a bit ghostly and it is likely not to be totally clean.

Despite all of this, don't be discouraged. An empty house rarely looks inviting, which is why estate agents like to shoot pictures of well-dressed homes and property developers kit out show homes. Remind yourself that this is a very special moment when you open the door to your first piece of Britain. This will never be repeated, and is really quite historic. You might even want a camera to hand to capture that time when you arrive in your home for the first time as its new owner.

Buying your new home and taking possession of it is a real milestone in your life, like losing your virginity, passing your driving test and having a baby. This defining moment only happens once and you deserve a massive pat on the back for having got this far. Everything might not be perfect, but it is yours.

CASE STUDY

DON'T BE MOVED TO TEARS

Gabrielle Martin, a fundraiser for a woodland trust, has been married to an army officer for nearly 30 years. She has moved more than 20 times in the UK and abroad, and is probably one of Britain's leading experts on how to move house.

But even Gabrielle admits she can get things wrong, even after all of her years of experience. Here's her account of a recent move into a new home in a development in south-west England.

'Nearly 18 months ago, I moved house. It was only 10 minutes down the road, but the experience still haunts me. If there were an A-level in moving from one place to another, my teacher would have noted with a frown: "Could try harder."

'Overall, our move wasn't too bad, but there are so many useful hints I picked up when it was all over (isn't hindsight a fine thing?), I wish I had thought everything through a bit more before the big day.'

Moving can be fun, however. Here are Gabrielle's ideas to make your move a joyous occasion.

- Talk to the house builder selling you your new home (if you're buying a brand-new home). Some offer removal services as a package deal, and most recommend good moving firms and also hand out a moving checklist. An estate agent can recommend some good removal companies, too, that will usually do you a good deal.
- Some good moving house websites, including www. moveme.com and www.iammoving.com have cropped up, offering change of address form letters to banks and utility companies, names of removal firms and other invaluable advice. Www.moveme.com even sends you a free moving gift box and a moving planner. This box certainly saved the day for me this time round.
- Turn yourself into one of those scary de-clutter experts. The more you throw out or give away, the more money you save. Removal firms estimate the cost of moving by how many items they have to shift.
- Talk to a local charity, which might be grateful for some of your de-cluttered clutter. Our neighbour runs an annual coffee morning for the Macmillan nurses charity and was more than happy to take various things off our hands, including a set of old golf clubs and a large, rather cumbersome desk.
- If you decide to store some items, first ask yourself if you really do want or need them. We have just thrown out a skip load (costing nearly £200) of 'junk' we couldn't part with when we packed up. If only we'd lost them back then, we'd be £200 richer.

- Note down the meter readings for gas, electricity and water for your old property the day you leave, and also note down the readings for all meters in your new house. Mistakes can be made and you don't want to be wrangling with a utility company over a bill for energy that you didn't use (which can be quite expensive).
- Ask the house builder the best way to move into your new home, if you're buying at a new development. Many will help by padding a lift especially for the move, or can select the simplest route into the building and up the stairs if there isn't a lift.
- And finally, treat yourself to a takeaway or try a local restaurant on the first night in your new home. How better to get to know a new neighbourhood? We discovered a great new little Thai place a few streets away and have been there many times since that first night in our new place.

After the move

The world doesn't stop spinning when you've moved into your new home. Life goes on, so here are a few things to think about once you've actually moved in:

- **Get to know your neighbourhood**
  It might be a completely new place for you, so get out there to familiarise yourself with the area. Take regular walks or cycle rides around the streets to get to know the names of the roads and where the local shops are. Also, find out where the libraries, churches, schools, pubs, restaurants, cinemas, clubs and theatres are. It's important you work out local transport routes and how to get to your local hospital, too. The local papers are a terrific source of information. Or, try knowhere.co.uk to find out

more about your area. Specialist websites for each area (such as, secret-london.co.uk for London) will give you personal recommendations for anything from cafés and shops to walks and arts events.

- **Get to know your neighbours**
  Be friendly and introduce yourself to your neighbours. A simple 'Good morning' can make all the difference and might be the start of some great new friendships. It's always a good idea to build up good relationships with your neighbours, so you can help each other out by taking in deliveries, looking after children, keeping an eye on your home when you're away and being available in case of an emergency.

- **Get to know your doctor and dentist**
  Register with a doctor and dentist as soon as you can. You should also seek out a good local optician. Ask your neighbours for recommendations, or go to the National Health Service website (nhs.uk) to the section on how to find a local doctor.

- **Get to know local tradesmen**
  You never know when you'll need the telephone numbers of a good plumber, electrician or heating engineer. Again, ask your neighbours and local shop owners who they would recommend. A good builders' merchant can help with suggestions, too.

- **Get to know local services**
  If you want to get your newspapers delivered, find a local newsagent. Equally, there might be a milkman delivering in your area (a rare event these days, so your milkman deserves your support). Keep an eye out to see what services are available and check your local press. And of course, it's important to keep a list of good local takeaway places. If you're too tired to cook from all that unpacking and redecorating, you can order from your new favourite Chinese or Indian restaurant.

- **Make sure your TV licence is up to date**
  In all the removals excitement, don't forget to register your TV licence at your new address. You don't want to be fined, or go through a lengthy process explaining about the move and why you hadn't informed the authorities.

PHIL'S TOP TIP

If you didn't notice a list of local businesses and services in your new home, why don't you type out a list of all the people whose contact numbers you would need. Send it to the vendor and he can fill in the numbers and give it to you or your estate agent. Tap the estate agent's brain, too. A good local agent will know loads about your new area and can give you the lowdown on what's happening where.

YOUR MOVING CHECKLIST

- [ ] Plan the date and time for the move
- [ ] Take time off work
- [ ] Book a van or removal company
- [ ] Inform authorities (such as utility companies, Electoral Roll, your employer and Inland Revenue) of your new address
- [ ] Clear out or sell unwanted items
- [ ] Check your insurer covers you for any damage while moving
- [ ] Check your removal company is insured for any damage that occurs
- [ ] Tell the removal company about any narrow roads or drive
- [ ] Contact the local authority to suspend a parking bay for the removal van
- [ ] Pack, making sure fragile items are well wrapped
- [ ] Label each box with a number or letter corresponding to the room where it will go
- [ ] Pack a 'moving box' (tea, milk, cleaning items) that you will need immediately
- [ ] Pack a bag for each person with a toothbrush and change of clothes
- [ ] Keep passports and other important items with you

- ☐ Check readings of utility meters in old and new homes
- ☐ Make beds first in your new home
- ☐ Toast your new home with a glass of bubbly and order a takeaway or visit a local restaurant to celebrate

PHIL'S CONTACTS BOOK

- Royal Mail offers a redirection service of your post – 08457 740740 (+44 1752 387116 if calling from abroad), www.royalmail.com
- Two websites where you can easily sell unwanted items are www.ebay.co.uk and www.amazon.co.uk
- British Association of Removers – over 500 removal companies listed as members – www.bar.co.uk
- Two websites with information and recommendations of removal firms – helpiammoving.com and uk-removal.co.uk

CHAPTER TEN
Maintaining Your Home

The work doesn't stop once the contracts have been exchanged and you've moved in – home ownership brings with it a responsibility to your property

A bit like giving birth, all the excitement seems to be centred round the new arrival, while the hard work is only now beginning. As tempting as it is to simply slump back and enjoy your new home (and you are allowed to do this for a day or two), you need to get it in shape and look after what is probably your primary asset.

If you concentrate on a few check-in details about a month after you move in (not unlike the concept of what you need to do or ask when you check in to a hotel), life will be all the easier with such attention.

Phil's check-in list: what to do now you're in your new home

- Double-check your contents insurance. Are you covered for all the new items you've bought, or are in the process of buying, since the move? Give special attention to any old or precious items – Aunty Mary's writing desk, a present for you when you moved in, might be worth more than you reckoned.

- Check the gas and electricity are connected and in the right name (yours or your co-owner's). I'd check this on the moving day itself, and again a month later to make sure your name is entered on the utility companies' computer database. They can be notoriously slow sometimes at updating information, and it's better to get this right now, rather than spending hours on the phone later trying to explain everything.

- Don't rush out and buy lots of new furniture and appliances right away. Establish your outgoings first and then you'll know how much you have to spend. Budgeting monthly is important and you might find friends and family are happy to give you some unwanted items, anyhow, or you can scour junk and charity shops, as well as websites, such as eBay (www.ebay.co.uk). There are some great bargains out there for first-timers.

- Again, unless you know exactly what you want, I'd wait a bit before doing any major decorating as well. If it's not too dreadful, I'd live with the previous owner's décor for while until you get a feel for what you can do. You can economise by bulk buying and painting all the walls in the same light, neutral colour – this is a neat trick for opening up small spaces, too. Then you can just add a bit of colour through the accessories (cushions, lampshades, etc) – and you can change smaller items later on to get a whole new effect for very little money.

- Make a will, or update your current one. Now that you have a major asset, you should write down officially who you will leave it to if something happens to you.

Household budget

Once you've settled in, try to work out a new budget for living in your new home. This doesn't sound like the most exciting way to spend your free time, but one evening in working out what you need to pay, allowing for extras, can be hugely productive and helpful. Getting into debt almost as soon as you move in won't be a good start, and you'll thank yourself later for drawing up a new budget list.

Try to stick to a new budget that includes all of your income, and then work out your costs. Your ongoing costs list could look something like this:

- Mortgage repayments
- Any other loans (maybe including paying back some money lent by friends or family to get you started)
- Insurance: mortgage payment protection, life and sickness insurance, buildings and contents insurance, car or motorbike insurance
- Council tax
- Utilities
- Food and drink
- Household expenses: energy bills, service charges, ground rent, telephone bills, TV licence
- Transport and travel: car tax, Tube and train fares, congestion and parking charges, resident's parking permit, petrol
- Clothing

Disposable income

Charles Dickens summed up the concept of disposable income brilliantly in his novel, *David Copperfield*. 'If a man had twenty pounds a year for his income and spent nineteen pounds nineteen shillings and sixpence, he would be happy, but that if he spent twenty pounds one he would be miserable.' Basically, if you can't stick to your budget and spend within your means, therein lies doom and gloom.

What is disposable income?

After you take away your costs from your income, the remainder is your disposable income. This sum is the amount you can spend on activities, holidays, presents and luxuries – and don't forget about savings. I would recommend that you really try to keep your costs tight and put away some savings for a rainy day, as your granny probably sagely suggests.

This might sound a bit boring and dreary – I know you're only young once – but if you're constantly overdrawn at the bank and worrying about whether you have any money or not, life's not much fun, anyhow. As time goes by, things generally get easier. Your salary should go up at some point and the capital on your property will accumulate over time. You shouldn't assume we live in a get-rich-quick world (the prosperous 1980s are long gone), but with a bit of patience your financial position will improve.

If you are at all worried about budgeting and being able to afford the basics, do talk to a sympathetic bank manager or financial advisor. Or, get hold of a sensible friend or family member who can talk you through how they budget and look after their finances.

PHIL'S TRADE SECRET

Just as many freeholders or residents in a building often club together to support a 'sinking fund' (a pool of money that can be used for emergency repairs or maintenance), I think it a good idea to do this for your own individual property.

While a sinking fund in a block of flats is used for large repair jobs to communal areas, such as the roof, your own little sinking fund could be for unexpected repairs on your new home. You might need to find cash for a broken-down boiler or a leaky shower in the future. If you've cannily put money aside, the shock when it comes to pay for the work won't be half as scary as it might be if you have no money in the kitty at all.

Budget for maintenance

I always think maintaining your home in general, no matter how rich or poor you are, is terribly important. Putting aside some money for regular maintenance (and you don't necessarily need all that much) is something every first-time buyer should do.

I'm a great believer in maintenance and get a bit fanatical about it. It's crucial you get used to carrying out small tasks to keep your new home up to scratch. This is such a good habit to acquire, making life easier when you come to sell your property, as well as making it better to live in while you're staying put. Here's my list for making sure your new asset doesn't lose its sheen:

PHIL'S TOP TIPS

HOW TO MAINTAIN YOUR HOME

- Keep the windows clean. This is a good way to make sure your wooden window frames (if you have wooden ones) don't start to rot. Get the name of the vendor's window cleaner, or you can find one through the local paper or displayed in the ads of the newsagent or local shop.
- Service the boiler. Major boiler repairs or replacing an ignored boiler can be costly, so get yours serviced annually. Most gas suppliers run service schemes where they come every year to check yours out.
- Install smoke alarms. These don't cost a great deal and are priceless if they save a life.
- Check out areas of your home you don't use on a daily basis. Is there any damp or mildew in the loft, basement or anywhere else? If so, get it sorted pronto before it turns into something nasty.
- Regularly walk around the outside of your house and check for leaks, stains on the walls, broken guttering or loose tiles. It's wise to do this before winter sets in, as strong winds can dislodge tiles.
- Get up on a ladder in the autumn to make sure fallen leaves haven't blocked the gutters, leading to water pouring down the outside walls and producing damp patches. While you're up there, replace split tiles and keep a watchful eye on pointing (mortar that has been placed between bricks to hold them together) and paint the exterior to keep the damp out.
- Remove heavy moss from the roof, particularly in the spring and autumn.
- Inspect painted metalwork every couple of years and renew it when it is in danger of starting to crack and peel.
- Tackle frost damage and slippery algae growth on stone and brick steps and garden paths.

- Fix cracked pipes and drains. These cause damp problems and look unsightly hanging off your home, or next to it.

If you live in a new development and are concerned about any maintenance issues inside your own home, or generally in communal areas, do report these to the management company as soon as possible. The longer such problems are left to fester, the more expensive and complicated they will be. Don't worry about nagging the company to do the work. It is important in the long run to hold onto the value of your home and the overall site.

How to economise

It can be difficult having enough money to pay all the bills, and having some spare to pay for emergencies and the odd treat, like a trip to the cinema or a takeaway pizza, particularly during the first few months in your new home. But, there are ways you can economise and accrue a bit more cash. Here are some of my ideas:

Reduce, reuse and recycle

You can save money by being less wasteful. Keep an eye out for two-for-one offers in supermarkets (but only gather up large amounts of food-stuffs and cleaning materials if you'll actually use them and they won't go to waste). Don't throw out new clothes you haven't yet worn (try altering them so you'll be happy putting them on). Or, why not swap unwanted items with friends – for free.

Save energy costs

Turn the thermostat down – even by one degree. It makes a difference, honest.

Save water

Run only what you need. Don't fill the kettle to the brim for one cuppa, and don't fill up a huge tub of water for a bath when a shower will do.

Energy-efficient appliances

These often cost a bit more to buy, but in the long run you could save money, because they are more efficient with shorter cycles that use less energy.

Energy-efficient home

At the time of going to press, the government wasn't exactly upping the number of grants to make your home more energy efficient, but this could change in the future when there's more money to spend. So, keep an eye out for new schemes that might be available.

Meanwhile, think of improving your home's energy efficiency to reduce bills by draught proofing (heavy curtains and simple draught excluders for doors can make more of a difference than you think) and insulating the loft. Again, this isn't expensive (you can do it for as little as a few hundred pounds) and this stops the heat from escaping needlessly.

Rent out a room

Taking up the legacy of Rupert Rigsby, the seamy but lovable landlord from 1980s' TV comedy *Rising Damp,* you might relish renting out a room or two in your house for a bit of extra cash. This not only brings in some extra cash from the rent, but having someone else sharing expenses and bills can save you money, too.

Thankfully, things have moved on from the days when lecherous and stingy Rigsby barged into tenants' rooms, with mangy moggy Vienna in tow, to collect a few quid for cubby-holes riddled with damp that he insisted was just condensation. Now, homeowners, including a number of first-timers, are letting out rooms, converted attics, outbuildings and entire floors and wings (for the wealthier among us) of their homes to help pay the bills, enjoy some companionship and drive the burglars away.

The government is encouraging homeowners to let spare rooms through its 'Rent a room' scheme, where you can earn rentals income up to £4,250 a year (or £81.70 a week). And, taking in a lodger does not affect your tax banding. For more information, visit www.direct.gov.uk/en/moneytaxandbenefits.

CASE STUDY

A PART-TIME LODGER

First-time buyer Florence Hoskins, who is in her early 30s, lets out an upstairs room in her Berkshire cottage to a management consultant from Northumberland during the week, reclaiming the room on weekends. She found her lodger through website www.mondaytofriday.com, one of several websites that link up landlords with weekday-only renters.

'After buying the cottage, I was keen to find ways to make some extra money. It was a bit of a struggle every month once I paid the mortgage, council tax and all the other bills. Letting a room to a lodger from only Monday night to Friday morning is perfect, as I have the house to myself on weekends, and when I'm away, the tenant can keep an eye on things,' says Florence.

To avoid having a dodgy Rodger the Lodger on the premises, Florence advises you always to get a reference, although she believes this method of taking in paying guests beats bed and breakfast. 'Tenants have a job, are more permanent than transient bed and breakfast customers and, frankly, it's a lot less work. You don't have to get up early to cook breakfast, nor change the sheets every day.'

Landlords pay £29.95 to register on the website for three months and lodgers pay £10 a month. And if you thought taking in a lodger was only an urban pursuit, there are many requests as well for people wanting to rent accommodation in rural areas.

'With business parks growing on the edge of towns and cities, and companies moving their quarters to converted farm buildings, a number of people like my tenant need somewhere to stay. They don't want to commute miles every day or uproot their families for short periods of time. Renting a room in someone else's home is generally cheaper and more appealing than a soulless hotel room,' Florence explains.

If you fancy your child marrying a doctor, you could even let your spare room to a medic from the UK or overseas through Doctor in the House (www.doctorhouse.co.uk). A recent favoured spot for medical practitioners is the Chalfonts in Buckinghamshire, not far from the clinics and hospitals of Harrow and Uxbridge, to counter those notions that this only applies to big cities like London or Manchester. To give you some guidance on costs, Doctor in the House charges £25 to check out your home and £42 a night for a single room and £66 for a double, taking a cut on a sliding scale, typically £15 from a £42 weekly rental.

One word of caution, however. You are not covered under the Housing Act with lodgers, as you are if you let out a flat or house. You do not have the same rights and could find it hard to lose a dodgy lodger, so draw up a tenancy agreement. The useful website Desktop Lawyer (www.desktoplawyer.com) provides reasonably priced standard contracts, or a solicitor can compile one for around £250.

Top ten lodgers

- Graduate students that vacate the premises during the summer
- Week-day-only, part-time renters
- The self-employed working from home to keep burglars at bay
- DIY freaks keen to mend your dripping tap

- Green-fingered tenants intent on cutting the hedges
- Gordon Ramsay-wannabes whipping up gourmet dinners
- Dependable medics handy in an emergency
- Child-friendly lodgers happy to baby-sit
- Counsellors who will listen to your woes
- Night-shifters rarely there when you are

Getting behind with the mortgage

I do hope this never happens to you, but sometimes people – especially hard-pressed first-time buyers – can fall behind with their mortgage repayments. Things happen – people lose jobs, they fall ill and go back to study. There can be a tendency when there's a financial problem to stick your head in the sand and hope it will go away. But the problem won't go away – it's likely to get worse – so do go to your lender and see what can be done. They might offer to:

- Give you a payment holiday
- Agree to lengthen or alter the terms of your loan
- Allow you to add the arrears (the unpaid payments) to the total mortgage debt
- Accept lower payments in the short term
- Convert a repayment mortgage into an interest-only mortgage

Make sure you look into all of the options and understand any consequences they might have. For instance, if you defer making a payment you could end up paying extra interest on the loan.

If you don't come to a suitable agreement with the lender, or fail to stick to the agreement you've made with the company, you will be sent a 'notice of default'. The lender might take you to court with the view to have you evicted from your home. This is known as making a 'claim for possession' and you will be sent paperwork from the court before a court hearing is heard.

These days, most lenders do their utmost to avoid having to take you to court and possibly, evict you. The government is encouraging lenders to help debtors as much as possible, due to the recent economic crisis. And even if you do receive a notice of default, do keep talking to your lender.

You should also get some help from an independent adviser, or you can contact your local Citizens Advice Bureau (a registered charity that over the last year helped 2.1 million people with 7.1 million problems), if you have one. Visit www.adviceguide.org.uk, or you can call a new national phone service on 0844 477 2020. This new phone service is being established across England and Wales over the next two years.

Another good source of help is government-backed Citizens Debt Advice. They give debt management ideas and solutions seven days a week. Visit www.debtadvicegroup.co.uk, or call 0800 116 4952.

PHIL'S TOP TIP

However bad things are, do not walk away and do not hand your keys over to the lender. You will then lose everything you have put in so far, which would be a terrible shame. It's never too late to get advice, so keep talking to the lender and anyone else who's helping you.

MAINTAINING-YOUR-HOME CHECKLIST

- [ ] Make sure the utilities (gas, electrics, etc) are connected and in your name
- [ ] Double-check you have enough insurance
- [ ] Update your will
- [ ] Draw up a household budget, including money to maintain your home

- [ ] Carry out regular maintenance, including servicing the boiler, checking guttering and roof tiles and inspecting metal paintwork
- [ ] Reduce, reuse and recycle to save money
- [ ] Think of renting out a room if pushed for cash
- [ ] If you fall behind with the mortgage, get help immediately

PHIL'S CONTACTS BOOK

- Check out www.nationwideeducation.co.uk – a valuable resource from a lender that produces a terrific first-time buyers' guide
- For advice, top tips and useful dos and don'ts on maintenance from the Society for the Protection of Ancient Buildings (SPAB), visit www.maintainyourbuilding.org.uk
- Citizens Advice Bureau (CAB) – adviceguide.org.uk – CAB is rolling out a new national phone service (already operating in Wales): 0844 477 2020
- Citizens Debt Advice – visit www.debtadvicegroup.co.uk or call 0800 116 4952

CHAPTER ELEVEN

Fixing up Your New Home

Bring on the builders

N ow you've settled into your new home, many of you will find this is a good time to get on with doing up a property that could benefit from some tender loving care.

You could do the work yourself, depending on your level of expertise, which will save you a load of cash. Or, maybe you have a friend or family member who is a qualified builder, or at least is skilful when it comes to plumbing or electrical work.

But it is more likely you will get the builders in to help you, or to carry out all of the work. It can be quite daunting calling in builders for the first time. How do you know they're not ripping you off? Are they any good at their jobs? And, what is a fair price to pay for the job they do?

Despite any misgivings about coping with builders, I believe that for certain jobs (such as electrical repairs, boilers and most plumbing tasks) there's no substitute for getting in someone who has had a great deal of practice at carrying out specialised work. You need to consider safety first, and I've seen many bodged DIY attempts that have put people in danger. So, please consider using a proper trained tradesman for jobs, such as rewiring, rather than risk electrocuting the inhabitants of the property.

Pros and cons for getting in a builder

Pros

- An experienced builder has specialised skills that will make your house look better, compared with an amateur (i.e., you) doing the work.
- A builder can do the work faster than you.
- If there is a crisis, a good builder will know how to troubleshoot and rectify the problem.
- A builder can come up with ideas and ways to get round dilemmas and save money.

Cons

- A good builder doesn't come cheap. Expect to pay from about £100 a day for basic building work, and from £200 for something a bit more refined.
- Having builders in the house can be disruptive. If you work from home, or have time to do the work yourself, you might want to tackle it.
- Building work can run on, especially if the builder is going between jobs instead of finishing your job off first. This can be frustrating and disturbing.

Phil's guide to dealing with builders

Don't be scared by the idea of dealing with builders. It can be a bit of a minefield for anyone, even if we've gone through the process many times before. At the end of the day, the same logic that you've learned about dealing with estate agents in an earlier chapter isn't all that different from how to deal with builders. Remaining calm and really listening to your builder goes a long way, as does regular communication and knowing when to stand up for yourself if things get ticklish.

Here's my guide to how to deal with builders for first-timers who've never had to deal with them before. This chapter gives you basic information to help you make decisions, and hopefully, it should offer you peace of mind as well. You need to safeguard your most important asset, after all.

Is it best to wait a while before getting builders in?

Although your instinct after moving in might be to heave a big sigh of relief and spend some time recovering from such an all-consuming experience as buying a property, planning to carry out small- to medium-sized projects to improve your asset is a good move. I find new homeowners, whether they're first-time buyers or not, tend to fall into two camps.

The first group is made up of the **'leave well enough alone'** buyers. They know they probably should get down to doing something about the ghastly outdated shower, for instance, but can't really summon up the energy to do anything about it. The danger is that once you've grown used to something you tend not to see its awfulness anymore.

And yet, there can be an argument about living with your home for a short while at least before you start tearing down walls and shifting things around. You do get a sense of the space and work out what you really like, and hate. Perceptive visitors often give insight into what you could do ('Have you thought of knocking out that cupboard and installing a small en-suite shower room at the end of the master bedroom?').

PHIL'S TOP TIP

The best jolt to get you out of the stupor you've fallen into is to invite people round to stay (mothers or mothers-in-law are particularly perceptive at spotting such awfulness, I find). Or, throw a party. Believe me, you'll see your crumbly home in a whole different light when you know your mates are about to take a look around it.

Despite the painful thought of having to do anything, I'd say just get on and do it. You've spent all that money so far on the property itself, and all its associated costs, so why are you hesitating now? Life is for living, so I wouldn't wait. And even if you're not flush with cash, there are things you can still do.

I recall one friend who loathed some built-in wardrobes in her new home. Her husband was definitely in the 'leave well enough alone' camp, which meant his promise to sort out the wardrobes was pretty unlikely to ever be fulfilled. So, my friend took an axe and punched huge holes in the wardrobe doors. This certainly motivated her husband into action to get the job done. Although this might be a rather dramatic way to spur someone on, it did work in this case.

I also know someone who is a perpetual DIY freak, with great ambitions to start projects, but not necessarily to finish them. His wife suffers years of knocked-down chimneys and torn up carpeting, but rarely sees the finished result. Be cautious about bashing something about if you'll end up having to live with it longer than you can bear.

Is it better to do all the building work immediately?

The second group of buyers can be just as problematic. I call this the **'let's do it all now'** brigade. Unless you are overly riddled with cash, it's unlikely most first-time buyers can do absolutely everything perfectly all in one go.

Also, aiming too high can be disappointing, and I've often seen people starting out spend far too much on one thing. Then, they run out of cash and everything grinds to a halt. There's nothing worse than walking into a state-of-the-art living room with wooden flooring and the latest flat-screen telly hanging on the wall, while the rest of the property looks like a crack dealer's den.

Spend on the basics: the infrastructure

I find first-time buyers sometimes lose the plot a bit and start spending money on lovely linen and stylish cutlery. Although the cosmetics are something most people would want to have, you need to allocate money for the basics first, in my opinion.

Spending money on the infrastructure (the actual structure, or the bones of the property) is worth far more in the long run, instead of worrying about the accessories. Once the basics are sorted you can save up for these extras. After all, what's the point of owning a beautiful pair of curtains if there's water dripping down the wall and soaking them, the wall and the floor from a leaky bathroom above?

Do not commit that classic first-time folly of getting the property repainted before you get basics, such as the electrics, fixed. I've observed too many incidents of a freshly painted wall being gouged open in order for the electrician to access the wires behind the wall. What a waste of time and money.

Get the basics sorted

- Mend, or replace, the boiler if it is very old and likely to pack it in soon.
- If the electrics are dodgy, get them mended, or rewire the property if need be. Now is a good time to install extra sockets.
- Good lighting can make all the difference, so think about where you need light. Even investing in a few lamps for reading and close work is a start.
- Decent plumbing is a must. Get the plumber in to look at leaking pipe work and joints before there are any floods.
- Solve any potential dry or wet rot problems.
- Put down good flooring – wood floors or carpets.
- Paint external window frames.
- Check the roof and mend any broken or slipped tiles. Replace any flashing around the chimney stacks if necessary, to keep the water out.
- If you have a chimney, get any repairs carried out to it and have it swept as soon as you move in. Make a note to get it swept annually.

Knowledge is power

Undertaking a new domestic building project can be alarming for those getting down to building work for the first time, so do your research (information is knowledge and knowledge is power, as they say) and ask as many questions as you need to.

Like anyone in a specified field, builders tend to use long and complicated contractual jargon at times, not to mention crazy terms for building parts and materials. If you're not sure what someone is saying it's better to ask there and then, or at least look up the word later on if it's not too late.

I think specialists appreciate someone asking what something means, rather than pretending they know what is being discussed. It gives the builder or tradesman a chance to impart his own knowledge and, generally, he will be happy to explain things to you.

Is your builder always right?

We hold certain professionals, such as doctors and solicitors, in high regard. But, are they always right? Of course not. One problem is there isn't always a definitive answer to a building problem, and often you don't really know the extent of the work until you start ripping up floorboards or knocking into a wall to take a good look.

You must trust your builder, though, or the whole relationship will collapse. He might not always be right, but you have to keep in mind that most, or perhaps all, of the time he knows a lot more than you do.

Should I employ an architect?

It's important to know when to ask for professional help. Architects, who take seven years to get a qualification, have a great understanding of how to use space well.

I would recommend you hire an architect if you are doing any major work to your new property. A good architect will know all of the planning regulations and whether what you want to do is possible. He will also know of clever ways to get round problems and make your home just that bit more special.

An architect does cost money, of course, although I don't think this should put off a first-time renovator. Some firms offer simple architectural advice from only a couple of hundred pounds, which could be money well spent.

If you don't feel you can afford an architect to manage an entire project, you could hire one upfront to help you deal with the planners (particularly if the job has complications) and maybe draw up some basic plans. You've cut out some of the hassle of dealing with the planning department (especially if it's an architect who has dealt with the local authority before), and the builder can work from the architect's drawings.

Where do I find an architect?
Word of mouth is a preferred option. Check if a friend, family member or neighbour knows someone they can recommend. A good local estate agent or the local planning department might know some good local architects, too.

Another trusted source is the Royal Institute of British Architects (RIBA, www.architecture.com). RIBA publishes a useful standard agreement called 'Small works (SW99)' for projects under £100,000.

Before employing anyone, get a clear idea of the costs involved. Rates do vary, starting at around £50 an hour. For a large project, you normally pay an architect from 10% of the total cost of the building work.

Finding a builder

Finding a good builder needn't be difficult. Word of mouth is probably the best way to locate a decent builder (I think a good recommendation is worth its weight in gold), so ask your friends, family members and neighbours who they would suggest. Another good source is the local press.

A reliable place to find a good builder is the Federation of Master Builders (www.findabuilder.co.uk, 0800 015 2522). This is a useful resource if you want to track down a builder with experience in your area. For older period buildings or a specialist job (such as getting a cracked stained-glass window repaired) the Guild of Master Craftsmen (www.guildmc.com, 01273 478449) is another good contact.

There are various websites, too (some are listed at the end of the chapter), that have databases of local tradesmen and builders. Be warned, however, that the supposed neutral recommendations by real punters aren't always what they seem. Frequently, the tradesmen pay for the listings and are known to also advertise elsewhere on the site, so I'm not sure how unbiased all of these recommendations are.

Check out the builder's other projects

Do ask if the builder has any qualifications, or past experience. Being able to take a look at another project he has just finished, or is currently working on, can be very revealing. Look for the following:

- Is the site well run?
- Is the site clean and tidy?
- Are the workmen sharp and getting on with their tasks?
- Is the workmanship of high quality?
- Are there plans and schedules hanging neatly on the wall?
- Does the site look safe?
- Is the foreman or main builder calm?
- Is there a good atmosphere with happy banter between the tradesmen?
- Did the builder proudly show you a particular piece of work he's thrilled with?
- Is there good attention to detail?
- Is the finishing at a high level?

Get help from those who've had builders in before

If you are still feeling nervous, which is totally understandable, why not ask a family member or friend who have had builders in before to come round and meet the builder? He or she can ask some questions that are probably more informed.

Get your friend or parent's opinion on the builder you are keen on hiring. If they have any misgivings, they can share them with you before you make your decision.

Better still, employing a trusted builder who has done a lot of work for your parents or a friend is a good idea. He will want to do the job well to keep in with a valued customer (your parents or friend), and if he gets it right, he can add you to his list of regular clients too.

Your building requirements

There are a number of questions you can ask yourself to help work out the best builder for the job, how much input you might want to make and how to focus more specifically on what you actually want to do.

- What do I want to do?
- When do I want to do it?
- Does the builder have a good reputation?
- How much do I have to spend?
- Will I use brand names?
- Are there cheaper alternatives I could use?
- Will I do some of the work myself, or get help from friends?
- How much time do I realistically have to carry out any work myself?
- Is there a deadline for the work?

Decisions, decisions, decisions

Don't be scared about making decisions. Some problems tend to solve themselves as you go along, anyhow, and others are easily solvable if you go one step at a time.

Tell yourself these decisions are not all that different from making decisions about having work carried out on the car, planning a holiday and buying furniture and furnishings for your home. At the end of the day, you know how much you have to spend and what you want to accomplish. There are risks involved, but you can manage these risks.

Be positive and calm in your decision-making. I find most problems occur when a novice is trying to do everything in a rush at the last minute. If you need to decide what kind of sink you want to put into the bathroom, for instance, don't try to do it the day before the builder needs the sink. You'll make the decision in a state of panic, and it is usually those hasty decisions that tend to go wrong.

Although things can sometimes go awry, you need to stand by your decisions. The trick is not to get upset and jump up and down. It's good to make your point known, but you're better off saving your energy to communicate with the builder to come up with a mutual solution to a problem.

Remind yourself that uncovering an unexpected difficulty is not necessarily the builder's fault. How was he to know that lurking below the carpet were rotting floorboards, particularly if you hadn't got him in earlier to take up some of the carpet to take a look? Be reasonable and realistic, and often, you will find that a solution to a problem can be quite creative, and not all that expensive either.

One-off tradesmen, or a building team?

A lot depends on the size and complexity of the job, but you will have to decide whether you opt for hiring separate one-off tradesmen (a plumber, an electrician, a plasterer, for example) and manage bringing them in at the right time yourself. Or, do you employ a builder who brings in his own tradesmen when they're needed?

One-off tradesmen

- It can be cheaper getting individual tradesmen (a plumber, electrician, carpenter, painter) to come in and do their bit if the job is simple, but a lot relies on them actually arriving on the day they said they'd turn up.

- The other downside is it gives the tradesmen the opportunity to blame one another when things don't happen.
- But, going down the individual tradesmen route does work; the job just generally takes longer.

A building team
- There's a lot to be said for getting in a building team – a builder with all of his tradesmen. The builder can manage the team, so you don't need to worry about who will turn up when.
- Going down this route can possibly cost more, although you might argue that it is worth having someone else manage the individual tradesmen. Also, with a building team you aren't paying each tradesman by the hour. If it takes them longer to do something, this isn't your problem.
- With a team of people in place who've worked with one another before, this should be the quicker route to get the work finished.

Getting a quote from a builder

Before you select anyone, I'd get quotes from at least three builders after you give them a straightforward brief about what you want them to do.

The wording of builders' quotes can be misleading, so be careful. Some builders only quote for the bare bones of the work, or exclude VAT, to make their quote appear to be the lowest. This usually means they will ask for more cash for those extras later on that you could argue should have been in the quote in the first place. So, don't be put off by a more expensive quote that includes everything. In these circumstances, often the middle quote is the most fair and realistic.

Getting a quote from a builder or tradesman is straightforward, but knowing the psychology behind how builders operate can be useful. Often, small jobs are not worth a builder's while. They can see right away how long a job will take and how much materials will cost. Your house might take an hour to get to, and then it's another hour for the builder to get home again. On top of that, they have to order materials and pick them up, so that's another hour gone. Your job might take only an hour to do, but the builder has to charge you for three hours, and this doesn't include anything towards his fuel, insurance, tools or profit.

For small jobs then, you might be better off hunting down a good local handyman, who can turn his hands to most things and is happy to get paid for only a few hours at a time.

Another suggestion is to use a handyman or individual good at one or two particular things when you need their services. I use a wonderful electrician, for instance, who often comes in the evenings or weekends after he's finished his main day job working with a larger building company. He's happy to spend a couple of hours fixing any problems before he goes home. This works for small remedial tasks, but perhaps might not be ideal for large and more complex jobs.

I'd also make sure you include simple demands, such as getting the builders to tidy up a bit at the end of the day (especially if you are living in your property when the work is being carried out).

Don't pay over the odds: striking a bargain with your builder

Building work on your home is a service purchase, just like any other. There is evidence from consumer surveys that many people pay too much for building work because they don't shop around and don't search for the best deal.

The bigger the job, the bigger possible overpayments, because builders' quotes vary and often, homeowners (especially those getting work done for the first time) don't bargain with builders to reduce costs.

A recent survey revealed big differences in quoted prices for basic building work. There were regional differences among the 245 builders across the UK that were called upon to quote for a simple three-sided brick dustbin enclosure.

The lowest quote was £346 less than the highest quote, and the majority of builders (66%) did not include VAT (value added tax, which currently is 20%) in their quotes. This is a standard trick, as I mentioned in the section on getting builders' quotes, making the quote look far cheaper than those that did include VAT.

The study also found homeowners often tended to take the first quote they got and didn't shop around for better deals. Very few bothered to play one quote off another to drive for a better deal. If you want to get the best deal:

- Never assume the first price quoted is the lowest you can get, and always get at least three different tradesmen to quote.
- Never assume that a builder's first offer is the final offer.
- Be prepared to haggle with your chosen builder, including telling him what others have quoted to bring the price down.
- Always talk with some previous clients of the builder to be reassured about the quality of work and service reliability.
- Itemise all of the work details in writing, specifying the standards expected, cost of materials and labour and the timeframe for the work.
- Always insist on VAT being written into the agreement.
- Never hand out cash before delivery. Hand over the money at the beginning of each stage, and as the builder needs it for **your** job.
- Always insist on a receipt for every payment, especially when you hand over cash.

Get references for a builder

It's important to get references for a builder as well. The reference could be as simple as: 'Here's a letter from Mrs Jones over the road, who was really happy with our work.' If that's the case, make sure you hot foot it round to Mrs Jones to ask her what she thought of the builder and the quality of the work, and you can take a good look at what her house looks like.

Or, you could ask for more detailed or professional-looking references, although often, simple and straightforward local references are more useful.

A colleague of mine managed to find a treasure of a builder after he peered curiously through the window of a neighbouring property. He thought, 'That looks great and I want to do something similar', so he rang the bell and introduced himself to his new neighbour.

She was only too happy to show him around her home and recommended her excellent builder. She even provided information about where she bought her ceramic tiles and gave him tips on what she would do differently next time round (which essentially was his project now).

We're all very envious he's had such an easy ride with his new builder, but he was just carrying out good local research, which netted such good results.

Is your builder insured?

More demanding projects do require properly insured builders (public liability insurance is a must in case there are any accidents), so check what level insurance each of the builders has.

What is public liability insurance?

Public liability insurance covers the workmen, or anyone else on the property, from a personal injury claim or property damage. There are different levels of cover, typically from £1 million to £5 million, covering all of the different trades.

Do ask the builder if he is properly insured and has public liability cover. It is reassuring for you, the builder and his team to know that if there is an accident or damage caused at some point, his insurance company will pay up.

I would suggest that you ask whomever you employ whether they have any insurance at all. Even if the job is a small one, it is comforting to know there is some insurance cover if something does go off beam.

PHIL'S TOP TIP

Make sure your insurance company is aware of the building works that are being carried out on your property. If something goes wrong and you haven't informed the insurers, they might be reluctant to part with any money.

Contracts and agreements

It is a good idea, and crucial I think for a larger job, to have some form of contract or agreement with your builder. The contract could be as simple as listing the items you want the builder to deal with, or a more detailed breakdown of the project.

A good starting point is asking someone else you trust who has had building work carried out what they did. If your friend could lend you the contract or agreement he drew up with his builder, you could copy it and use it as a basis or template for your own document.

There are some brilliant websites with contract formats you can download for free, which I think can be very helpful. Two of these websites are: www.fmb.org.uk (the Federation of Master Builders' site), and building-contract.co.uk. You can tailor your contract accordingly, as you might not need all the categories that are listed.

PHIL'S TOP TIP

The more detail you can put into writing, the less room there is for miscommunication with your builder. Don't expect him to be a mind reader. He's not the magician Derren Brown, so why should he know what's in your head?

Make sure you set out the following in the contract or agreement:

- An itemised breakdown of all of the work you want the builder to do
- Any specific instructions relating to individual items, such as a certain sliding door you want in the living room, or the type of paint you have chosen
- The timescale (also known as the project schedule) and anticipated finish date, if appropriate
- The agreed fee for doing the work (make sure you include VAT)
- The terms you have agreed for the builder to be paid for any extra work, or an over-run (this could be an hourly rate, or you could negotiate as you go along)
- You might want to put in a penalty clause if the builder doesn't finish on time (although a good builder might take umbrage at this and it could case bad feelings from the start)
- If you have agreed on a specialist to carry out any of the work, then put this into the agreement as well

CASE STUDY

LEARN TO LOVE YOUR BUILDER

In a smart Cheshire town, first-time buyers Valerie and Roger Casey wanted to add a £35,000 extension to their new house. They found their builder listed in the phone book, and although the Caseys were thrilled with his work early on, unfortunately they fell out with the builder partway through the job.

Despite recognising that jobs often run over, Roger, a chef in a nearby hotel, says, 'We were really upset that what was believed to take about three months still wasn't completed after nearly seven months. It was dreadful. The drains were uncovered, which was smelly and dangerous, the windows leaked and our builder disappeared. We hadn't seen him in six weeks and he didn't answer our calls.'

Roger admits that perhaps the couple never really built up a trusting relationship with the builder – 'We were always leaning on him and didn't always listen to him properly, to be honest' – and that finding a builder in the phone book without any recommendations or references was possibly a bit foolhardy. 'We should have been tipped off, I guess, when we asked to see some examples of the builder's work and he was reluctant to show us.'

The most important thing would have been to talk to other people the builder had worked for, Valerie, a human resources manager, suggests, 'But we were both under a lot of stress and didn't get round to it. We should have asked them whether there were any problems, but it's a bit late for that now.'

The Caseys have since employed another builder to finish off the work, and have been more rigorous this time round. 'We asked for references, saw an earlier job he carried out in the next town and really thrashed everything out with him. He's doing a great job, so hopefully, we won't be suffering any of the mistakes from last time,' Roger adds.

His advice to other first-time buyers in the same situation? 'Don't be nervous just because you haven't employed a builder before. And don't nod your head sagely when you don't have a clue what the builder's on about. It can get you into hot water, like it did with us'.

And where did the Caseys find their new builder? This time they talked to their neighbours and friends, one of whom came up with the contact number for the builder. Word of mouth makes all the difference when choosing the right person for the job.

PHIL'S TOP TIPS

FOR A FIRST-TIME BUILDING PROJECT

- **Manage the project**

  Set out the terms of the contract, when you are paying what and the project schedule.

- **Fix the price for the job**

  Don't offer to pay an hourly or a daily rate, unless the job is very small. If you opt for a fixed price, you can say, 'I want that amount of work done for that amount of money in that amount of time'. It's totally straightforward and everyone knows the boundaries.

- **Manage your money throughout the build**

  It's not just about having a budget and spending it. It's about spending it in the right way. A good reference is *The Architects' Guide* published by RIBA (Royal Institute of British Architects, architect.com), which outlines what's expected of the homeowner and how best to manage your funds.

- **Brief your builder properly**

  Otherwise, the builder will nod politely and just try to work it out as he goes along. Ultimately, you'll be disappointed – and so will he. And, you could find yourself paying for costly mistakes.

- **Have a contingency (emergency) fund of at least 10%**

  Every time the builder mentions a figure, it's a good idea to mentally add on an extra 10%. Hopefully, you won't need to spend all of the contingency fund, but it is best to be prepared, as things happen and costs creep up.

- **Make as many choices about design as you can before the builders arrive on site**

  If you can make your decisions during the planning stage, the project will be less stressful and probably more cost-effective.

Once you start changing your mind it will cost time and money, two things a builder working at a fixed rate hates. You're also handing the builder an easy way to up his prices: 'Of course, you can have that, mate, but I'll have to charge you more.'

- **You don't need to buy all of the sanitary ware for the bathrooms and appliances for the kitchen instantly**
  But, do remember that the size of the toilet or fridge, for instance, can have a knock-on effect as to how big a space needs to be to accommodate an item, or how big the pipes will need to be connected to a sink.

- **Do your research as early as possible**
  It takes time browsing the Internet and visiting shops and showrooms. Rushing around at the last minute won't contribute hugely to the project.

- **Spend money in the right places**
  Use your common sense and spend money on a new boiler, rewiring and the plumbing. Upgrade the boiler instead of installing a sauna. Get the heart of the house in shape and the rest will follow.

- **Communicate well with your builder**
  Unless you can afford to pay an architect or project manager to look after the building work, I think you need to be on site as often as you can (at least twice a week). This doesn't mean turning up to yell at workmen and throw your weight around. If you treat your builder and his crew properly, they'll respond in kind. You want them to respect you and feel enthusiastic about the job, rather than dreading being there – and you.

- **Keep the builders on their toes**
  Pick up quickly on things that aren't right (using the wrong colour mortar, or putting a window in the wrong place). It's far cheaper sorting out problems right away, instead of having to tear things out to rectify difficulties later on.

- **Really listen to your builder**

  If there's a reasonable cause for delay – maybe a delivery of materials has been held up, or the taps you want are out of stock – you might need to expect the job to take longer, and even pay him more money for something that isn't his fault in some instances.

- **Be picky about the finish**

  If you make a builder do those final important touches too fast, you'll probably be unhappy with the finer detail. There's nothing worse than paying for a job and then having to get it done all again a few years later, because you pushed the workmen too hard first time round and the result wasn't good.

- **Allow some extra time at the end of the job**

  Just as you have to budget an extra 10% for most building work, you also need to allocate more time (usually, it takes a third longer than you originally scheduled for a large job) to realistically finish everything off.

- **At the end of the job, hold back a minimum of 5% until you compile a snagging list**

  If you've employed an architect, he will look after the snagging (a list of small problems that need to be rectified by the builder before you'll sign off on the job) for you. Make sure you include the 5% holdback in the contract, so the builder knows he won't be paid the final instalment until he sorts out all of the glitches you've discovered. This applies mainly to larger jobs.

- **Even though you think you've seen the last of the builders…**

  …you might well see them again in six months' time once everything has settled in. Small cracks can appear in the paintwork, due to changing temperatures. This is common, so don't panic. A good builder will get his decorator to touch up the cracks. If he won't return to sort things out, you've got every right to get someone else in and pay him from the 5% of the money you've kept hold of for the snagging.

BUILDING CHECKLIST

- [ ] Work out whether you're doing all (or some of) the work, or whether you need a builder
- [ ] Find an architect, if required
- [ ] Get quotes from three builders
- [ ] Find a builder (or individual tradesmen)
- [ ] Fix a price
- [ ] Check out the builder and get references
- [ ] Make sure the builder has insurance
- [ ] Brief the builder
- [ ] Draw up a contract with the builder
- [ ] Sort the basics first: plumbing, electrics, boiler, flooring, etc
- [ ] Have a contingency fund of 10% for emergencies
- [ ] Hold back 5% for snagging (sorting out problems at the end of the job)

PHIL'S CONTACTS BOOK

- Royal Institute of British Architects (RIBA) – 020 7580 5533, architecture.com
- Royal Institution of Chartered Surveyors (RICS) – 0870 333 1600, www.rics.org
- Federation of Master Builders (FMB) – 0800 015 2522 www.fmb.org.uk
- The Guild of Master Craftsmen – 01273 478449, www.guildmc.com
- Building-contract.co.uk – useful website with free contract templates
- The Building Skills Academy – 01635 52207, www.buildingskillsacademy.co.uk
- Planning Inspectorate – 0117 372 6372 (England), 029 2082 3866 (Wales), www.planning-inspectorate.gov.uk

- Planning Portal – www.planningportal.gov.uk
- Royal Town Planning Institute – 020 7960 5663, rtpiconsultants.co.uk

CHAPTER TWELVE

Selling Your Home

You've been a first-time buyer – chances are that in the not-too distant future you're going to be a first-time seller too...

Most first-time buyers don't really think of becoming first-time sellers. But, one day you will want to move on to the next property when you've outgrown your first home. Circumstances change – you need to move for a job, a partner has moved in, a child has arrived – marking that cosy flat or small cottage even cosier.

You should really think about how you will sell from the start. I know it's hard to get your head around selling a property when you're going through the anxious task of buying a first home. Yet, you should ask some simple questions about how you will sell the property. You might need, or want to, sell it on in a hurry for various reasons and this saleability factor should be one of the buying criteria.

What the buyer wants

A good idea is to put yourself in the buyer's shoes for a moment. It's probably safe to assume that the buyer of your first property will be similar to you: a single person or young couple just starting out, an older person or couple buying a first home or perhaps a young family moving into their first place.

And yet, just because you like your first property, will someone else like it too? You need to ask a set of questions identifying what concerns the next owner could have. Would he want to:

- Live on a busy road?
- Listen to Tube or train rumble?
- Reside in a basement flat that could attract burglars?
- Climb several sets of stairs to a top-floor flat (if there's no lift)?
- Live in an ex-council property?
- Live on a big estate without any character?
- Be more than 10 minutes away from a transport link (bus stop, train or Tube station)?
- Live near a green space (a park, common or woodland)?

But, if your home isn't in an ideal spot close to transport or close to greenery, don't panic. In this chapter I'll show how you (and the agent) can point out its positive points.

First steps to selling a home

While a few people choose to market and sell their property themselves, it's not something I would advise you to do. Real estate agents are vastly more experienced than the average person at selling homes, and can act as a buffer between you and your potential buyers, as well as negotiate the best price for your house.

What does an agent do?

- Carry out a valuation of your property
- Put together the sales particulars with photographs
- Advertise your property in the local, and sometimes national, press, online and perhaps in specialist magazines (a period property in *Country Life* magazine, for example)
- Send letters or emails to interested applicants
- Make appointments and conduct viewings for potential buyers
- Negotiate the selling price
- Help manage the sale until it completes

Choosing an estate agent

Before you troop into the offices of any of your local estate agents, I would advise looking on the Internet first to get an idea of:

- Who is selling homes in your area
- What level of property (low, mid or high end) they are selling
- What price they are selling at

Also, check out how many properties similar to yours are for sale, and for roughly how much.

Armed with these facts, go and talk to the agents that you think deal with your type of home within the price bracket for your property. There's no point talking to a very high-end estate agent about your humble studio flat, for instance.

I would recommend you talk to at least three agents. Get those you get on with and that you think could do the job of selling your home round to see the property. Ask the agents to value it and tell you how they intend to sell your home to get the best possible price.

Which agent (or agents) should I choose?

Choosing an agent is very subjective. Some people get on better with one agent over another, and some prefer different selling methods to others. Here are my tips on what to look for in an estate agent:

- Find someone you can trust.
- The agent's office should be clean and orderly.
- Make sure there is enough staff to do the job.
- The staff should be friendly and helpful.
- An agency with its own website, and that advertises property on other websites (such as, Findaproperty, Rightmove, Primelocation and Findanewhome for new homes).
- Make sure the agent is a member of a professional body (the National Association of Estate Agents, Royal Institution of

Chartered Surveyors or The Guild of Professional Estate Agents). All agents are bound by the Estate Agents Act 1979, whether they belong to a trade organisation or not

- Someone who is confident, but not too cocky
- Someone who knows the area well
- Enthusiasm for the job
- Honesty when dealing with you and the buyers
- A flexible agency that remains open in the evenings and on the weekends to show buyers your home

Selling methods: sole, joint or multiple agents

There are three different ways to sell a property through an estate agent or agents. You can choose an agent as your:

- Sole agent (the only agent you employ)
- Joint sole agents (two estate agents market the property and split the fee)
- Multiple agents (you employ two or more agents)

Sole agent

Pros
- The agent's commission will be lower (about 2% plus VAT).
- With only one agent, it is easier to monitor what happens (for instance, when the market is taken off the market when it's under offer).
- The sole agent could be more motivated, as you've just chosen him.

Cons
- You sign a contract for a period of time with only one agent (typically, four to six weeks, although you can negotiate).
- If you're not happy with the service, you have to wait until the

contracted period is up before you can switch or take on any
more agents.

Joint sole agents

Pros
- With two agents, your chances are doubled of finding a buyer.
- With two agents competing against one another, it could spur
  them on to find a buyer (and beat the other agent).

Cons
- An agent might put in less effort if he feels the other agent could
  come up with a buyer first.
- The winning agent has to split his fee with an agent who may
  have done very little.

Multiple agents

Pros
- With several agents, more people get to see your property.
- Despite all the effort several agents are putting in, you only have
  to pay the agent that sells your home.

Cons
- You have to deal with two or more estate agents.
- Having several agents could make you look desperate,
  suggesting the house has a problem or it is overpriced.
- The commission is higher (about 3.5% plus VAT).
- The property could appear on different agent websites at
  different prices, confusing potential buyers.

Agent's commission

Before you've selected your agent (or agents) and the method of selling,
you can negotiate on the commission. It is good to see what sort of deal

the agent is willing to strike with regards to the level of commission. At the same time, don't be too aggressive in getting the commission down. If you've driven a very hard bargain and the commission is very low, the agent will have little incentive to sell your property.

PHIL'S TOP TIP

Another idea is to incentivise the agent. You could say, for instance, 'If you sell my property for more than £300,000, I will offer you a £500 bonus on top of the commission.' This is perfectly legitimate and might just give the agent that added spark to market your place with gusto.

Negotiate the contract

After choosing your agent (or agents), you will need to work out the contract with the agent. I would advise not putting your property on for too long with any one agent. Try to get the agent to agree to the minimum period – usually, four weeks.

If you are pleased with the agent's efforts – gauged generally by the number and quality of viewers he has sent round to see your home – you can extend the contract further. And if you're not satisfied with the service thus far, you don't have to renew the contract. You can then talk to other agents about giving them a contract to sell your property.

What's my home worth?

It's a common misconception that a seller should simply choose the agent that comes up with the highest price for the property. Although it's flattering to be told your home is worth more than you imagined, there's a lot more to selling a place than slapping a high price tag on it.

It can be puzzling, especially for a first-time seller, working out what the value of a property might be, as you probably discovered when you were buying your home. An accurate valuation involves taking a long, hard, objective look at a property, and takes into account:

- Supply and demand – more eager buyers than sellers out there pushes up prices, and, of course, the reverse is true. Know the market.
- How quickly the seller wants to move – the faster you want to get on, the lower the price to spur on a fast sale.
- Improvements that have been made by the seller, which add to the value of the home (high-value improvements include adding an extra bedroom or bathroom, loft conversion or extension).

So, how does an agent value a property?

Agents normally value a home by making comparisons (they call it 'comparables') with recent sales of similar homes in the neighbourhood. There can be a conflict between the need for an agent to win business and coming up with a sensible price. Greed can get the better of many a seller, with a number of agents overpricing.

A good agent probably has a pretty good idea of the value of a property. Pricing to get the business, however, often has nothing to do with reality. Yet there are different tricks to selling, not all of them involving high prices. For instance, sometimes putting a property on at a lower price will attract more viewers through the door, which can push the price up if viewers start bidding against each other.

Whatever price an agent comes up with needs to be examined. Ask the agent:

- How he arrived at the price?
- Has he pitched it high or low?
- What marketing techniques has he in mind related to pricing?
- How many sales has he made over the last three months, and at what price?

PHIL'S TRADE SECRET: SETTING THE PRICE
A trick of the trade is to think of two figures – the lowest figure you are willing to accept and the perfect price you would ideally like to achieve for your home. Most buyers like to be able to knock something off the asking price, so somewhere between the low and high figures might be about right.

The danger of pricing too high

Be careful of pricing too high. The problem is that reducing the price later if the property doesn't sell can make it appear flawed. And reducing the value by small amounts slowly can be agonising, as the property will be hanging around on the market for far too long. Buyers will steer clear of the property altogether, assuming there's something terribly wrong with it, or it was hugely overpriced in the first place, reducing trust in the seller and agent.

What's included in the sale

You need to think about what fixtures and fittings you are prepared to leave behind for the new owner. First of all, it's important to understand the difference between a fixture and a fitting.

- A **fixture** is an item permanently fastened to the property and is regarded as part of the property. For instance, fitted carpets, wooden flooring and fittings screwed to walls are usually identified as fixtures. If you remove them, they would leave marks on the walls and could even significantly damage the building.
- A **fitting** is an item that is easily removable, such as a chair, sofa or table.

Typically, most fixtures are left behind. This can be used as a bargaining tool when negotiating the sale. If you don't want to take your carpets and curtains, you can be seen to be generously throwing them into the sale, while perhaps the buyer (possibly a first-time purchaser like you were recently) will appreciate being given these extras. Don't be upset, however, if the buyer declines your seemingly kind offer.

Your solicitor will send you a 'fixtures, fittings and contents form' and to save arguments later on, you should fill in as accurately as possible what you intend to leave behind and take away with you. There can be grey areas when it comes to defining fixtures and fittings – are shelves and curtain rails fixtures or fittings, for example – so it is sensible to be as clear as possible to save falling out with your buyer at a later stage.

Energy Performance Certificate

Remember these? I said on page 156 that you should ask to see the property's Energy Performance Certificate (EPC) when you're interested in a property, and now that you've come to see your home you (or your agent) will need to order an EPC before you start marketing the property. The EPC must be available for potential buyers to examine at the earliest opportunity, and certainly before the exchange of contracts. The EPC is held at the estate agent's office and any buyer can ask to see it. As I said earlier, an Energy Performance Certificate explains how energy efficient the property is and indicates how your home could be moved up a bracket, or more, to conserve energy.

The EPC used to be part of the home information pack, but the rest of the pack has been jettisoned. The exception to the rule is Scotland, where the EPC is part of the Home Pack, or Home Report.

An EPC costs from about £30 and there are a number of firms (some useful websites include epc.direct.gov.uk and www.energy-performance-certificates.org) that send people to your home to carry out an energy-efficiency check.

They are looking for energy-saving measures, such as double glazing, central heating and good insulation. You get a tick for every good energy measure and the results are calculated on a computer model to determine an energy grading for the house.

It's a moot point whether a poor EPC would actually stop someone buying your property. And yet, I suspect an eco-friendly home with lower utility bills could be more attractive in the future if energy costs rise further.

Marketing information

The next stage is to give the estate agent information about your home that he can use to write up what is called the 'particulars'.

This could be as simple as a brief description of your property with a picture, or as complicated as a glossy brochure with a number of colour photographs. As your property is likely to be at the lower to mid end of the scale, the agent probably won't recommend compiling an expensive brochure. It is important the agent uses the information and pictures to advertise your home on his and other websites, too.

The written details should include:

- What your property is (one- or two-bedroom; rural or city centre; terrace, semi-detached or detached)
- The number of bedrooms
- The number of bathrooms
- The number of reception rooms (living room, drawing room, sitting room)
- Extra rooms, such as a study, nursery, playroom, dining room, snug, media room, hall or conservatory
- Any outside buildings, spaces or structures (barn, garage, shed, greenhouse, carport, parking space, pool, tennis court, stables)

- Price — **asking price**: a definitive price

  guide price: a suggested price for buyers

  in the region of: a price bracket, from £150,000– 165,000, for example

  offers over, or **in excess of**: the seller will only consider prices offered over a certain level (for instance, offers over £350,000 means offers only over that amount)
- Floor plan
- Square footage (it might be in square metres too)
- High-resolution colour photographs (preferably, an exterior shot and a couple of interior views)
- Virtual tour – a video tour of your home is generally reserved for the top of the market, but it might be worth considering if your property is unusual or a niche property (a rare Arts & Crafts or highly contemporary home, for instance)

You will want the agent to show you the written details, floor plan and photographs, and he shouldn't hand anything out to anyone until he gets your approval first.

Check that the agent has:

- Portrayed your property fairly and accurately, but in the best light possible
- Emphasised any outstanding features (such as an original Victorian fireplace), off-street parking (in a driveway or underground car park) or the fact that there's a garden
- Emphasised practical information, including close proximity to good travel links and ample storage
- Used good colour photographs shot while the sun was shining
- Provided the correct measurements of the property for the floor plan

Viewings

If there's a shortage of your type of property and high demand from buyers, don't be surprised if your property doesn't get as far as having particulars and web links produced for it before viewers start coming round. Your agent should have a database of potential buyers who have registered already and are keen to have a property like yours. It's a good sign that the agent knows what he's doing if he insists on getting people around right away.

Whenever possible, let the agent conduct the viewings. I think it's more professional to let a trained agent show people your property. The potential buyer will feel more relaxed not having the homeowner present and they can talk to the agent more candidly. If you do have to be there (maybe you work from home), be polite and say hello, but then let the agent get on with his job carrying out the viewing. Resist the temptation to extol the virtues of your home or ask the person viewing what they think of it.

Preparing your home for viewings

A lot has been written about how you should bake bread and light scented candles so wonderful smells drift around the house. Personally, I think these are gimmicks that will make the buyer wonder if you are hiding something terrible, such as a blocked sewer or mildew growing somewhere.

The key thing is to make sure the house is as spotless as you can get it. There's nothing worse than a dirty property, which totally puts people off. Always make sure loos and sinks are sparkling clean, beds are neatly made and the children's toys or any other items are tidied away. I know this can be hard to do before every viewing, but it is very important.

De-cluttering a house isn't a ploy. Losing as much heavy furniture, piles of old newspapers and unwanted paraphernalia is a fantastic idea. It not only makes your property look light and bright, but less clutter also gives the effect that your property is roomy and airy.

Instant de-clutter tips

- Hide toys in colourful toy boxes or secrete them under your child's duvet (a duvet looks lumpy anyhow, so no one will be the wiser).
- Put large items, such as a pushchair, bicycle or golf clubs, in the back of the car to free up space.
- Store newspapers and magazines in attractive boxes or smart magazine racks.
- Conceal shoes, extra duvets and pillows on top of wardrobes or under beds.
- Make sure towels are hung in an orderly fashion in bathrooms.
- Remove and store items (such as the food processor, ice-cream maker and bread machine) that you don't use daily from the kitchen counter.
- Although some personal items make the place look homely, put away some photographs and children's drawings to give a sense of neatness.

PHIL'S TOP TIP

If a potential buyer comes to see your home at night, make sure the house is warm, lit well and has the right atmosphere. An open blazing fire (if you have a fireplace) and soft music playing won't appear to be such a gimmick, as you could be legitimately relaxing at the end of the day.

My house isn't selling: what do I do?

Whatever you do, don't panic. All you need is one person to cross the threshold and fall in love with the place. If you are concerned, you must talk to the estate agent and ask him for any advice on what you could do to tempt a buyer into making an offer.

Here are some other tips that might help too:

- Lower the price. If you aren't getting much interest, perhaps your property is overpriced. If it comes down in price a bit, you could attract a new group of buyers.
- Ask friends and family what they think you can do to make your home more inviting. They are likely to be less polite than an agent who needs your business.
- Check out what I call the 'kerb appeal': how your home looks when people approach it for the first time. As those first seconds when they first turn up are all-important, look at it with fresh eyes. Trim the hedge, mow the lawn, fix the gate, paint the front door and put out some nicely planted pots of flowers. It can make all the difference.
- Offer the agent new photographs of the property, or ask him to take some more. If the spring bulbs have come up since you put your home on the market, or you've managed to paint the windowsills, it could appear brighter. Even if you don't change the photos on the particulars, you can at least put new pictures up on the agent's and other websites.

Other ways to sell

Selling at auction
If you want to be rid of something a bit out of the ordinary, in need of modernisation or anything else that's hard to value, selling at auction might be a good option. Other pluses for a seller include:

- It's an easy way to sell
- It's quick – as soon as the hammer falls, the deal is done
- Competing buyers can push the price up as they bid against each other

How to sell at auction

The whole process of selling at auction is very straight-forward. The auction house will value the property and recommend a 'guide price'. Photographs and details will be gathered together for the auction catalogue – a booklet that lists all the 'lots' (properties) for sale. This is issued to prospective buyers about three to four weeks before the auction, and gives buyers time to view your property and arrange surveys.

You might not always make much money, however. By the time you pay the auction house its commission (about 2.5% of the sale price) and a sum to put your property into the cata-logue (about £300–1,500), there might not be a great deal more profit than if you'd sold through down the more tradi-tional route with an estate agent (known as 'private treaty').

Sale by tender

Another alternative is 'sale by tender': estate agents can ask buyers to send in written competitive bids for a property, and the agent can help a seller choose the best bid. The best bid might not be the highest one, as you want someone who can painlessly complete the deal as soon as possible.

Accepting an offer

It's always puzzling, especially for a first-time seller, when you get an offer right away on your home. Is it because you've priced it too low, so someone is snapping it up straightaway? Should you leave it on the market a bit longer to see if someone offers more? These are questions that could haunt you for some time.

Ask your agent for guidance, obviously. You could accept the offer with the proviso that the buyer sells his property within a certain time limit (say, six to eight weeks).

I've also seen sellers keep the property on the market with the verbal promise (it's only verbal, so it's not official) that if someone else makes an offer they'll let the original interested buyer know. I think it's good to be kind to people who show interest, but if you can hold out for a while you might find someone willing to put in a higher offer.

Once you do accept an offer, your property is now 'under offer' and a sign to this effect (or a 'sold' sign) could be erected on your property. You see 'under offer' banners across homes on property websites too.

First-time sellers can get very excited at this stage, but remember, the deal has not been done yet. There is nothing official about the sale until contracts have been exchanged.

Accepting an offer: what happens next

After you accept the offer, you need to contact your solicitor so he can start the conveyancing process. He will be:

- Getting 'office copy entries' (a copy of the deeds for unregistered properties)
- Getting the title deeds for the property
- Sending proof of the title to the buyer's solicitor, to show you are the owner of the property
- Answering what are known as 'preliminary enquiries' from the buyer's solicitor
- Preparing the contract
- Getting everything in place for you to sign the contract
- Exchanging contracts with the buyer's solicitor

The mortgage valuation

The next step is for the buyer's lender (if the buyer needs a mortgage) to send out someone to value your property. The lender will book an appointment, and the valuer will check that your home is worth the amount of money that is being loaned.

The valuation could be anything as simple as a 'drive by' (they literally come and look at front of the property and don't go inside) valuation through to a more detailed examination. If the property's hard to value, the valuation might take a bit more time.

Some buyers might want a survey carried out too. This is when a surveyor comes round to look at the structure and at various items, such as whether there's any damp, dry or wet rot, and any other defects that could affect the price – or the actual sale itself. He could turn up with a ladder (to check out the roof and the guttering) and a damp meter to check for damp, so don't be alarmed by his tools of the trade.

Is no news good news? What to do if you hear nothing

In my opinion being met with a wall of silence from the buyer and/or his solicitor usually isn't good news. The property could have been valued below the agreed sale price after the surveyor spotted some defects and the buyer could be getting cold feet.

This is the time to get your solicitor to chase up the buyer's solicitor to find out what is going on and what he can do to help speed up the process. Miscommunication has scuppered many a sale, so talking to the other side is a wise idea.

Of course, the buyer might have eyed up another property and he's hedging his bets. If the buyer pulls out because they fancy another place there isn't a great deal you can do. In your favour is the fact that the buyer will already have to pay legal fees and money spent on a valuation and/or survey, so pointing out the financial losses might make the buyer reconsider.

Renegotiating the price

Of course, the buyer could come back and offer a reduced price. If this happens, I would get the buyer to justify why they want to offer less and hopefully, your solicitor can carry out negotiations with the buyer's solicitor to keep things on track.

If you think you are about to lose the sale, you could renegotiate the price downwards – a difficult step, I know, when you're upset and annoyed. However, if something has come up from the survey that shows that the buyer could be justified in asking for a reduction, you might have to swallow your pride and consider negotiating. In one case, I remember a buyer's solicitor discovering plans for a possible rail link just behind the property. Wearing my house finder's hat, I had to advise the buyer to offer less as there was a risk that these plans could one day go ahead.

Once your solicitor has gathered all the facts, you will need to find a way to negotiate, working out a suitable compromise if you still want the sale to proceed. It pays to stay calm and reasonable, even if you're not feeling very reasonable at the time. You can suggest sharing the costs of a problem as well – maybe offering to pay half of a £1,000 estimate to fix the roof, for instance.

Exchange of contracts

Much of the information in chapter 7 also applies here, so do take the time to read over it again. I would like to reiterate that it's important that you keep on top of your solicitor and make sure that they aren't holding up the sale.

And make sure that you don't hold up the sale either – do be forthcoming with any further information that the buyer's solicitor wants.

Completion day

Most completions go ahead without any disasters. But sometimes, money is delayed somewhere in the chain (someone doesn't receive money for the sale of his house down the line, causing a knock-on effect), but this is rare. Here's what to expect on completion day:

- You leave a set of keys to your property with your estate agent or solicitor to hand them over to the buyer once all the money has been received. Sometimes, you will hand the keys directly to the buyer, depending on what's been agreed. But, do not hand the keys over until your solicitor confirms that it's okay (no matter how much the buyer begs you, because the money might not have been transferred yet).

- A time will have been agreed (usually about mid-day or early afternoon) when you will have to be out of the property.
- You must take all of your possessions out of the property by this agreed time. If you're struggling for some reason (maybe the removal van was delayed, or you have more belongings than you realised), you might be able to leave some of your things locked in the garage, or a similar space, until the following day. Remember, you have to get the new owner's permission for this arrangement.

CASE STUDY

FIRST-TIME SELLING NEEDN'T BE STRESSFUL

After four years in a starter studio flat in St Albans, Simi Bond knew it was time to move on. 'I loved my little home my mum jokingly called it my "cosy cupboard" – but despite its diminutive size, it was ideal for me,' she explains.

Simi, who works in finance, said the small, but orderly, studio eventually became too cramped, however, especially when Simi got engaged and her fiancé was spending more time with her.

'A studio is not really meant for two people,' admits Simi, 'and the situation wasn't helped by the fact that I'd accumulated quite a bit of stuff since I moved in. I had a pair of skis and my suitcases tucked along the wall by the fold-up bed, which my fiancé complained about. He found himself tripping over them all of the time, but there wasn't really anywhere else to keep them. And, I won't even go into the piles of books on the floor, and my make-up and toiletries that were spilling out of the minute bathroom cupboard.'

It was time to sell, so Simi decided to put her much-loved first home onto the market. 'I walked past a couple of estate agents when I went to the station every day to get the train into London, so one day I left the office a bit early to get back to St Albans and check them out.'

Simi talked to three agents on her way home and gathered up important information, such as how much commission the agents charged and whether there was demand currently for a property like hers. She also made sure the agents weren't so top-end that they would be uninterested in showing her little home to potential buyers.

Luckily, all three were interested – her home was the perfect pad for first-time buyers and investor landlords alike. 'The proximity to the station – it's only a five-minute walk – was a big plus, the agents told me, as was the parking space that I bought when I got the studio flat.'

The most confusing part of the process for Simi was trying to decide if she should just go with one sole agent, or have several agents try to sell her studio flat. As she wasn't in a huge hurry to sell – she could stay with her sister in a village just outside St Albans until she and her fiancé found a larger place to move on to – she decided to put the property on with one agent and see how it went.

'I was amazed how many people were shown around by the agent within a day of the property going onto the agent's website, as well as on www.findaproperty.com and www. rightmove.com. Studio flats are popular, and the agent gave me good advice on how to present the property. He told me to store the skis, luggage, books, some of my clothing and kitchen items, such as the coffee-maker and bread machine, at my sister's so the place didn't look too cluttered,' says Simi.

Within a week, Simi had an offer at only £250 below the asking price. 'I accepted the offer, as the agent pointed out that the possible buyer was someone with cash who could get on with the whole deal fairly quickly. She was also flexible as to when I would have to complete, because she was so keen to get her hands on the flat.'

Simi says the process wasn't totally without stress. 'I remember a lot of phone calls between the two solicitors. The buyer wanted a lot of information about service charges, the sinking fund and how the management company operated, which was fair enough. I asked a lot of those questions when I bought too.'

Simi advises first-time sellers to keep paperwork, bills and invoices filed neatly, so it is easy to access everything when a buyer wants details of costs.

'I'm ashamed to say I wasn't as organised as I should have been, so it took a while to gather everything together. The buyer was pretty patient, though, all things considered.'

Other tips from Simi include making sure the estate agent draws up a good floor plan – 'Everyone wants to see a floor plan, and some agents are better than others about providing one' – and that he shoots decent photographs, too. Simi had shot some of the property on a sunny day that were used for the particulars instead of the agent's, that were taken when it was grey and drizzly.

'It was hugely tempting to be there when viewers came round, but the agent firmly suggested I leave and let him get on with his job. I'd go out for a coffee down the road, or round to my sister's whenever someone turned up. As my place was so small, it would have been crazy to have me there in the way as well. Besides, it would have made my studio flat appear even smaller, which wouldn't have been good.'

The whole process took three months from when the buyer first made an offer right through to the completion date. The only hitch, Simi said, was her finding all of the right paperwork and waiting for responses to queries from the freeholder and managing company. 'My solicitor was terrific, though, and he did chase them up constantly so I didn't lose the sale.'

Now, Simi lives in a larger two-bedroom flat about a mile from her first home.

'I really miss it sometimes – it was so convenient and close to the station – but it's also fantastic having all this extra space. I can have people to stay in the spare room/study, and my skis no longer clutter up the living room.

'My fiancé is thinking of renting his flat, which is just outside St Albans, and moving in with me. I feel selling was the right thing to do and it feels great to be moving on and getting on with my life.'

SELLING CHECKLIST

- [ ] Think what a buyer wants
- [ ] Choose a selling method (sole, joint sole or multiple agents)
- [ ] Consider alternatives (such as selling at auction)
- [ ] Choose an agent (or agents)
- [ ] Hire a solicitor
- [ ] Negotiate a contract with the agent
- [ ] Negotiate on the commission for the agent
- [ ] Decide what's included (fixtures and fittings) in the sale
- [ ] Provide information for particulars/brochure and photographs
- [ ] Get an Energy Performance Certificate
- [ ] Prepare your home for viewings
- [ ] Accept an offer
- [ ] Get a solicitor to start the conveyancing process
- [ ] The buyer gets your property valued by a lender
- [ ] Exchange contracts
- [ ] Completion of the deal
- [ ] Hand over the keys when the solicitor says to
- [ ] Remove your possessions from the home
- [ ] Move out

PHIL'S CONTACTS BOOK
- The Law Society (England & Wales) – www.lawsociety.org.uk
- The Law Society of Northern Ireland – www.lawsoc-ni.org
- The Law Society of Scotland – www.lawscot.org.uk
- The Council for Licensed Conveyancers (CLC) – www.conveyancer.org.uk
- National Association of Estate Agents (NAEA) – 01926 417794, www.naea.co.uk
- Royal Institution of Chartered Surveyors (RICS) – 0870 333 1600, www.rics.org
- The Guild of Professional Estate Agents – 020 7629 4141, www.propertyplatform.co.uk
- www.zoopla.co.uk – lists prices a property's sold for over recent years
- The British Association of Removers – www.bar.co.uk

APPENDIX A

Planning Permission

I f you do raise the cash to buy your wreck, remember that you will need to get planning permission to improve the property before you start any work. The planning system is in place to protect the environment where we live in towns, cities and the countryside. The central government comes up with a national planning policy with guidelines, but the main responsibility comes down to local councils (or planning authorities). Essentially, planning permission is asking whether you can do a simple, or sometimes more complex, piece of building work.

Each authority creates a local development framework that outlines how planning will be managed in an area. The local planning authority decides whether development – anything from adding a new bathroom to your home right through to the building of a massive shopping mall – should proceed or not.

To find out more about the planning process and the rules governing what you can and can't do, go to the brilliant website www.planningportal.gov.uk. This is a concise and easy-to-understand guide to planning permission and building regulations approval. Different projects are dealt with, including adding on an extension or a conservatory, using an interactive process where you click on different parts of a house to get more detail. There's also a 'green' house you can navigate round to get eco-friendly tips. The guidance given in this chapter is based on what is suggested for homeowners in England. You will need to check for any variants on planning in Scotland and Wales.

Most projects that will change the building in a major way need planning consent, and if you're in a conservation area you mustn't do anything that dramatically changes the look of the outside of the building, or the landscape (such as cutting down trees), without getting permission. And, if the property is listed, you will need to apply for permission for work that could change the special characteristics of the building.

Keep in mind that getting planning permission is separate from building regulations approval. Basically, planners tell you what you are allowed to do and building regulations inspectors make sure you have carried out the work properly to the correct building code.

The local authority planners need to respond to your application within eight weeks, and if they turn down your application, you can appeal. But, there is no guarantee you will win your case. What could occur is you will be asked to resubmit altered plans and a compromise might be reached.

You will deal with the local council in your area. Start the process by looking at the council website to get an idea of local planning guidance. Remember, every council interprets government legislation in its own way. One planner might be in favour of contemporary design, for instance, while another elsewhere could be less enthusiastic.

Planning rules for your home

Outlined below are current planning rules for different areas and aspects of your property. These rules apply to houses, and you will have to consult your local authority to see if the same rules are in force for flats. Also, these planning rules were up to date when this book went to press, but could alter in the future, so do check that information is still correct when you come to seek permission to carry out any building work.

Paving your front garden

You will not need planning permission if a new or replacement driveway of any size uses permeable (or porous) surfacing, such as gravel, permeable concrete block paving or porous asphalt. You also won't require permission if the rainwater is directed to a lawn or border to drain away naturally.

If the surface to be covered is more than five square metres, planning permission will be needed for laying traditional, impermeable driveways that do not provide for the water to run to a permeable area.

Why all the attention to more porous materials? New rules have been introduced about paving your front garden since serious flooding in 2007 caused disruption to people's lives, several deaths and damage estimated at about £3 billion. In many cases, flooding occurred because drains couldn't cope with the amount of rainwater flowing into them. The effects of climate change mean that this kind of heavy rainfall and flooding could occur more often in the future.

The drains in most urban areas were built many years ago and weren't designed to cope with increased rainfall. More water is entering the drains from new developments, and paving front gardens adds to the problem. Although paving over one or two gardens might not seem to make a difference, the combined effect of many people in a street or area doing this can increase the risk of flooding.

The harm caused by paving gardens is not limited to just flooding. Hard surfaces such as concrete and asphalt collect pollution (oil, petrol and brake dust) that is washed off into the drains. Many drains carry rainwater directly to streams or rivers, where the pollution damages wildlife and the wider environment.

In older areas, the rainwater may go into the foul water sewer, which normally takes household waste from bathrooms and kitchens to the sewage treatment works. These overflow into streams and rivers in heavy rainfall. As more water runs into foul sewers from paved areas there are more frequent overflows, passing untreated sewage into watercourses.

Loose gravel

This is the simplest type of construction to pave your front garden. A surface layer of gravel or shingle covers the driveway sub-base, and gravel with different shapes and colours is available to make the surface more decorative. A strip of block paving or asphalt at the entrance can limit the loss and spread of gravel from the drive.

Hard permeable and porous surfaces

Hard surfacing that allows water to soak into it can be built with porous asphalt, porous concrete blocks, concrete or clay block permeable paving. The material has open voids across the surface of the material, or around the edges of blocks, that allow water to soak through.

To work effectively, permeable surfaces should be laid over a sub-base differing from traditional hardcore with a lot of fine material (sand and silt) in it that allows water to pass through it easily. For permeable and porous driveways, different sub-base materials are required that allow water to pass through, and also store the water for a while if it cannot soak into the ground as fast as the rain falls.

Rain gardens and soakaways

An area of garden can be formed into a **rain garden**, widely used in America, but a relatively new concept in the UK. A rain garden has a depression to collect and store rainwater running from conventional impermeable surfaces (asphalt, concrete and block paving), before slowly allowing it to soak into the ground or to flow to the drains.

The depressions can be located along the edge of the drive, or as a larger area in the garden, at a low point. The depression can be planted with suitable plants to help slow run-off, or gravel or cobbles can be used as decorative features. There may be a gravel-filled trench below it to increase storage capacity and allow water to soak into the ground more easily.

Soakaways are a similar idea, except that water is piped into a gravel-filled trench or special container and allowed to soak into the ground. In some areas, many houses have roof downpipes connected to soakaways. They are more suitable for houses with larger front gardens, as they require space and need to be located a suitable distance from buildings.

Wheel tracks

To keep hard surfaces to a minimum, a driveway can be created that has just two paved tracks where the wheels of a vehicle go. These can be surfaced with blocks, asphalt or concrete, but to provide a durable construction they should have a sub-base below.

The area between and around the tracks can be surfaced in gravel or planted with grass or suitable low-growing plants. Water must drain from the tracks into the surrounding permeable area.

Fences, gates and garden walls

You will need to apply for planning permission if you want to erect or add to a fence, wall or gate if:

- It will be higher than one metre and is next to a highway used by vehicles (or the footpath of such a highway); or over two metres high elsewhere.
- Your right to put up or alter fences, walls and gates is removed by a direction or planning condition.
- Your property is listed or in the curtilage of a listed building.
- The fence, wall or gate, or any other boundary involved, forms a boundary with a neighbouring listed building or its curtilage.

You don't need to apply for planning permission to take down a fence, wall or gate, or to alter or improve an existing fence, wall or gate (no matter how high it is), if you don't increase its height. **In a conservation area**, however, you might need conservation area consent to take down a fence, wall or gate.

And, you won't require planning permission for hedges, unless a planning condition or a covenant restricts planting (for instance, on an open plan estate, or where a driver's sight line could be blocked). Although building regulations do not apply, the structures must be sound and maintained regularly.

Garden walls

If the garden wall is classified as a 'party fence wall' (a wall you share with a neighbour), and depending on the type of building work you intend to carry out, then you must notify the adjoining owner of the work in respect of the Party Walls Act of 1996. However, this does not include wooden fences.

What is the Party Wall Act?

The Party Wall Act is a framework for preventing and resolving disputes in relation to party (shared) walls, boundary walls and excavations near neighbouring buildings. As recommended in the leaflet drawn up by the government (you can download it at communities. gov.uk/publications/planningandbuilding/partywall), I think neighbours along a party wall should consider themselves joint owners of the whole of a party wall, instead of an individual assuming he's the sole owner of a half or part of a wall. This considerate way of looking at things will solve a lot of hassles, and ultimately, save time and money in the long run.

Basically, you and your neighbour (or neighbours) will have to agree on how work will be carried out to the party wall, and to the timing of the work. You have certain rights, which include being able to:

- Insert a damp proof course through the wall
- Raise the height of the wall and increase its thickness
- Demolish and rebuild the wall
- Underpin the thickness of the wall
- Protect two adjoining walls by putting a flashing from the higher over the lower wall

Anyone wanting to carry out work on a party wall has certain duties he must adhere to. You must:

- Tell all adjoining owners about the proposed work
- Not cut into your side of the wall without telling anyone
- Not cause any unnecessary inconvenience
- Provide temporary protection for adjoining buildings and property, when necessary
- Take responsibility for making good any damage caused, or the neighbour might want you to pay in lieu and he'll sort out the damage himself
- Share the cost of the wall with the neighbours if it is demolished and rebuilt

If you can afford it, I would recommend paying for the total amount of the work, particularly if relations with the neighbour, or neighbours, is a bit prickly. Also, the adjoining neighbour could stop the work through a court injunction or by other legal redress if he isn't happy and believes you're doing something incorrectly.

PHIL'S TOP TIP

Obviously, it's crucial that you talk to the neighbours before you give them written notice of any work to be done. Getting them on side early in the proceedings is very important to iron out any snags or concerns through friendly discussion. The adjoining neighbours might not be able to stop what you're doing, ultimately, but they certainly can delay the process, which could hold up the rest of the building work, too.

You don't necessarily need to take professional advice, although it might make sense if what you intend to do is complicated or controversial. If the adjoining property is empty, or the owner unknown, you can address the notice of work to be carried out to 'The Owner' and make sure you display it conspicuously on the premises.

Officially, you need to give two months' notice and this is then valid for a year (so don't give notice too early, or your usable time will lapse). A counter-notice from a neighbour needs to be served within one month, and do put any agreements in writing.

If there's a dispute, an independent surveyor (one not employed by you or the neighbour) will draw up what is called an 'award', outlining what will happen and who will pay. Usually, the building owner doing the work pays, but not in every case, and he must give notice when he needs access to the neighbour's property.

It won't be a surprise that keeping calm and using as much common sense as possible will go a long way. You could even point out to your neighbour that this might be a good time for him to carry out any work he wishes to do on his side of the party wall at the same time as you do your work. The costs could be shared, guaranteeing a saving for both of you, and any disruption occurs at roughly the same time.

Garden and boundary walls should be inspected from time to time to see if any repairs are necessary, or whether a wall needs rebuilding. These walls are among the most common forms of masonry to collapse, and unfortunately, they're one of the commonest causes of death by falling masonry, according to the government. Your insurance may not cover you if the wall has been neglected, so you've been warned.

> *Besides the general deterioration and ageing of masonry walls over the years, walls may also be affected by:*
>
> - An increase in wind load, or driving rain if a nearby wall is taken down
> - Felling of nearby mature trees, or planting of new trees close to the wall
> - Changes leading to greater risk of damage from traffic
> - Alterations, such as additions to the wall, or parts of the wall being removed (for a new gateway, for example)

Doors and windows

Planning permission is not normally required for repairing, fitting or replacing doors and windows (including double glazing). However, if the building is listed, or is in a conservation area (or other designated area), you should consult with your local planning authority. And, if you're a leaseholder, you may need to get permission first from your landlord or the management company looking after your building.

Building regulations for doors and windows

Since 1 April 2002, building regulations have applied to all replacement glazing, to increase thermal performance and other areas, such as safety, air supply, means of escape and ventilation.

You could use an installer registered with a Competent Person Scheme (BSI, CERTASS or FENSA). This means an installer registered with an organisation approved by the Secretary of State will be approved to carry out the work to comply with building regulations, without involving local authority building control. When the work is completed, you will receive a certificate showing that a registered installer did the work. More information about the Competent Person Schemes can be found on the Communities and Local Government (CLG) website: communities.gov.uk/planningandbuilding/building regulations/competentpersonsscheme.

Alternatively, you could use an unregistered installer or do the work yourself, in which case approval can be sought from the relevant Building Control Body — see www.planningportal.gov.uk/building regulations/howtogetapproval/wheretogetapproval — through your local authority or an approved inspector. They will check the replacement windows or doors for compliance and, if satisfied, issue a certificate of compliance.

Access to buildings

When replacing main entrance doors in a dwelling unit that has been constructed since 1999, it's important to ensure that the threshold remains level, otherwise the works will not comply with the building regulations as it would be making the threshold worse than it was when constructed. This is to enable a wheelchair user to have continued access to the dwelling.

External walls

You do not need to apply for planning permission for repairs, maintenance or minor improvements, such as painting your house. If you live in a listed building, however, you will need listed building consent for any significant works, whether carried out internally or externally.

If you live in a conservation area, a National Park, an Area of Outstanding Natural Beauty or the Broads, you will need to apply for planning permission before cladding the outside of your house with stone, artificial stone, pebble dash, render, timber, plastic or tiles.

Extensions and additions

An extension or addition to your house is considered to be permitted development, not requiring an application for planning permission, subject to the following limits and conditions:

- No more than half the area of land around the 'original house' would be covered by additions or other buildings. *The term 'original house' means the house as it was first built, or as it stood on 1 July 1948 (if it was built before that date). Although you may not have built an extension to the house, a previous owner may have done so.*
- No extension forward of the principal elevation or side elevation fronting a highway.
- No extension to be higher than the highest part of the roof.
- Maximum depth of a single-storey rear extension of three metres

beyond the rear wall for an attached house, and four metres beyond the rear wall for a detached house.

- Maximum height of a single-storey rear extension of four metres.
- Maximum depth of a rear extension of more than one storey of three metres beyond the rear wall, including the ground floor.
- Maximum eaves' height of an extension within two metres of the boundary of three metres.
- Maximum eaves and ridge height of extension no higher than the existing house.
- Side extensions to be single storey with a maximum height of four metres, and width no more than half that of the original house.
- Two-storey extensions no closer than seven metres to rear boundary.
- Roof pitch of extensions higher than one storey to match existing house.
- Materials to be similar in appearance to the existing house.
- No verandas, balconies or raised platforms.
- Upper-floor, side-facing windows to be obscure-glazed (so as not to overlook the neighbours), with any opening to be 1.7 metres above the floor.

On designated land (*designated land includes National Parks, the Broads, Areas of Outstanding Natural Beauty, conservation areas and World Heritage Sites*):

- No permitted development for rear extensions of more than one storey
- No cladding of the exterior
- No side extensions

Basements

The planning regime covering the creation of living space below ground in basements is evolving and under review at the time of this book going to print.

Converting an existing residential cellar or basement into a living space is in most cases unlikely to require planning permission, as long as it's not a separate unit, or unless the usage is significantly changed or a light well is added, altering the external appearance of the property.

Excavating to produce a new basement, which involves major works, a new separate unit of accommodation and/or alters the external appearance of the house, such as adding a light well, is likely to require planning permission.

If you live in a listed building, you are most likely to need consent for internal or external work. In all circumstances, you are advised to contact your local planning authority for guidance on local policy before starting any work.

PHIL'S TOP TIP

Basement conversions are becoming controversial in some places, with residents complaining there are too many being carried out and they could result in problems with flooding in the future. A study was carried out by the Royal Borough of Kensington & Chelsea in London recently that found the link between basement conversions and flooding couldn't be proven, yet the debate still continues.

Conservationists wonder whether having so many basement conversions carried out, particularly in dense towns and cities, could have an effect on a locale. With fewer places for water to run off, they worry that with heavy rainfall there might be backed-up drains that can lead to flooding (not dissimilar to concerns about people paving their front drives).

With this in mind, I'd recommend you carry out your research rigorously, talk to as many informed people as you can (architects, builders and estate agents on your patch, in particular) to gauge opinion. Some councils will be happier about granting permission than others, and seeing some basement conversions in your neighbourhood might be a wise idea.

Boilers and heating

Planning permission is not normally required for installation or replacement of a boiler or heating system if all the work is internal. But, if you live in a listed building you should check with your local planning department.

And, if the installation requires a flue outside, it will normally be allowed within permitted development if the conditions outlined below are met.

* Flues on the rear or side elevation of the building are allowed to a maximum of one metre above the highest part of the roof.
* If the building is listed or in a designated area and even if you enjoy permitted development rights, it's advisable to check with your local planning authority before a flue is fitted. Consent is also likely to be needed for internal alterations.
* In a conservation area or in a World Heritage Site, the flue should not be fitted on the principal or side elevation if it is visible from a highway.

If the project also requires an outside building to store fuel or related equipment, the same rules apply to that building as for other extensions and garden outbuildings.

Ceilings and floors

Planning permission is not generally required to replace a floor or ceiling. However, if you live in a listed building you should contact your local planning department.

Changes of use requiring a planning application

Other than for the permitted changes of use listed above and changes where both uses fall within the same use class, planning permission is generally required for a material change of use. Also, most external building work associated with a change of use is likely to require planning permission.

Change of use

You might want to seek change of use when a property listed for one use (for instance, as a pub in use class A4 – see overleaf for an explanation of the different classes) could possibly be changed into a different use class (such as residential, so you could convert it into a home).

How does change of use help me get a home?

It depends on the circumstances and the views of the local planners, but permission might be granted to allow you to convert a pub, church, village hall, café or even an office into a residential home, or homes. In a downturn when there are a number of vacant business premises, a local authority might be more amenable to turning an unloved and unused space into a residential dwelling.

PHIL'S TRADE SECRET

If you think laterally and get something moved within a class use band to a category more likely to get permission (such as a pub or chapel), this could be a canny move to pick up a property at a reasonable price.

Estate agents call these dwellings 'white elephants', as they're not really residential homes as we know them, but equally, they're not wholly commercial any more either. A country house might have been turned into training premises for a company, for example, and you might be able to convert it back to its original use as a home. There might be a few too many whiteboards, nasty carpets and utilitarian bathrooms, but don't forget, they can be easily ripped out and replaced with something more homely.

However, do not ever buy a property that is in a business use class, hoping you will get permission later on to make it into a home. This is a risky thing to do, as you can never be certain the local planning department will give you permission to change the use of the property. I've noticed, however, that a number of office blocks, which were standing empty and starting to deteriorate due to the recession, have been converted into flats now.

There will be a great deal of consultation that will need to go on with the planners, and only those with patience, time and probably a certain amount of cash should consider going down this route to get onto the property ladder. It can be hugely rewarding, however, to convert an unusual building into an interesting place to live. Most of us have driven past converted schools, chapels and maybe even lighthouses, and wished we could live there. I think this would be a highly ambitious project for a first-time buyer, but nothing's impossible.

Use classes

The Town and Country Planning (Use Classes) Order 1987 (as amended) puts uses of land and buildings into various categories known as 'use classes'.

The following list gives an indication of the types of use that may fall within each use class. Please note that this is a guide only and it's for local planning authorities to determine in the first instance, depending on the individual circumstances of each case, which use class a particular use falls into.

- **A1 shops**
  Shops, retail warehouses, hairdressers, undertakers, travel and ticket agencies, post offices (but not sorting offices), pet shops, sandwich bars, showrooms, domestic hire shops, dry cleaners, funeral directors and Internet cafés
- **A2 financial and professional services**
  Financial services, such as banks and building societies, professional services (other than health and medical services), including estate and employment agencies and betting offices
- **A3 restaurants and cafés**
  For the sale of food and drink for consumption on the premises – restaurants, snack bars and cafés
- **A4 drinking establishments**
  Public houses, wine bars or other drinking establishments (but not nightclubs)
- **A5 hot food takeaways**
  For the sale of hot food for consumption off the premises

- **B1 business**
  Offices (other than those that fall within A2), research and development of products and processes and light industry appropriate in a residential area
- **B2 general industrial**
  Use for industrial process other than one falling within class B1 (excluding incineration purposes, chemical treatment, landfill or hazardous waste)
- **B8 storage or distribution**
  This class includes open-air storage

- **C1 hotels**
  Hotels, boarding and guesthouses where no significant element of care is provided (excludes hostels)
- **C2 residential institutions**
  Residential care homes, hospitals, nursing homes, boarding schools, residential colleges and training centres
- **C2A secure residential institution**
  Use for a provision of secure residential accommodation, including use as a prison, young offenders' institution, detention centre, secure training centre, custody centre, short-term holding centre, secure hospital, secure local authority accommodation or use as a military barracks
- **C3 dwelling houses**
  This class is made up of three parts:
  - C3(a) covers use by a single person or a family (a couple whether married or not, a person related to one another with members of the family of one of the couple to be treated as members of the family of the other), an employer and certain domestic employees (such as an au pair, nanny, nurse, governess, servant, chauffeur, gardener, secretary and personal assistant), a carer and the person receiving the care and a foster parent and foster child
  - C3(b): up to six people living together as a single household and receiving care (for instance, supported housing schemes, such as those for people with learning disabilities or mental health problems)
  - C3(c) allows for groups of people (up to six) living together as a single household. This allows for those groupings that do not fall within the C4 HMO definition, but which fell within the previous C3 use class, to be provided for, i.e. a small religious community may fall into this section, as could a homeowner who is living with a lodger

- **C4 houses in multiple occupation**
  Small shared dwelling houses occupied by between three and six
  unrelated individuals, as their only or main residence, who share basic
  amenities such as a kitchen or bathroom

- **D1 non-residential institutions**
  Clinics, health centres, crèches, day nurseries, day centres, schools, art
  galleries (other than for sale or hire), museums, libraries, halls, places of
  worship, church halls, law courts, non-residential education and training
  centres

- **D2 assembly and leisure**
  Cinemas, music and concert halls, bingo and dance halls (but not
  nightclubs), swimming baths, skating rinks, gymnasiums or an area for
  indoor or outdoor sports and recreations (except for motor sports, or
  where firearms are used)

- **Sui generis**
  Certain uses do not fall within any use class and are considered 'sui
  generis'. Such uses include: theatres, houses in multiple occupation,
  hostels providing no significant element of care, scrap yards, petrol
  filling stations, shops selling and/or displaying motor vehicles, retail
  warehouse clubs, nightclubs, launderettes, taxi businesses, amusement
  centres and casinos.

Changes of use not needing planning permission

In many cases involving similar types of use, a change of use of a building or land
does not need planning permission. Planning permission is not needed when
both the present and proposed uses fall within the same 'class', or if the Town
and Country Planning (Use Classes) Order says that a change of class is permitted to another specified class (see table opposite).

For example, a greengrocer's shop could be changed to a shoe shop without
permission, as these uses fall within the same 'class', and a restaurant could be
changed to a shop or a estate agency as the Use Class Order allows this type of
change to occur without requiring planning permission.

Most external building work associated with a change of use is likely to
require planning permission.

From	To
A2 (professional and financial services) when premises have a display window at ground level	**A1** (shop)
A3 (restaurants and cafés)	**A1** or **A2**
A4 (drinking establishments)	**A1** or **A2** or **A3**
A5 (hot food takeaways)	**A1** or **A2** or **A3**
B1 (business) (permission limited to change of use relating to not more than 235 square metres of floor space)	**B8** (storage and distribution)
B2 (general industrial)	**B1** (business)
B2 (general industrial) (permission limited to change of use relating to not more than 235 square metres of floor space))	**B8** (storage and distribution)
B8 (storage and distribution) (permission limited to change of use relating to not more than 235 square metres of floor space)	**B1** (business)
C4 (houses in multiple occupation)	**C3** (dwelling houses)
Casinos (sui generis)	**D2** (assembly and leisure)

Additionally, a planning application is not required for change of use in the following circumstances:

- from A1 or A2 to A1 plus a single flat above
- from A2 to A2 plus a single flat above

These changes are reversible without an application only if the part that is now a flat was, respectively, in either A1 or A2 use immediately before it became a flat.

Conservatories

Adding a conservatory to your house is considered to be permitted development, not requiring an application for planning permission, subject to the limits and conditions listed below.

- No more than half the area of land around the 'original house' (see definition earlier in this chapter) would be covered by additions or other buildings.
- No extension forward of the principal elevation or side elevation fronting a highway.

- No extension to be higher than the highest part of the roof.
- Maximum depth of a single-storey rear extension of three metres for an attached house, and four metres for a detached house.
- Maximum height of a single-storey rear extension of four metres.
- Maximum depth of a rear extension of more than one storey of three metres, including the ground floor.
- Maximum eaves' height of an extension within two metres of the boundary of three metres.
- Maximum eaves and ridge height of the extension no higher than the existing house.
- Side extensions to be single storey with maximum height of four metres and width no more than half that of the original house.
- Roof pitch of extensions higher than one storey to match existing house.
- No verandas, balconies or raised platforms.
- On designated land (as defined earlier in this chapter), no permitted development for rear extensions of more than one storey, no cladding of the exterior and no side extensions.

Decking

Putting up decking, or other raised platforms, in your garden is within permitted development, so you needn't worry about not applying for planning permission, providing:

- The decking is no more than 30 centimetres above the ground.
- Together with other extensions and outbuildings, the decking or platforms cover no more than 50% of the garden area.

Demolition

In most cases you will not need to ask for planning permission to get the wrecking ball out to knock down your property or any of its outbuildings, unless the council has made an Article 4 direction restricting the demolition or alterations you could normally carry out under permitted development rules.

If you decide to demolish a building, even one that has suffered fire or storm damage, it does not automatically follow that you will get planning permission to build any replacement structure or will be allowed to change the use of the site. Where demolition of any kind of residential property is proposed, the council might want to first agree the details of how you intend to carry out the demolition and how you propose to restore the site afterwards.

You will need to apply for a formal decision on whether the council wishes to approve these details before you start demolition. This is what is called a 'prior approval application' and your local council will be able to explain what it involves.

Listed buildings and buildings in conservation areas

Technically, you do not need to make a planning application to demolish a listed building, or to demolish a building in a conservation area. However, you may need listed building or conservation area consent. The government planning portal website outlines whether you will need approval first (see www.planning portal.gov.uk/permission/responsibilities/beforeyoustart/otherpermissions).

You should discuss your proposed plans with your local planning authority before you take any decision to demolish buildings in sensitive locations to avoid the risk of legal action being taken against you. You could have an enforcement notice served on you, be fined and even end up with a criminal record if you do something illegal, so I'd recommend getting advice from the planners and specialists, such as a good architect or builder.

Permitted development rights

You can make certain types of minor changes to your house without needing to apply for planning permission. These are called **permitted development rights**. They originate from general planning permission granted not by the local authority, but by Parliament.

Bear in mind that permitted development rights that apply to many common projects for houses do not apply to flats, maisonettes or other buildings.

In some parts of the country known as designated areas, permitted development rights are more restricted. If you live in a conservation area, a National Park, an Area of Outstanding Natural Beauty or the Norfolk or Suffolk Broads, you will need to apply for planning permission for certain types of work, which do not need an application in other areas.

Permitted development rights withdrawn

You should also note that the local planning authority may have removed some of your permitted development rights by issuing an Article 4 direction. This will mean that you have to submit a planning application for work, which normally does not need one.

Article 4 directions are made when the character of an area of acknowledged importance would be threatened and are most commonly found in conservation areas. You will probably know if your property is affected by such a direction, but you can check with the local planning authority if you're not sure.

Listed property

There are also different requirements if the property is a listed building. With regards to listed property, it's generally a good idea to contact your local planning authority and discuss your proposal before any work begins. The planners will be able to inform you of any reason why the development may not be permitted and if you need to apply for planning permission for all or part of the work.

Garage conversion

Planning permission is not usually required, providing the work is internal.

Sometimes, permitted development rights have been removed from some properties with regard to garage conversions, so you should contact your local planning authority before going ahead with your plans, particularly if you live on a new housing development or in a conservation area. And, where work is proposed to a listed building, listed building consent may be required.

Kitchens and bathrooms

A planning application for installing a kitchen or bathroom is generally not required, unless it's part of a house extension. However, if your property is a listed building, you should consult the local planners.

Greener homes

Being eco-friendly might not be the first thing that comes to mind for cash-strapped first-time purchasers. But if you can find the money upfront, you will probably save cash in the long run. Also, when it comes time to sell, it could be a good selling point that your home costs less to run.

Advice from the Federation of Master Builders (www.fmb.org.uk), which is pretty sensible, is to look for A-rated (energy-efficient) kitchen appliances and aerated taps, which reduce water use. If mains gas is available, use it for cooking as well as heating. If it's not, consider an electric induction hob, which saves energy over a conventional electric or halogen hob.

If you're undertaking a bathroom renovation, think about the amount of water you're going to consume. You can reduce this by buying low-flush toilets, showers and basin taps, and a smaller capacity bath. If you've got enough cupboard space, you might even have room to fit a grey-water recycling unit, which will use water from your bath and shower to flush the loo.

Loft conversion

Planning permission is not normally required to convert the attic space. However, permission is required where you extend or alter the roof space so it exceeds specified limits and conditions.

A loft conversion for your house comes under permitted development, not requiring an application for planning permission, subject to the following limits and conditions:

- A volume allowance of 40 cubic metres additional roof space for terraced houses.
- A volume allowance of 50 cubic metres additional roof space for detached and semi-detached houses.
- No extension beyond the plane of the existing roof slope of the principal elevation that fronts the highway.
- No extension to be higher than the highest part of the roof.
- Materials to be similar in appearance to the existing house.
- No verandas, balconies or raised platforms.
- Side-facing windows to be obscure-glazed and any opening to be 1.7 metres above the floor.
- Roof extensions not to be accepted under permitted development rules in designated areas.
- Roof extensions, apart from hip to gable ones, to be set back, as far as practicable, at least 20 centimetres from the eaves.

PHIL'S TOP TIP

You must remember that any previous roof space additions must be included within the volume allowances listed above. Although you may not have created additional space, a previous owner may have done so in the past.

Protected species

Work on a loft or a roof may affect bats. You need to consider protected species when planning any work. A survey may be needed, and if bats are using the building, a special licence will be required to move them.

Whatever you do, don't get caught out trying to get rid of the bats yourself. You could end up in serious trouble, as bats and their roosts are protected by law. It is illegal to kill, injure or take a wild bat, or intentionally or recklessly damage, destroy or obstruct access to the roost.

Contact your local statutory nature conservation organisation (for England, naturalengland.org.uk) for advice. Another good contact is the Bat Conservation Trust: Bat Helpline 0845 1300 228, www.bats.org.uk.

Outbuildings

Rules governing outbuildings apply to sheds, greenhouses and garages, as well as other ancillary garden buildings, such as swimming pools, ponds, sauna cabins, kennels, enclosures (including tennis courts) and many other kinds of structures for a purpose and incidental to the enjoyment of a dwelling house.

Outbuildings are considered to come under permitted development, not needing planning permission, subject to the following limits and conditions:

- No outbuilding on land forward of a wall forming the principal elevation.
- Outbuildings and garages to be single storey, with maximum eaves' height of 2.5 metres and maximum overall height of four metres with a dual pitched roof, or three metres for any other roof.
- Maximum height of 2.5 metres in the case of a building, enclosure or container within two metres of a boundary of the curtilage of the property.
- No verandas, balconies or raised platforms.
- No more than half the area of land around the original house would be covered by additions or other buildings.
- In National Parks, the Broads, Areas of Outstanding Natural Beauty and World Heritage Sites, the maximum area to be covered by buildings, enclosures, containers and pools more than 20 metres from the house to be limited to 10 square metres.
- On designated land, buildings, enclosures, containers and pools at the side of properties will require planning permission.
- Within the curtilage of listed buildings, any outbuilding will require planning permission.

Patio

Elsewhere around your house there are no restrictions on the area of land that you can cover with hard surfaces at, or near, ground level. However, significant works of embanking or terracing to support a hard surface might need a planning application.

If you live in a listed building, you will need listed building consent for any significant works, whether internal or external.

Porches

Adding a porch to any external door of your house is considered to be permitted development, not requiring an application for planning permission, provided:

- The ground floor area (measured externally) won't exceed three square metres.
- No part will be more than three metres above ground level (height needs to be measured in the same way as for a house extension).
- No part of the porch will be within two metres of any boundary of the dwelling house and the highway.

Roof

You don't normally need to apply for planning permission to reroof your house, or insert roof lights or skylights.

The permitted development rules allow for roof alterations without the need for planning permission, subject to the following limits and conditions:

- Any alteration to project no more than 150 millimetres from the existing roof plane.
- No alteration to be higher than the highest part of the roof.
- Side-facing windows to be obscure-glazed and any opening to be 1.7 metres above the floor.
- The permitted development regime for solar panels has different limits on projections, and in relation to protected areas.

Trees and hedges

Many trees are protected by tree preservation orders, which means that generally, you need the council's consent to prune or fell them. In addition, there are controls over many other trees in conservation areas.

If you are unsure about the status of trees that you intend to prune or fell (or you simply require further information), you should contact your local council.

PHIL'S TOP TIP

The use and nature of hedges can sometimes be controlled through planning conditions and legal covenants, so make sure your solicitor does a thorough check when carrying out searches on the property.

You don't normally need permission to plant a hedge in your garden and there are no laws saying how high you can grow your hedge. However, you are responsible for looking after any hedge on your property and for making sure it's not a nuisance to anyone else.

If a hedge does adversely affect the owners or occupiers of an adjoining domestic property, then they can take action through the High Hedges complaints system introduced by the Anti-social Behaviour Act of 2003. The complaints system specifies the type of hedge (typically, fast-growing Leylandii hedging) and the adverse effects that it covers. Anyone with concerns about the effect a hedge is having on their property should contact the local council to see whether the High Hedges complaints system is applicable to their circumstances.

Working from home

You do not necessarily need planning permission to work from home. The key test is whether the overall character of the dwelling will change as a result of the business.

If the answer to any of the following questions is yes, then permission will probably be needed:

- Will your home no longer be used mainly as a private residence?
- Will your business result in a marked rise in traffic or people calling?
- Will your business involve any activities unusual in a residential area?
- Will your business disturb your neighbours at unreasonable hours or create other forms of nuisance, such as noise or smells?

Whatever business you carry out from your home, whether it involves using part of it as a bed-sit or for bed and breakfast accommodation, using a room as your personal office, providing a child-minding service, or using a space for hairdressing, dressmaking or to teach music, you need to ask: is your home is still mainly a home? Or, has it turned into business premises?

The same questions need to be asked with regards to using buildings in the garden for repairing cars, or storing goods connected with a business, for instance.

If you're in doubt, you can apply to the council for a Certificate of Lawful Use for the proposed activity to confirm it is not a change of use. This saves you paying higher business rates and also helps sell the property later, as some potential buyers might be nervous about the business tag.

Wind turbines

The planning regime for installing wind turbines is complex and still evolving. At present, in most cases you'll need to apply for planning permission from your local authority to add a domestic wind turbine to your house or grounds surrounding your home.

It's up to each local authority to decide what information you may need to provide with your application. It may be helpful to contact your authority before applying to discuss the following planning issues connected to a wind turbine:

- Visual impact
- Noise
- Vibration
- Electrical interference (with TV aerials)
- Safety

As this book was going to press, the government was carrying out a consultation process on possibly extending permitted development rights to domestic wind turbines. Do check with your local authority to determine what the position might be following the consultation.

Complaints: Redress Schemes and the Property Ombudsman

Approved redress schemes

Any businesses carrying out estate agency work under the Estate Agents Act 1979 (EAA 79) must belong to an approved redress scheme (even if they don't call themselves an estate agent). Estate agents that don't join an approved scheme will be subject to a £1,000 penalty charge, which can be repeated if necessary, and will ultimately be banned from carrying out estate agency work if they refuse to join a scheme.

Find your estate agent's redress scheme

There are two estate agents' redress schemes. Ask your estate agent which scheme the firm belongs to.

Members of The Property Ombudsman (TPO) scheme must display the TPO logo and have copies of the TPO consumer guide available in their offices. Members of the Surveyors Ombudsman Service (SOS) should provide you with a copy of their complaints handling procedure, which will outline if the firm is a member of the SOS.

The Property Ombudsman

You can complain to The Property Ombudsman if you're unhappy with the services provided by an estate agent who is a member of the TPO scheme.

Before you complain to the Ombudsman, however, you must have complained to the firm and given them a fair chance to sort out the problem.

Using a member estate agent to buy or sell your home

All estate agents are required to register with an Estate Agents Redress Scheme that has been approved by the Office of Fair Trading (OFT) and which investigates complaints against estate agents. The Property Ombudsman (TPO) is one of the schemes approved by the OFT.

Many estate agents have in addition voluntarily agreed to follow the TPO Code of Practice for Residential Estate Agents, approved by the OFT under its Consumer Codes Approval Scheme. Estate agents signing up to this Code of Practice are required to provide additional consumer protection that goes beyond that required by law. They can be recognised by the joint TPO/OFT approved code logos, which they display. Registered agents, who do not voluntarily accept the Code of Practice obligations of the TPO Scheme, are not entitled to show the OFT-approved code logo.

What does The Property Ombudsman do?

The Property Ombudsman provides a free, fair and independent service for dealing with unresolved disputes between TPO registered agents and those who are buying or selling, or potentially buying or selling residential property in the UK. The Ombudsman is a member of the British and Irish Ombudsman Association and follows the standards and rules of the Association. The Ombudsman is totally independent of estate agents and reports directly to the TPO Council, which has a majority of non-industry members.

What has the TPO member agent agreed to do?
- An agent is required to have professional indemnity insurance to ensure that any compensation awarded to you can be paid.
- An agent is required to have an in-house complaints system with written procedures, and should be able to inform you how to refer any unresolved dispute to the Ombudsman and co-operate with any investigation by the Ombudsman.
- An agent agrees to pay compensation, in full and final settlement of a complaint, if this is awarded by the Ombudsman and is accepted by you as the complainant. This award must be paid promptly.
- The maximum that the Ombudsman can award is £25,000.
- In the rare case that an agent fails repeatedly to follow the rules of the scheme, the agent can be reprimanded, fined or expelled from the TPO. In the case of expulsion, local media, the OFT and other organisations will be informed.

What rules must a registered agent follow?

Estate agents must meet all their legal obligations when acting as estate agents. These include:

- **Making financial checks**
  An estate agent must ask you, if you are the seller of a property, to provide proof of identity, as required by the Money Laundering Regulations 2007. The estate agent may also ask buyers for similar information to ensure that their records are complete, and especially if they are providing the buyer with another service, such as help in arranging a mortgage.
- **Duty of care**
  An estate agent must always work in the best interests of the client, that is to say the person who is paying for the estate agency services (usually, the seller). An estate agent should also treat fairly, and with courtesy, all those involved in the proposed sale or purchase. If the estate agent, or one of his staff, has any personal or business interest in the property, you, as buyer or seller, must be told as soon as possible in writing.
- **Impartial advice**
  An estate agent will offer appropriate advice, explanations and assistance to all regardless of age, race, religious belief, gender, sexuality, ethnicity or disability.
- **Terms of business**
  All estate agents must give you written terms of business with an explanation of terms used. The estate agent must also explain all fees and charges and tell you if any fee will be payable if you withdraw your instructions to sell the property.
- **Fees and charges**
  An estate agent must inform you in writing, before you agree to use his service, what fee (including VAT) is payable and when the fee is due. It must be stated clearly whether the fee is a fixed price regardless of the achieved selling price, or whether it is calculated as a percentage based on that achieved selling price.
- **Marketing your property**
  The estate agent must describe the property as accurately as possible and not misrepresent the details.
- **Energy Performance Certificate**
  The estate agent must ensure that he holds an appropriate Energy Performance Certificate (you used to have this in a home information pack, but the rest of the pack has been abandoned) for the property he is marketing.

- **'For Sale' boards**
  Boards must not be displayed in areas where this is not permitted. The estate agent must also ask if the seller wants a 'For Sale' board to be displayed and ensure that only one board of the correct size is displayed for each property.
- **Access**
  If the estate agent holds the keys, staff from the agency must accompany those who are viewing and anyone else requiring access on behalf of the buyer, unless the seller gives authorisation to the contrary.
- **Viewings**
  The estate agent must follow the seller's instructions on how viewings should be conducted.
- **Offers**
  The estate agent must record all offers received and pass a written copy of the offer promptly to the seller. The estate agent must not conceal or misrepresent offers made on the property to the seller, and where relevant to prospective buyers.
- **Services to buyers**
  If the estate agent offers services to the buyer, he must inform the seller in writing of those services.

How do you tell if an estate agent is a member of the TPO?

An estate agent must tell you that he is registered with the TPO scheme as soon as possible, and before you agree to use his services. You can recognise a registered estate agency by the OFT-approved code logo or the TPO logo displayed in the window of the office or on its letterhead. Member agents are required to display copies of the TPO consumer guide in their office and make copies available free of charge on request. In addition, the agent will send copies of the consumer guide to you at various stages of the sale and purchase process.

If you have a problem, tell the agent that you have a complaint and want them to look at it under their internal complaints procedure. The Ombudsman will not consider your complaint unless you have done this first.

When the agent has finished considering your complaint under his internal complaints procedure, he should inform you in writing of the outcome. If you're still dissatisfied, you can refer your complaint to the Ombudsman. Please contact the Ombudsman's office if you aren't sure whether he can look at your complaint.

If the agent persistently ignores or fails to address your complaint within a reasonable time, you should refer your complaint to the Ombudsman, who will assist you to progress your complaint. And, if the agent has been dealing with your complaint for eight weeks or more, and it remains unresolved, then you may take your complaint directly to the Ombudsman.

What complaints does the Ombudsman consider?

Your complaint may be considered by the Ombudsman if you believe that the agent has:

- Infringed your legal rights
- Failed to follow the rules and obligations set for agents under any code of practice to which they may subscribe
- Treated you unfairly
- Been guilty of maladministration (including inefficiency or unnecessary delay)

Also, your complaint will be dealt with if you think any of the above list were dealt with in a way that results in you losing money or suffering avoidable aggravation, distress and/or inconvenience.

What complaints will not be dealt with by the Ombudsman?

Broadly speaking, the Ombudsman cannot deal with your complaint if:

- Your complaint is not against the TPO scheme member agent.
- Your complaint is being, or has been, dealt with by a court, or similar body.
- Your complaint is about a survey and/or a formal valuation of the property.
- Your complaint is about obtaining a mortgage, or about the work of a solicitor.
- Your complaint refers to something that happened before the estate agent was registered with the TPO, or more than 12 months before you complained in writing to the agent.
- You refer your complaint to the Ombudsman more than six months after the date of the agent's final viewpoint letter.

What will the Ombudsman do?

The Ombudsman can consider complaints about the TPO member agent from actual or potential buyers and sellers of residential property. The Ombudsman's office will send you a complaints form with guidance on how you may present your side of the case to the Ombudsman. At the same time, you will receive full information about how the Ombudsman will try to resolve the dispute between you and the agent or, if this is unsuccessful, how he will reach a fair and reasonable decision.

You can accept or reject the Ombudsman's final decision. If you accept his award of financial compensation, you do so in full and final settlement of your dispute with the agent. If you reject his final decision, it and the award will lapse, and you are free to do as you wish, including taking legal action against the agent. Your legal rights will not have been affected by the Ombudsman's decision.

Any request for an oral hearing will be considered by the Ombudsman (or his appointed deputy) by reference to the issues to be determined, and in particular, the extent to which the complaint raises issues of credibility or contested facts that cannot be fairly determined by reference to documentary evidence and written submissions. In deciding whether there should be a hearing, and whether it should be in public or private, the Ombudsman will have regard to the provisions of the European Convention on Human Rights. The Ombudsman will give reasons in writing, if he declines to grant a hearing.

What if you're not happy with the Ombudsman's decision?

If you are dissatisfied with the way your complaint has been handled, you can bring your concerns to the attention of the Ombudsman. If you are still unhappy, you may at the end of the process raise your concerns with the Independent Reviewer. His remit is to consider complaints about the service and not about the merits of the Ombudsman's decision.

Glossary

Advance Another term for the mortgage loan, and the amount your lender agrees to give you.

Agreement in principle Initial document from your lender that gives you an idea of the amount you are likely to be lent. This is not a guarantee, but is often needed when dealing with estate agents so they have an idea of the size of your mortgage and if you can afford a property.

Annual percentage rate (APR) Interest rate you would pay over the period of a year. It helps you compare the cost of borrowing between different mortgage lenders. It takes into account interest to be paid, the length of the repayment term and any other charges.

Arrears When payments haven't been paid on the due date, they're said to be in arrears.

Asking price The amount the seller values his property at and wants to get if it's sold. You can negotiate on the asking price if you think it's too high.

Bank Organisation that offers a range of services (current and savings accounts, loans and mortgages).

Bank of England Government bank responsible for setting interest rates, issuing bank notes, maintaining a stable financial economy, and also, a lender for commercial banks.

Base rate Interest rate set by the Bank of England used as a benchmark by lenders to set their own charges, which would generally be higher. The base rate is reviewed throughout the year and can fluctuate (go up and down).

Beneficial joint tenants The property is jointly owned (you don't own a specific share in the property), and if you die the property goes to the other owner.

Broker A person who gives advice on a mortgage (also called a mortgage broker). Some are wholly independent of lenders, and some aren't.

Building society A financial company that offers similar services to a bank (such as letting you save or lending you money), but it is owned by its members (customers).

Buildmark The Buildmark 10-year warranty and insurance cover provided by the National House Building Council covers the majority of new homes built in the UK. Homeowners receive an NHBC booklet, which contains information about the warranty.

Capital The amount of money you have actually borrowed, or still owe on your property (not including the interest or other charges).

Capital and interest mortgage Where you pay off part of the capital (the amount borrowed) as well as interest each month (as opposed to interest only). This usually means everything (capital and interest) will have been fully paid off by the end of the agreed term.

Capped-rate mortgage A mortgage where you have a guaranteed maximum amount that you have to pay each month. Your payments may go up or down under that amount, as interest rates increase or decrease, but you wouldn't have to pay above that maximum even if the interest rates rise higher.

Cashback mortgage A mortgage that gives you an extra lump sum of cash at the beginning of your mortgage for you to spend on anything you like (but usually the house), mostly linked with variable rate mortgages. It's not a free gift and does need to be paid back (it will be added to your overall mortgage).

Claim for possession A legal claim made by the mortgage lender for possession of a mortgaged property, because the borrower hasn't paid his mortgage loan.

Collared mortgage A type of mortgage usually in combination with a capped or tracker mortgage where there's set upper and lower levels (the 'collar').

Collateral Something of value that's offered as a guarantee against a loan (with a mortgage, it's the home itself).

Completion The finalisation of the sale when all the monies are passed over and the buyer has legal rights to the property. Completion day is when all money is transferred and the buyer can access the property.

Contract The buyer and seller of a property enter into a contract that only becomes binding when both parties have signed it and the purchaser has handed over the agreed deposit to the solicitor.

Conveyancing The legal transfer of a property from one owner to another.

Credit score A score given to a person based on their credit worthiness (how big a risk for you managing to keep up repayments), often carried out through a credit agency.

Covenant A restriction or condition affecting the property, such as not being allowed to build an extension, which must be complied with.

Deeds All the legal documents relating to the property.

Deposit A part payment of the agreed purchase price paid by the buyer on exchange of contracts (or conclusion of missives in Scotland).

Detached house A detached house is a separate house not attached to another property.

Disposition, or feu disposition A legal document (in Scotland only) which transfers ownership of a property to the buyer.

Early repayment charge Amount of money you might have to pay a lender if you move your mortgage to another lender or pay it earlier than the agreed term.

Energy Performance Certificate (EPC) Sellers in England and Wales are required to provide a copy of a valid Energy Performance Certificate (EPC). It gives details about the energy efficiency of the property, using ratings from A to G, where A is the most and G the least energy efficient.

Equity The difference between the value of the property and what you owe as a mortgage.

Exchange of contracts The contracts are in fact two identical documents – one signed by the seller and the other by the purchaser. When these are exchanged, both sides are legally bound to complete the transaction. (In Scotland, this is known as a missives conclusion.)

Fixed-rate mortgage A mortgage where the rate of interest stays fixed for an agreed period of time, allowing monthly payments to remain the same throughout.

Flat Individual unit in a building (sometimes known as an apartment).

Financial Services Authority (FSA) An independent non-governmental body that regulates the financial services industry in the UK.

Freehold The full ownership of both the property and the land on which it stands.

Gazumping When the seller accepts a buyer's offer and then later rejects it to accept a higher offer from another buyer.

Gazundering When the buyer demands a price drop from the seller at the last minute (usually due to declining values in the area).

Ground rent This applies to leasehold properties and is a sum paid annually to the freeholder by the leaseholder.

Guarantor A person who guarantees you'll pay the mortgage repayments (often a parent or other relative).

Guarantor mortgage A type of mortgage where a guarantor ensures the lender will pay the mortgage repayments, but you don't necessarily jointly own the property.

Home contents form Lists details of the physical condition of a property's fixtures and fittings (such as curtains, carpets and kitchen appliances) that the seller is including in the sale, or excluding, or willing to negotiate over.

Home information pack Sellers of properties in Scotland need to create a home information pack (HIP) before the property can be marketed. HIPs contain information about energy performance, legal documentation and other details.

Insurance
- **Buildings insurance** covers the actual bricks and mortar of your home and covers you for any damage (from fire, floods and wind, for instance) to your building. Is sometimes called 'home insurance' when grouped together with contents insurance.

- **Contents insurance** covers all of your possessions in your home, with any valuable items, such as jewellery, specified and covered by an 'all risks' policy that applies even when the items aren't in the home.
- **Income protection** gives regular monthly income if you can't work because of accident or illness.

Interest The amount of money that's charged on money borrowed.

Interest-only mortgage A type of mortgage where each month you only pay interest on what you've borrowed. It usually means lower monthly payments, but at the end of the agreed mortgage term you still owe the entire amount borrowed.

Interest rate The percentage showing how much money you will have to pay as interest (usually linked to the Bank of England's rates and can move up or down).

Joint mortgage A type of mortgage when you buy a property with someone else (parents or a partner, for instance), where the property's jointly owned.

Land certificate A certificate issued by the Land Registry as proof of ownership.

Land Registry fees Land Registry fees (or land registration fees) are paid through your solicitor to register your ownership of the property with the Land Registry. The Land Registry is a government department that records registered land in the UK, or ownership, along with details of that land, such as mortgages or sales. The government fixes the scale of fees.

Lease A contract that conveys land from one person to another for a specified period (for instance, 99 years), usually in return for rent.

Leasehold Land held under a lease for a number of years on which annual ground rent is paid.

Lender The mortgage company or financial institution (typically, a bank or building society) that loans you the money for a home (a mortgage).

Loan-to-value The amount of money you have as a loan compared to the value of the property (how much it's worth), usually in a percentage form.

Local authority search Carried out by your solicitor, the search determines if your new home is likely to be affected by any planning decisions.

Maisonette A home on two levels with internal stairs and, often, its own entrance at street level.

Management company A management company is sometimes employed to take responsibility for maintaining the main structure, common parts (for instance, stairs and hallways) and landscaped areas. A management company might also look after gyms, pools, roads, street lighting, open spaces and car parks on a larger development. The company recovers its costs from each owner through a service, or maintenance charge. In Scotland, the term used is factoring company.

Missives The name given to a contract (in Scotland only). Missives are letters exchanged by the purchaser (making an offer for the property) and the seller (accepting the offer).

Mortgage Most people will need to take out a mortgage, or loan, to buy a home. There are many different types, which a mortgage advisor can explain.

Mortgagee The lender.

Mortgagor The borrower, whose property is secured for the loan.

Mortgage indemnity insurance/guarantee Your mortgage lender usually will require additional security if the loan is in excess of 70–80% of the purchase price. This involves a once-only payment that can normally be added to your overall mortgage. The amount of the payment varies with the amount borrowed and the term of the loan.

Mortgage protection policy An insurance policy often arranged in conjunction with a mortgage. It is taken out to ensure the loan will be paid off should the borrower die before the end of the mortgage term. Insurance is also available to protect your repayments in the event of redundancy, and sometimes, illness.

Mortgage valuation survey Prior to your lender making a mortgage offer, your lender will have the property valued for 'mortgage purposes'. You will pay a fee that is variable depending on the purchase price.

National House Building Council A non-profit making body, whose role is to both protect the homebuyer and help the building industry to construct quality new homes. NHBC inspectors carry out spot checks and regular examinations on all new properties at various stages of construction. The NHBC also provides a 10-year Buildmark warranty.

Negative equity This happens usually when house prices fall and the value of the property is less than the amount you owe as a mortgage.

Offset mortgage A mortgage that allows you to save on the interest you will pay on your mortgage debt by 'offsetting' any savings you (or perhaps your family or friends) have linked to your mortgage.

Purchase price The amount or cost of the property you're buying.

Registered land The title for land, including buildings on the land, registered at the Land Registry, legal ownership of which is guaranteed.

Repayment mortgage Each month you pay off part of the 'capital' (the amount borrowed) as well as the interest. This usually means that everything, capital and interest, will have been fully paid off by the end of the agreed mortgage term.

Searches Used to denote the physical and written procedure for determining any adverse effects in or on a particular property, whether already in effect or planned to take place.

Seller The present owner of the property (also called the vendor) who wants to sell it.

Semi-detached house A semi-detached house (or a semi) is a pair of houses built side-by-side.

Settlement In Scotland only, the end of the home-buying process, when the deeds of the new property and other documents are handed over in return for the agreed price.

Shared ownership A way to help people get onto the property ladder if they can't afford to buy a property alone. Shared ownership allows you to own a 'share' in a property with another party, usually a housing association. You pay the association rent for their share of the property.

Stamp Duty The full term is Stamp Duty Land Tax with regards to property (opposed to shares), but generally known as Stamp Duty. A government tax on the purchase price of a property paid for by the buyer. Typically, your solicitor automatically handles payment on your behalf.

Sold subject to contract Sold subject to contract (STC) means that the seller and the buyer are proceeding with the sale, but the paperwork is not yet complete.

Survey An inspection of a property by a qualified surveyor carried out before buying a property.

Tenants in common When you jointly own the property, but you own a share of the value that you can give away, sell or leave to someone else if you die.

Title The rights and liabilities that are attached to the property.

Title deeds Legal documents describing the rights and liabilities attached to the property and that prove ownership of the property.

Title report Solicitor's certificate confirming that the title to the property is acceptable. A lender must have one before an advance cheque for the mortgage monies can be issued.

Tracker mortgage A tracker mortgage is a variable mortgage linked with the interest rate from the Bank of England. If interest rates go up or down, then so will your payments.

Transfer deed Legal document transferring ownership of land.

Under offer A property is 'under offer' when the seller has accepted an offer from the buyer, but not yet exchanged contracts.

Utilities Public services we need everyday, such as gas, water and electricity.

Valuation The inspection that checks the value of a property to see how much it is worth.

Variable-rate mortgage A mortgage where payments can move up or down depending on the movement of the interest rates of the mortgage lender.

Will A will is a legal document that allows a person to make decisions on how his or her estate will be managed and distributed after his or her death. As a homeowner, it's advisable to make a will, or alter an existing one. Your solicitor can advise you and help draw up your will.

Resources

General

www.amazon.co.uk
www.direct.gov.uk
www.ebay.co.uk
www.gumtree.com
www.hmrc.gov.uk
www.loot.com
www.moneysavingexpert.com
www.nationwideeducation.co.uk
www.royalmail.com

Builders

Federation of Master Builders, www.fmb.org.uk

Builders' contracts

building-contract.co.uk
Federation of Master Builders, www.fmb.org.uk

Finding an architect

Royal Institute of British Architects (RBA), www.architecture.com

Finding a builder

Federation of Master Builders, www.findabuilder.co.uk, 0800 015 2522
Guild of Master Craftsmen, www.guildmc.com, 01273 478 449

Buying with a partner, friend or relative

Sharedspaces.co.uk
Sharingaccommodation.co.uk

Conveyancers

Council for Licensed Conveyancers, www.conveyancer.org.uk
The Law Society (England & Wales), www.lawsociety.org.uk
The Law Society of Northern Ireland, www.lawsoc-ni.org
The Law Society of Scotland, www.lawscot.org.uk

Debt advice

Citizens Advice Bureau, adviceguide.org.uk, 0844 477 2020
Citizens Debt Advice, debtadvicegroup.co.uk, 0800 116 4952

Estate agents

National Association of Estate Agents, naea.org.uk, 01926 496800
The Guild of Professional Estate Agents, propertyplatform.co.uk, 020 7629 4141
The Property Ombudsman, tpos.co.uk

Government-shared-ownership schemes

www.direct.gov.uk
www.shared-ownership.org.uk

Household budget calculators

Most banks and financial websites offer budget calculators.
Here are some good ones:
- Goodwithmoney.co.uk
- www.nationwide.co.uk
- www.thisismoney.co.uk

Lodgers

www.direct.gov.uk/en/moneytaxandbenefits

Lodger contract
Desktop Lawyer, www.desktoplawyer.com

Finding a lodger
Doctor in the House, www.doctorhouse.co.uk
www.mondaytofriday.com

Mortgages

Association of Independent Financial Advisers, aifa.net
British Bankers Association (BBA), www.bba.org.uk
Building Societies Association (BSA), www.bsa.org.uk
Council of Mortgage Lenders, www.cml.org.uk, 020 7437 0075

New builds

Building warranties

National House Building Council (NHBC), nhbc.co.uk, 0844 633 1000

Planning permission

Planning Inspectorate, www.planning-inspectorate.gov.uk, 0117 372 6372 (England),
    029 2082 3866 (Wales)
Planning Portal, www.planningportal.gov.uk
Royal Town Planning Institute, rtpiconsultants.co.uk, 020 7960 5663

Property websites

www.findaproperty.com
www.primelocation.com
www.rightmove.co.uk
www.upmystreet.com
www.zoopla.co.uk

Removal companies

British Association of Removers, bar.co.uk
Helpiammoving.com
Uk-removal.co.uk

Rent-to-buy

Acorn Property Group, www.acornpropertygroup.org

Stamp Duty, including Disadvantaged Areas Relief and Zero-carbon Homes

www.hmrc.gov.uk

Surveyors

Royal Institution of Chartered Surveyors (RICS), www.rics.org, 0870 333 1600

Index

Also from Vermilion by Phil Spencer

Adding Value to Your Home

Whether you want to give your kitchen a bit of a facelift, install some new lighting in your bathroom or dig down into your basement, *Adding Value to Your Home* offers clear advice on enhancing your property. Showing you how to attract the most attention from buyers and what will make your house sell quicker and for more cash, this book is packed full of practical advice, clear information and real-life case studies.

From simple DIY projects or insulating the loft, to coming up with a well-planned and well-executed extension, *Adding Value to Your Home* is here to help you understand what could work best for you, and what will make the overall feel of your house more valuable in the eyes of a potential buyer.

£12.99   9780091935368

Order direct from www.randomhouse.co.uk